Higher Education

*A Worldwide Inventory
of Centers and Programs*

Philip G. Altbach
and
David Engberg

Center for International Higher Education
Lynch School of Education, Boston College

ORYX PRESS
2001

The rare Arabian Oryx is believed to have inspired the myth of the unicorn. This desert antelope became virtually extinct in the early 1960s. At that time, several groups of international conservationists arranged to have nine animals sent to the Phoenix Zoo to be the nucleus of a captive breeding herd. Today, the Oryx population is over 1,000, and over 500 have been returned to the Middle East.

© 2001 by The Oryx Press
4041 North Central at Indian School Road
Phoenix, Arizona 85012-3397
http://www.oryxpress.com

Published simultaneously in Canada
Printed and bound in the United States of America

∞ The paper used in this publication meets the minimum requirements of
American National Standard for Information Science—Permanence
of Paper for Printed Library Materials, ANSI Z39.48, 1984.

Library of Congress Cataloging-in-Publication Data
Altbach, Philip G.
   Higher education: a worldwide inventory of centers and programs / Philip G. Altbach
and David Engberg.
      p. cm.
Includes index.
   ISBN 1-57356-480-X (alk. paper)
   1. Education, Higher—Research—Directories. 2. Education, Higher—Study and
teaching—Directories. 3. Universities and colleges—Directories. I. Engberg, David II.
Title.
LB2326.3 A48 2001
378'.0025—dc21
                                                                    00-066666
                                                                    CIP

TABLE OF CONTENTS

ACKNOWLEDGMENTS

We are especially indebted to our colleagues in the field of higher education who responded to our requests for information. Without the assistance of colleagues around the world, we would not have been able to compile this inventory. Several organizations were especially helpful to us in identifying potential respondents. The Center for Higher Education Policy Studies (CHEPS) at the University of Twente was especially generous in providing us with their list of organizations. We are indebted to Peter A. M. Maassen and the CHEPS staff. The International Association of Universities in Paris assisted us with our journals list. Toru Umakoshi of the Center for Higher Education at Nagoya University in Japan and Ulrich Teichler and Jürgen Enders of the Gesamthochschule Universität Kassel in Germany also assisted us. Dr. Xiangming Chen of the Institute of Higher Education at Peking University, Beijing, China, helped us with our coverage of China. Jan Sadlak of the UNESCO European Center for Higher Education in Romania assisted us in checking some entries. At Boston College, Yoshikazu Ogawa and Kevin Sayers were involved with the project, as was Salina Kopellas.

This project is part of the research program of the Center for International Higher Education at Boston College. Our work is funded in part by the Ford Foundation, and we are indebted to Jorge Balán for his continuing support. The International Education Research Foundation of Los Angeles also assisted in the funding of the inventory.

INTRODUCTION

This international inventory is a guide to higher education programs, centers, and related agencies. The book is a pioneering venture in that it is the first such international inventory in the field of higher education ever undertaken. While the goal was to create a comprehensive inventory, as an initial effort this project is inevitably incomplete. Nevertheless, we hope that it will be but the first in a series of efforts to bring the higher education research community together.

The book is divided into three main sections. The first is an essay that gives an overview of higher education research and training, providing a context for the programs and centers listed in the inventory. The second section is the inventory itself. The final section is a listing of journals in the field of higher education worldwide. Our intention has been to describe the growing worldwide network of institutions and programs devoted to higher education. As postsecondary education has become a major policy concern in every country, there has been an expansion of research, service, and training programs intended to serve higher education systems and institutions. This book is the first effort to capture this growing network of organizations. We hope that it will become a useful resource for the emerging community of specialists in higher education worldwide.

The Essay

Only in the past half century did higher education become an area of research and scholarly attention, although the roots of the field extend further back. Training programs for higher education administration are also of recent origin. The essay attempts to provide a brief summary of the development of the field and a discussion of current trends in research and training. It is intended as a kind of "road map" for a field of research and training that is rapidly expanding and maturing.

The Inventory

The main contribution of this book is the higher education inventory. Data for the inventory were collected over a period of two years, from 1998 to 2000. To facilitate the response process, respondents were able to reply through an on-line survey form, e-mail, or regular post. Approximately 265 requests for information were initially distributed to universities, research centers, and regional and international organizations. Persistent efforts were made to contact the relevant agencies, and to be as comprehensive as possible in coverage. All told, the inventory contains 187 centers, institutes, and programs. The response data were then edited for clarity and to conform to our specific categories. In some cases, incomplete information was received. Using available resources we have tried to complete all listings as much as possible. Nevertheless, some listings remain less complete than others. The inventory is alphabetically organized by country.

Criteria

We used the following categories to identify the programs and centers to be listed:
- academic programs—degree-granting programs located in universities that offer postgraduate degrees in the field of higher and postsecondary education;
- institutes and centers—such places may be located in universities, government ministries or departments, or they may be freestanding. Some may be focused on research, while others may be engaged mainly in data collection.

Definitions

Defining our target institutions was not an easy task. We used the following categories as a guide to including centers, programs, and institutes:

Academic programs

a. At least one FTE (full-time equivalent) faculty member who concentrates on higher education—this might mean two or more faculty who have only a partial commitment.

b. At least four graduate courses (postbaccalaureate) or the availability of the most-advanced degree, usually the doctorate—in some countries, programs offering only the master's degree did not qualify for inclusion in the inventory.

c. Academic programs are generally housed in a university.

Centers or institutes

a. There should be a specific focus on research or policy in the field. We have excluded from the inventory centers or institutes that deal exclusively with institutional research.

b. The staff should include at least one full-time professional, and at least two professional support personnel.

c. The center or institute should have its own budget.

d. The center or institute may be housed in a university, in a government or private agency, or may be freestanding. Funding may come from a variety of sources.

e. The center or institute may have an academic program, a training program, or both.

The Questionnaire

The questionnaire requested the following information:

- the name of the center, institute, or program;
- full address, e-mail, fax, and other contact information;
- a short statement about focus, including key research interests and purposes;
- publications emanating from the center, institute, or program;
- the names of full-time and part-time staff members, with an indication of their research and teaching interests;
- an abbreviated list of major books used in academic programs, research projects undertaken, and major funding sources;
- courses offered (for academic programs); and
- numbers of students enrolled and degrees offered (for academic programs).

Coverage

This inventory is worldwide in scope, but obvious variations exist among the regions and countries. More than half the listings are from the United States. There are several reasons for this imbalance. Without question, the United States has the largest research and training enterprise in the field of higher education. Indeed it is the only country with a well-developed graduate degree-level training program in the field. The bulk of the American listings are for training programs. It also proved easiest to obtain responses from the U.S. Since the questionnaire and the responses were in English, it was clearly easier for academic systems that use English to respond. Additionally, we had a fully comprehensive list of academic programs in higher education in the United States. We estimate that the United States is home to about half of the programs and centers in the field. If one eliminated its graduate training programs, the United States would decrease its worldwide share dramatically.

China, by contrast, is underrepresented in this inventory. This was done purposely. We know that there are about 400 centers and institutes of higher education in Chinese universities today. Most focus only on the specific university and have little national or international role. Working with Chinese colleagues, we selected what are considered to be the main centers in China, and many of these responded to our questionnaire.

There are national and regional organizations dealing with higher education issues in many countries. In the United States alone, there are perhaps 50 such groups in Washington, D.C., representing the interests of parts of the higher education community to the federal government. These range from the Association of Jesuit Colleges and Universities, to the Council of Graduate Schools, and the American Association of University Professors. The United Kingdom has organizations representing university vice chancellors, international education programs, and other groups. In Japan, the private universities have their own organization. Many of these groups sponsor research or publications, and some of the larger ones, such as the American Council on Education, have research staff. We have not, however, included such organizations in this inventory. We have also excluded most of the international groups that represent specific higher education interest groups, such as the International Federation of Catholic Universities.

It should be noted that our response rate from centers and programs that do not use English as a primary language was no doubt lower than for those that use English frequently.

The Journals List

This volume includes a listing of journals focusing directly on higher education. Our goal is to provide as complete a listing as possible in all languages. We have included national as well as regional and international journals. The information provided includes the publisher, editor, frequency of publication, and relevant addresses. This list is current as of the beginning of 2000.

While we have been especially concerned to cover research-oriented journals, we have also included as many other periodicals as possible. The listing is, of course, not a complete one. Our coverage is more thorough for journals appearing in English and for those published in North America. We have actually purposely excluded many of the higher education journals published in China. Only a few of these journals are circulated nationally within China, and we have listed these. Purely local university-based publications were not included.

Yoshikazu Ogawa, a member of the staff of the Center for International Higher Education at Boston College, was mainly responsible for supervising the preparation of the journals list.

Related literature

This inventory is related to two volumes that analyze current trends in higher education research worldwide. These books are;

- Jan Sadlak and Philip G. Altbach, eds., *Higher Education Research at the Turn of the New Century* (New York: Garland Publishing and Paris: UNESCO, 1997).
- Ulrich Teichler and Jan Sadlak, eds., *Higher Education Research: Its Relationship to Policy and Practice* (Oxford, UK: Elsevier; Paris: International Association of Universities, 2000).

Philip G. Altbach
David Engberg
Chestnut Hill, Massachusetts
June 2000

CHAPTER 1

Research and Training in Higher Education
The State of the Art

Philip G. Altbach

In most countries, higher education has become a large, complex enterprise. As universities and other postsecondary institutions have grown, they acquire elaborate administrative structures that need major expenditures of public and, often, private funds.[1] Perhaps most important, postsecondary education is recognized as a central element in modern society. Universities are considered engines of the postindustrial age and of the knowledge economy. Moreover, higher education has become big business. Single academic institutions employ thousands of people and educate tens of thousands—or in some cases hundreds of thousands. Degrees in a multiplicity of specialties from ancient history to biotechnology are offered. In 1971 Eric Ashby characterized the American academic system as offering "any person, any study," in describing its diversity and scope.[2] Several decades ago, Martin Trow looked at the progression of higher education from elite to mass and finally to universal access.[3] In the industrialized nations, at least, mass access has been achieved, and a few countries—most notably the United States and Canada—have moved to semiuniversal access, enrolling half of the relevant age group. Many others, mainly in Europe and the Pacific Rim, educate 40 percent or more of the age group. Developing countries lag behind, but the main growth in the coming decades will be in this part of the world.[4]

In this context, there is a great need for expertise and data about all aspects of higher education and for a sophisticated understanding of the nature of academic institutions. Academic institutions require thoughtful and competent leadership. Research on higher education and training in the art and science of administration and institutional leadership are critical to the future of the university. Policymakers outside academic institutions, in government and in the private sector, who increasingly wield power over the future of academe, need knowledge and analysis in order to effectively coordinate complex institutions and systems.[5]

An Emerging Field

The field of higher education research is relatively new and undeveloped. Researchers have traditionally been reluctant to study the institution in which they work. Until the mid 20th century in most countries, academic institutions were small and enjoyed considerable autonomy. Government-mandated systems of higher education did not exist. Universities, though considered to be important, were seldom major social institutions. In a few cases, such as the Humboldtian reforms in Germany in the early 19th century where academic institutions became important institutions in national development, universities were somewhat peripheral. Social scientists preferred to focus their scholarly attention elsewhere, especially on subjects that might yield generalizable theories. Those interested in pedagogy and education were typically concerned with primary and secondary schools, and not with higher education. As a result, postsecondary education was ignored by researchers in the field of education as well as by social scientists.

The lack of interest on the part of academic institutions and agencies responsible for funding higher education research about academe meant there was little funding or support for research. Universities had a traditional pattern of governance and organization. University administrators were recruited from the ranks of the senior professoriate, very few of whom sought careers in administration. The complex administrative structures now found in most academic institutions did not exist. No training was provided to those who undertook leadership positions.

The reasons for the paucity of data, research, and analysis concerning higher education tell us something about the origin of the field. Few people claim that the study of higher education is a full-fledged academic discipline. Therefore, the infrastructures that go along with a scientific discipline—academic departments, professorships, and the like—are largely nonexistent.[6] In part because higher education has no disciplinary base, it has never had a clear academic home. In the United States, Britain, Canada, Australia—countries with an Anglo-Saxon academic tradition—and some others, the study of higher education has been incorporated into the research and teaching activities of universities, mainly in schools of education, where it is often considered peripheral to the main missions of these schools.

Only recently has a perceived need emerged for professionally educated administrators and other staff in postsecondary institutions. The growth of a group of midlevel administrators specifically trained in the field of higher education has been a development limited mainly to the United States, Canada, and Australia. Senior academic administrators continue to be drawn from the ranks of the professoriate and slowly gravitate to administration as a career. In contrast, in Germany there is a cadre of senior university managers appointed by government directly from the civil service who have responsibility for certain elements of university administration and management, especially in finance and nonacademic areas. These top administrative officials have little or no background in higher education. The lack of an institutional base has limited the growth and institutionalization of higher education as an academic specialty, although the growth in the number of professional middle managers in higher education has contributed to the expansion of the field of higher education studies.

The study of higher education is an interdisciplinary endeavor, which has been both a strength and a weakness. It is a strength because researchers in many social science disciplines—including but not limited to sociology, political science, psychology, economics, and history—have contributed very significantly to the development of research on higher education. Researchers in the field of educational studies have slowly begun to develop an interest in higher education; curriculum specialists, educational planners, and others now work on postsecondary issues. The small number of researchers focusing on higher education made the emergence of a distinctive field more difficult. In part because it is an interdisciplinary field, higher education research has no established methodology. It borrows from other fields. Again, this is both a strength and a weakness. Interdisciplinarity has made possible original and quite innovative research. On the other hand, it has hindered the creation of a permanent research community.

Until quite recently, there has been relatively little demand for data and analysis of higher education by potential users. Academic institutions themselves have been governed according to traditional norms and were fairly small, until after World War II. Governments tended to permit academic institutions considerable autonomy, even where state funds largely paid for postsecondary education. When decisions were made, research-based data and analysis were not seen as relevant for decision making.

Funding stimulates research, and until recently, little money was available for research on higher education. The few exceptions were short-lived and not sustained. For example, major reform efforts in Britain (the Robbins

Commission) and in Sweden (the U-68 Report) stimulated some research.[7] More recently, government initiatives, such as the Thatcher government's abolition of the binary system in the 1980s or the more recent Dearing Commission were not accompanied by major research studies. The Carnegie Foundation for the Advancement of Teaching in the United States and the Leverhulme Trust in Britain sponsored major studies of higher education in order to understand academic systems undergoing changes and facing considerable challenges in the aftermath of the expansion of the 1960s.[8]

Within the field of higher education, several subject areas do have a fairly strong research base. For example, the economics of higher education has become an especially central topic in a period when the allocation of resources is of great concern. The Institut de recherche sur l'économie de l'éducation in Dijon, France and the Institute for Research on Higher Education at the University of Pennsylvania have both focused on economic issues in higher education beginning in the 1980s as funding became problematical. Funding issues have received attention from commissions in several countries.[9]

Gathering international statistical information relating to higher education has been seen as a priority by UNESCO, which has been engaged in this area for several decades.[10] The Organisation for Economic Cooperation and Development (OECD) and the World Bank have also been engaged in compiling statistics. In the United States, the National Center for Educational Statistics of the U.S. government has recently developed initiatives to ensure the availability of accurate international statistics concerning higher education. National agencies in many countries collect national statistics, but few efforts exist to link these statistics or to ensure comparability among them.[11] Consistent, and reliable comparative statistical information concerning higher education is currently unavailable. With academic systems worldwide facing similar problems and with international student and staff mobility on the rise, more consistent statistical data are needed.

Comparative studies in higher education are also an identifiable trend in the literature, in part to provide national policymakers with a basis for comparison. Two recently published major international analyses of trends are contributing significantly to current discussions of comparative higher education. The World Bank's 1994 policy review for higher education[12] stimulated a good deal of discussion and controversy, including a volume of critiques.[13] UNESCO also completed an overview of higher education trends worldwide.[14] As part of the preparation for the UNESCO study, several reports were prepared.[15] The Task Force on Higher Education and Society issued a useful report on higher education in developing countries in 2000.[16] Truly comparative research is both difficult and expensive, and not surprisingly there are few comparative studies.[17] More common are compilations of case studies around a specific theme.[18]

Much of the research and data concerning higher education have not been formally published in standard books and journals and may be considered part of a "gray literature" that is difficult to access and often not available in library or other collections. These data often relate to individual academic institutions and are circulated only within the institution. Governmental and other reports are frequently issued only for limited audiences, and there is no effort to disseminate them more widely. Similarly, many of the studies commissioned by the World Bank are kept confidential and are unavailable to the research community.

After almost a century of intellectual development as a field of research, higher education has, however, built up a sizable literature, a network of communications, and a community of researchers. Those responsible for planning and administering higher education institutions and systems are beginning to recognize the need for data and interpretation. Yet, the field has no widely accepted theories. Policymakers and administrators often do not find research produced by the research community directly applicable. Nonetheless, the field has grown and matured.

A Higher Education Research Infrastructure

The field of higher education research has expanded in large part because conditions have created a need for such research and the means with which to conduct it.[19] The objective circumstances of higher education have changed: expansion of enrollment, staff, and budgets; a focus on the research mission of the universities; and the value of higher education to postindustrial society have all increased the attention paid to higher education in most societies. The following are some of the factors that have contributed to the development of higher education research and to the increasingly complex infrastructure of the field.

As academic institutions expand, they need more information about themselves—such as enrollment trends, statistics concerning student achievement, and data concerning faculty and staff. This data gathering is referred to as "institutional research" and is focused on a single institution but may be relevant to a wider audience.[20] Institutional research offices exist in thousands of academic institutions worldwide—they are common in larger universities in countries such as the United States, Britain, Australia, and Canada and are of growing importance in Europe and Japan. Elsewhere, institutional research is less well organized, but it is commonly carried out as part of the administrative work of universities.[21] Networks of researchers in this field are well organized in North America and Europe.[22] The output of the institutional research offices of individual universities probably constitutes the largest part of research on higher education. However, much of this research is only of local interest, and little of it is made available to a wider audience.

University-based centers or departments with a focus on higher education have been established in a small number of countries to educate higher education professionals and researchers. These departments and academic programs, located mainly in academic institutions in Anglo-Saxon countries, have also been the source of a considerable amount of research. There are probably close to 200 university-based programs worldwide. In the United States alone, close to 100 universities have programs in higher education located in schools of education that provide postbaccalaureate degrees. While many of these U.S. programs are small and without a research emphasis, several have contributed significantly to research in the field—chief among them the University of California at Los Angeles, Pennsylvania State University, the University of Michigan, the University of Pennsylvania, and several others. Prominent European examples are the Center for Higher Education and Work at the Gesamthochschule-Universität Kassel in Germany, the Center for Higher Education Policy Studies at the University of Twente in the Netherlands, and the Institute for Higher Education Studies at the University of London. The centers in Kassel and Twente, for example, have conducted significant research for the European Union and a number of agencies, and have published many research studies. These centers, unlike their American counterparts, do not provide degree-level training for professionals. The Research Institute for Higher Education at Hiroshima University, a similar center at Tsukuba University in Tokyo, and a half dozen new higher education centers at the major national universities are Japanese examples (including Nagoya and Kyoto universities). The prominent Chinese institutions are the Institute for Higher Education at Peking University and the Institute of Higher Education at Xiamen University, although there are more than 400 higher education research institutes around the country. Some of these university-based centers focus mainly on research, others on teaching.

Outside the English-speaking countries, however, there are few academic programs offering degree study in higher education, although the numbers are growing. Some university-based institutes are government funded. For example, the National Center for Postsecondary Improvement, now located at Stanford University in the United States, is funded by the federal government for the purpose of research on improving higher education.

Governments require national data and research for planning in higher education, the allocation of funds, and related purposes. In some countries, national research institutes have been established with funding made available for higher education research and data collection.[23] In some places, government-sponsored agencies assist with higher education reform and innovation. These agencies have responsibility for collecting statistical information on higher education, and some have a research mission as well. Research institutes vary greatly in size, purpose, and orientation. Some are linked with academic institutions, while others are attached to ministries of education. In Japan, for example, the Hiroshima University center is funded by the national government for the purpose of data collection and analysis on Japanese higher education as well as on overseas trends.

State planning and coordinating agencies have been established in many countries, and these organizations sometimes sponsor research and collect statistics to help them in their work. These agencies were established in the 1960s and more recently—during the period of expansion of higher education—to meet the need for relevant information and analysis. Not surprisingly, the former "socialist" countries of Central and Eastern Europe and the former Soviet Union, with their centrally planned economies, established large higher education research agencies to provide the data needed for centralized planning and development, as well as for coordination with other economic and political entities.[24] The Higher Education Funding Council for England (HEFC) is the governmental body responsible in that country for allocating funds to academic institutions and also conducts limited research. Scotland has a similar agency. In the United States, most state governments have coordinating bodies for state-supported higher education, which in some cases do collect and publish research as well. The U.S. federal government, through such agencies as the National Center for Educational Statistics, collects data, publishes analyses of higher education developments, and commissions some research. The Indian University Grants Commission has a research function and a responsibility for allocating research and other funds from the national government to higher educational institutions. The semigovernmental Korean Council on University Education has funding and coordinating responsibilities and also sponsors some research. Other countries have similar agencies and organizations.

University associations in many countries engage in research domestically and to some extent internationally. In the United States, the American Council on Education, the National Association of State Universities and Land Grant Colleges, the Council of Graduate Schools, and many other entities have made research and the dissemination of information part of their missions.[25] The German Hochschulrektorenkonferenz sponsors publications and supports some research. The Association of Indian Universities publishes books and journals and supports some research. These are just a few examples of university-sponsored organizations that conduct research and analysis as well as representing the interests of academic institutions to government and the public. On a regional basis, the Association of African Universities and the European Rectors Conference disseminate information and occasionally conduct research. The International Association of Universities has promoted research and dissemination at an international level.[26]

International and regional organizations are among the most effective in bringing together specialists on higher education as well as providing a forum for discussing higher education issues. UNESCO, established in 1946, has from the beginning been involved with postsecondary education—sponsoring many conferences, stimulating research, and publishing books and reports. It has also established regional offices that focus on higher education, including the UNESCO European Center for Higher Education and the Center for Higher Education in Latin America and the Caribbean (CRESALC). In recent years, the World Bank has sponsored research and issued publications concerning higher education. While much of its research concerns World Bank loans and projects and thus is unavailable to the public, a growing number of studies have been published and now constitute some of the best sources for research on higher education on developing countries.[27] OECD, an agency representing the industrialized nations, has long been involved with higher education research and related activities, and has produced a series of country-based studies that provides useful analysis.[28] The OECD also sponsors the Institutional Management in Higher Education initiative and a journal, *Higher Education Management*. Some parts of the world, such as Southeast Asia, do not have active regional organizations, while others, such as Latin America, have a range of research-based groups.[29]

The perceived need for data and analysis has spurred a plethora of organizations and agencies that provide information. Many are new, reflecting the emerging nature of the field, and exist at institutional, national, regional, and international levels. There is relatively little interaction or cooperation among them. Almost the entire infrastructure of higher education research is a post–World War II phenomenon—a product of expansion in the 1960s and of the emphasis on accountability and assessment as postsecondary education experienced financial problems in the 1980s and 1990s.

The Information Infrastructure in Higher Education
With the proliferation of research centers and agencies concerned with higher education administration, coordination, and policy, a network of publications and other means of communicating the knowledge base in higher education has developed. In many countries journals relating to

higher education have been launched that are aimed at researchers and other professionals in the field. The listing of journals included in this inventory provides an indication of the scope of publications. While their circulation is usually limited, these journals do provide access to relevant research, current data, and analysis on the field. There are also many publishers who consistently publish books and monographs in the field of higher education. The Internet has stimulated the development of websites devoted to higher education, which are now significant sources of data and analysis. A few journals are now available on-line to subscribers as well, although there are no solely electronic journals in higher education as yet.

It is not possible, in the context of this essay, to discuss all of the national, regional, and international publications in the field. However, it is useful to focus on selected sources of information. As noted earlier, much of the higher education research base is not easily accessible either because it has not been published or has been issued by institutions only in limited editions. This "gray literature" is generally not included in standard indexes or reference sources. Much of the material deals only with specific academic institutions, but some are institutional planning documents and studies, reform reports, and similar policy-related materials with wider relevance. Unfortunately, there is no clearinghouse or data center for "gray literature" in higher education. The ERIC (Educational Resources Information Center) bibliographies and database, sponsored by the U.S. Department of Education, is the single largest source of bibliographical information; it includes some of this below-the-radar literature. However, ERIC collects mainly American material and is of limited relevance to the rest of the world.

In addition to ERIC, several bibliographical sources in higher education exist. *Contents Pages in Education*—a journal that covers scholarly and research journals in education, including higher education—is an important worldwide resource, although it is limited to publications in English. Several abstracting journals dealing with higher education publications in Britain and the United States have good coverage of their respective countries. However, as pointed out earlier, these publications include only material published in journals or, in some cases, books.

Additional contributions to the research literature can be found in two encyclopedias on higher education in an international context.[30] These reference volumes provide not only worldwide coverage of higher education but also include "state-of-the-art" essays on key topics in the research literature. They are benchmarks for the field, showing that the study of higher education has come of age and has produced a coherent and reasonably comprehensive body of research. An earlier international encyclopedia, published in 1976, helped to establish higher education studies as a field of inquiry.[31] There are also several national encyclopedias or handbooks.

The number of research and other journals focusing on higher education has expanded in the past several decades. Most of the internationally circulated journals in the field have been established since the 1960s. Just in the past few years, new internationally focused specialized journals dealing with assessment, quality issues, technology, and teaching in higher education have been founded, reflecting important new trends in the field.[32] A number of well-established more broadly focused internationally circulated magazines and newspapers relating to higher education provide news, commentary, and reporting on research and policy initiatives. The most important of these are the *Chronicle of Higher Education* in the United States, the *Times Higher Education Supplement* (*The Higher*) in Britain, and *L'monde d'éducation* in France. All three publications have significant international circulation, and all report on international developments as well as national news. There are also many national periodicals with similar aims— for example, *University News* in India, *Das Hochschulwesen* in Germany, *Universitas* in Italy, *Universidades 2000* in Mexico, and others.

There are a small number of internationally circulated research journals in higher education. These publications set the standard internationally for research and disseminate key scholarship in the field. All are published in English, and most are edited and published in the United States or Western Europe. *Higher Education, Higher Education Management, Minerva,* and *Higher Education Policy* are the most explicitly international of the journals. Other periodicals are *Studies in Higher Education* and *Higher Education Review* (Britain), the *Journal of Higher Education, Review of Higher Education,* and *Research in Higher Education* (United States). *Higher Education in Europe* and the *European Journal of Education* focus on higher education from a mainly European perspective.

Hundreds of national journals also exist. In general, these do not circulate outside the country of origin. Among the most important of these journals, are the *IDE Journal* in Japan, *Universidad Futura* in Mexico, the *Canadian Journal of Higher Education,* and *Change* and *Lingua Franca* in the United States.[33] Others, such as the *Journal of Higher Education* in India and the *South African Journal of Higher Education* are less well known internationally but publish valuable material. There are approximately 400 journals devoted to higher education in China alone—all but a half dozen published by individual universities and seldom circulated outside the sponsoring institution.[34]

The publication of books on higher education has also increased significantly. Several publishers now specialize in books on higher education. Examples include Jessica Kingsley Publishers, Pergamon Press, and the

Open University Press in Britain, Routledge/Falmer Publishers, Jossey-Bass, Oryx Press, Agathon Press, and the Johns Hopkins University Press in the United States; Tamagawa University Press in Japan; Campus Verlag in Germany; and Lemma Publishers in Holland, among others. Research institutions and other organizations also publish books and monographs in the field—these include the Research Institute on Higher Education at Hiroshima University in Japan, the Russian Research Institute on Higher Education in Moscow, the American Council on Education in the United States, and others. The Society for Research into Higher Education in the United Kingdom has perhaps the largest series of books in the field of higher education, published in cooperation with the Open University Press.

A Map of the Field
Although the field of higher education studies did not exist until after the Second World War II, a small but insightful literature on higher education has existed and has shaped thinking about the nature of higher education. For example, Hastings Rashdall's history of the medieval university remains a classic of scholarship.[35] The Arab scholars who established the Al-Azhar University in Cairo thought about higher education, as did those responsible for the establishment of universities in medieval Europe.[36] Philosophers such as John Henry Newman[37] and sociologists Max Weber[38] and Emile Durkheim[39] analyzed higher education. Psychologist G. Stanley Hall is said to have taught the first academic course on higher education, at Clark University, in 1893.[40] Visionary academic leaders, from Alexander von Humboldt to Robert M. Hutchins, have articulated their views on the development of the university. Plato and Aristotle discussed advanced education in their writings, and Confucius had a profound impact on the nature of higher education in China and East Asia.

One of the first formal policy-focused studies was Abraham Flexner's influential report on American medical education, which inspired significant policy reforms in the training of physicians.[41] Later, Flexner wrote one of the first books using a comparative approach to study higher education and recommend policy. His *Universities: American, English, German* was aimed at stimulating reforms in American higher education.[42] One of the first government-sponsored reports on higher education was conducted as part of a reform effort in 1911 at the University of Calcutta in India. This document, and several others commissioned to shape higher education policies in colonial areas, influenced the later use of official reports on higher education.[43] There is a rich literature on the history of higher education, focusing especially on the history of individual universities.

This brief review indicates that although the research has been scattered and lacking in focus, influential work of high quality has been produced in the century or more prior to the emergence of a field of higher education studies in the mid-20th century. Scholars and researchers worked within the confines of their disciplines, although with little if any communication across fields of study. Thus, higher education was hardly a neglected subject, although it did not emerge as a field of scholarly and research analysis until quite recently.

At approximately the same time that higher education was developing as an interdisciplinary field, researchers in other subspecialties were dealing with topics relating to the higher education enterprise. For example, the sociology of science grew dramatically as researchers turned to analyzing how research networks in the scientific disciplines work, how research is carried out, and how scientists and researchers measure productivity and influence in science. This subfield established its own journals and other infrastructures. The sociology of science and the history of science relate only indirectly to higher education studies.[44] Researchers in the two disciplines rarely come into contact, and the science studies literature is seldom used by higher education scholars. Similarly, the subfield of bibliometrics, which examines the impact of research and the diffusion of scholarly work, is not generally consulted by researchers in the field of higher education.

The links are closer between the field of higher education and that of science policy studies. The journal *Minerva*, especially during the editorship of Edward Shils, straddled both fields and attempted to address the concerns of researchers in both areas. Others, such as *Technology and Society*, cover this intersection of fields. However, there has been little cross-fertilization, and only a limited number of researchers pay attention to both fields. Science policy is central to higher education now because it seeks to examine research networks that extend beyond the universities—for example to university-industry linkages.

More integrally related to higher education is the community of researchers involved with planning for college and universities. This field has its own professional organizations and a small research network.[45] Higher education management has also emerged quite recently as a distinct subspecialty, but in this case there are strong links with higher education research. The OECD's *Higher Education Management* journal provides an international perspective on this topic. *Planning in Higher Education*, an American journal, and *Tertiary Education and Management*, published in Britain, also focus on administrative and leadership issues. Because of the increasing complexity of academic institutions and the growing professionalization of university administration, there is a growing interest in management issues. So far, there seem to be few links between the broader field of management studies and higher education.[46] Management studies and business administration actually have a special relevance to higher education.

Another strand of research relates to international study and international students. The internationalization of higher education has become a topic of interest in many countries. The European Union, through TEMPUS and other programs, has fostered international study and scholarly exchange. There are more than one million students studying outside their home countries and numerous visiting scholars and researchers. The issues relating to international study are of increasing relevance in a globalized academic environment.[47] Organizations such as the National Association for Foreign Student Affairs in the United States, the European Association for International Education, the Canadian Bureau of International Education, and other groups sponsor research—much of it applied and intended to improve international education programs and exchanges.[48] A new publication, *Journal of Studies in International Education*, provides a focus for this research area. The Institute of International Education has published a series of studies focusing on international education issues.[49]

The international centers of the field control most of the publications, and the major research paradigms originate mainly in the major English-speaking nations, which play a central role in defining the foci of the field. Other parts of the world are to a considerable extent peripheral in terms of setting research agendas and determining major trends. Approximately 75 percent of the world's internationally circulated research in the field of higher education emanates from the United States, Britain, and Australia. In the 1990s, the research communities in such countries as Japan, the Netherlands, China, and Germany did, however, grow in size and scope. Initiatives on the Pacific Rim and, to a lesser extent, in Latin America are indications of growth of higher education research and analysis and the establishment of centers and institutes.[50] While the major English-speaking countries continue to dominate the research networks, the balance is changing as other countries build up research capacity in higher education. The field of higher education displays the same geographical inequality as most scientific disciplines, although probably to a lesser extent than in many fields.

Institutional Research

Institutional research is in greater demand as academic institutions grow and as accountability becomes a more central part of governmental agendas worldwide. Data collected as part of institutional research is rarely reported outside the institution and is frequently restricted.[51] For the most part, institutional reporting on such issues as trends in enrollments, student achievement, and fiscal arrangements have little relevance to a wider audience despite the importance of this data for institutional planning and assessment. Although in some cases institutional research data would have applications beyond the direct and immediate institutional needs, their potential is almost never exploited. For example, the comparison of institutional trends within sectors in a country, regionally, or internationally, might be useful. The idea of "benchmarking" institutional trends in higher education is beginning to be implemented in many countries, and institutional research data are useful in this exercise.

The institutional research community is well organized in only a few countries; outside of Europe and North America, few international links exist. Outlets for publication and analysis of data based on institutional research are limited in numbers. In the United States, the Association for Institutional Research provides a professional forum for the research community, although there is a lack of coordination between the institutional researchers and the wider higher education research community. The European Association for Institutional Research recently broadened its mission to encompass higher education research. There are no international journals on institutional research and few forums for international discussion in this field other than at conferences held in the United States or Europe. Institutional research is coming into its own as a subfield of higher education research, and is increasingly part of the mainstream.

The Education of the Administrative Estate
Academic administration has become increasingly complex. As institutions have become larger and more complex, providing many more services and offering more specialties, the need to provide skilled management and administration has grown as well. It is no longer possible for amateurs without training or a serious interest in administration to run modern universities.

Senior academic leaders, including presidents, rectors, vice chancellors, and deans still come from the ranks of the senior professoriate. They typically have no specific training for the administrative roles they perform, and most who assume these offices return to teaching and research after serving one or two terms. The United States is somewhat unique in that many senior academic administrators enter into administrative careers, going from one senior post to another, often at different institutions, and do not return to the professoriate.

The situation is different for the large and growing number of middle-level managers in higher education, and it is here that major expansion has taken place. It is not surprising that the United States, with the largest, most diversified and complex academic system, developed this new profession first. There has been a recognition that this new cadre of administrators require training for their jobs. The field of higher education administration developed after World War II, and by 2000, more than 100 American universities offered graduate level specialties in higher education.[52] The first subspeciality in higher education was that of student personnel administration—which provides training for those responsible for counseling and guidance, student extracurricular activities, and administering dormitories and other student facilities. Later, training for general academic administration and the development of such subspecialties as financial administration, and university legal affairs evolved. Today, higher education programs are offered as graduate (postbaccalaureate) degrees, and serve both entry-level students seeking administrative careers as well as seasoned administrators wishing to upgrade their skills and qualify for higher office. Traditionally, higher education graduates were hired for lower- and middle-level management positions in colleges and universities, as well as posts in government agencies dealing with higher education, think tanks, and related jobs. Institutional researchers often hold graduate degrees in higher education. In recent years, higher education graduates have assumed presidencies and other upper management positions, especially in the community college sector and in lower-ranking four-year institutions.

As of 2000, higher education administration is a well-established field. The programs are housed in schools of education in many of the top universities in the United States. Faculty members in these programs provide much of the published research on higher education and are often called on to serve as consultants and advisers for postsecondary institutions.

Similar programs have been established in several other countries, although growth has been surprisingly slow given the expansion in the number of administrators worldwide. The major English-speaking countries of the United Kingdom, Canada, and Australia now have university-based programs that provide training for academic administrators. A few other countries, such as Japan, are beginning to provide training for administrators, and others are beginning to think about it. It is likely that this field will continue to grow in response to the need for career-level administrators knowledgeable about higher education and schooled in the application of management theory, legal issues, student psychological development, and other social science–based disciplines.

Future Trends

Higher education research is recognized as useful in analyzing the challenges facing higher education institutions. Yet, many in government and in academic administration feel that higher education research does not directly address the day-to-day problems faced by managers in postsecondary education. This is probably an inevitable and unresolvable tension in the field. Some of the research produced by higher education scholars examines fundamental issues such as the relationship of academe to government or is designed to build up the methodologies or knowledge base in the field. This type of research is thus largely irrelevant to the search for immediate solutions to problems faced by academic institutions or systems. Practitioners and the public are often impatient for results. At the same time, at least some of this broadly based work is a necessary underpinning for more applied research. In fact, the tension between the two poles in the field is, in many ways, a strength. Those in control of research funding are insufficiently committed to the work of building a solid knowledge base, methodological rigor, and theoretical perspectives in the field. At the same time, there is often an unnecessary distance between university-based researchers and the "users" of research in academic administration or government agencies.[53]

The following trends may characterize the future development of the field of higher education studies:

1. The field will expand into countries and regions where it is now either weak or nonexistent. Recognition of the value of information and analysis about postsecondary education will stimulate continued growth in the field. There will be an expansion of the sources of information—journals, books, and newsletters, etc.—in these new research communities.

2. The current centers of research in higher education may lose some of their dominance, in part because of financial cutbacks in higher education and in part because of the development of new research communities in other regions. Despite these trends, the traditional centers in the field will in all likelihood retain their influence.

3. There is a growing focus on the process of teaching, learning, and assessment in higher education. Instruction, the central element in higher education, is imperfectly understood. In part to improve learning and create better ways to measure the results of higher education, there has been increased interest in the evaluation of teaching, measurement of instructional results, and assessment.

4. The gulf between institutional research and other research on higher education remains considerable. The field would benefit from better links between institutional research and the broader research community. The tension between basic and applied research in higher education will continue, with some confusion regarding the audience for research in the field.

5. Higher education is definitely an interdisciplinary field of inquiry. It will not emerge as a separate scientific discipline.

6. The recognition that academic institutions require a trained cadre of administrators will mean the expansion worldwide of university-based training programs in higher education. Some programs may offer academic degrees and require a rigorous curriculum of studies. Others may consist of shorter courses, seminars, or other academic experiences. This will contribute to a larger research community, since many of the faculty members appointed to teaching positions in these programs may also engage in research.

7. Large-scale research, either within one country or internationally, will be limited due to lack of funds.

8. A better balance between the research agenda of higher education researchers and the users of that research will strengthen the research community. There is a tendency for funding agencies to provide support for research that will yield specific answers to questions of immediate concern. In the long run, this approach weakens the knowledge base. This conflict between "basic" and "applied" research is by no means limited to the field of higher education.

9. Strengthening regional and international networks for reporting data and research will improve communication and expand the field. Organizations, databases, and publications that bring together researchers from different countries will also expand. In short, there is a need to build better networks in the higher education research community. Regionally based publications, both journals and books, require additional support.

10. Comprehensive, comparable, and accurate international data concerning higher education are central to both research and for policy development. Stronger international organizations can provide a basis for improved data collection.

11. Bringing currently peripheral research communities, such as those in smaller countries or in regions without any tradition of research in the field, into the international mainstream is a key priority.

12. Better integration of the institutional research community as well as institutional research into the higher education research system will help this largely ignored part of the higher education research community to

become part of the mainstream. In Europe, the European Association for Institutional Research (EAIR) has linked the two streams in the field.

13. Improvement of links between the higher education research community—now located in faculties of education in universities, in government agencies, and in independent research centers—and with researchers in the social sciences will strengthen the field of higher education.

Conclusion
Higher education research and training in the field have developed impressively over the past three decades. The organized infrastructures of a research area have emerged. There is a research community in government, academe, and in research organizations that has impressive geographical scope and increasing sophistication. The field has contributed significantly to a broader understanding and recognition of the importance of the university and more specifically of the complexities of academe in a period of expansion. It has contributed insights into the specific policy needs of academic administrators and political authorities. Higher education has legitimized itself as a research area within educational studies, gaining acceptance among those who are responsible for the leadership of higher education. A small but growing number of social scientists have taken on higher education as an area of research. This, too, has improved the literature and has helped to provide an analytical base.

In a number of countries, university-based training programs for academic administrators have been established. These programs have contributed to the expansion and legitimization of higher education research. Some of the graduates of these programs become researchers in the field—although most go into academic administration or policymaking positions, where they make use of research results. This trend is likely to extend to other countries, as there is a demonstrated need for professionally trained administrators for large postsecondary institutions and systems.

The research output in the field ranges from what the social scientists would call "middle-range theory" to the most applied data gathering pertaining to a specific problem at a single university. Social scientists from a number of disciplines have attempted to theorize about the nature of the university, about the dynamic of leadership in higher education, and about the nature of teaching and learning. However, there are few accepted theories that apply generally to postsecondary institutions. The quality of the research is also mixed, as is probably inevitable for a field in its early stages of development.

The field of higher education research is poised for change. It is gaining importance and legitimacy in parts of the world traditionally underserved. Expansion will be slower in the traditional centers as resources have become limited although research is still needed. The field has achieved a measure of legitimacy in the academic community, and it is now accepted as important by policymakers in national as well as regional and international organizations.

Notes

1. This essay is a revised and updated version of Philip G. Altbach, "Research on Higher Education: Global Perspectives," in *Higher Education Research at the Turn of the New Century: Structures, Issues and Trends*, ed. Jan Sadlak and Philip G. Altbach (New York: Garland, 1997), 3–24. See also Ulrich Teichler and Jan Sadlak, eds., *Higher Education Research: Its Relationship to Policy and Practice* (Oxford: Pergamon, 2000).
2. Eric Ashby, *Any Person, Any Study: An Essay on Higher Education in the United States* (New York: McGraw-Hill, 1971).
3. Martin Trow, "The Expansion and Transformation of Higher Education," *International Review of Education* 18, no. 1 (1972): 61–83.
4. *Higher Education in Developing Countries: Peril and Promise* (Washington, D.C.: World Bank, 2000).
5. For an earlier consideration of similar topics, see Philip G. Altbach, "Perspectives on Comparative Higher Education: A Survey of Research and Literature," in *Higher Education in International Perspective: A Survey and Bibliography*, ed. Philip G. Altbach and David Kelly (London: Mansell, 1985), 3–54. See also Jan Klucyczynski, "Research on Higher Education in European Socialist Countries," in *Higher Education Research at the Turn of the New Century: Structures, Issues and Trends*, ed. Sadlak and Altbach, 55–88.
6. See Paul L. Dressel and Lewis B. Mayhew, *Higher Education as a Field of Study* (San Francisco: Jossey Bass, 1974) for a discussion of the origin of the field in the United States and of the debate about higher education as a discipline. For one of the few other studies of the development of the field, Xu Yu, "The Development of Higher Education in China" (Ph.D. diss., State University of New York at Buffalo, 1995), which focuses on similar debates in China, where many of the first generation of researchers attempted to establish higher education as a discipline.
7. Lord Robbins, *The University in the Modern World* (London: Macmillan, 1966).
8. In the early 1970s, under the leadership of Clark Kerr, the Carnegie Commission on Higher Education sponsored more than 50 volumes that provided an impressive research base for American higher education. The Commission also issued a number of policy-oriented reports. At the end of the decade, again under Kerr's leadership, the Carnegie Council on Policy

Studies in Higher Education sponsored additional studies and reports. These impressive efforts were funded by the Carnegie Foundation for the Advancement of Teaching. The Foundation continues to be actively involved in sponsoring research, and has a special interest in policy-oriented studies. At about the same time, the Leverhulme Trust in Britain sponsored a dozen or more volumes relating to British higher education in the aftermath of the Robbins Report.

9. See, for example, *The Report of the National Commission on the Cost of Higher Education: Straight Talk about College Costs and Prices* (Phoenix, Ariz.: Oryx, 1998).

10. See *World Education Report, 1993* (Paris: UNESCO, 1993) for some international statistical information. See also UNESCO's *Statistical Yearbooks* for a range of information relating to education and other cultural developments.

11. See *Higher Education in Developing Countries: Promise and Peril,* for a very useful statistical appendix covering enrollments and related issues worldwide.

12. *Higher Education: The Lessons of Experience* (Washington, D.C.: World Bank, 1994), and Jamil Salmi and Adriaan M. Verspoor, eds., *Revitalizing Higher Education* (Oxford: Pergamon, 1994).

13. Lene Buchert and Kenneth King, eds., *Learning from Experience: Policy and Practice in Aid to Higher Education* (The Hague: Center for the Study of Education in Developing Countries, 1995).

14. *Policy Paper for Change and Development in Higher Education* (Paris: UNESCO, 1995).

15. For example, see *Trends and Issues Facing Higher Education in Asia and the Pacific* (Bangkok: UNESCO Principal Regional Office for Asia and the Pacific, 1991), and *Higher Education in Africa: Trends and Challenges for the 21st Century* (Dakar: UNESCO Dakar Regional Office, n.d.).

16. *Higher Education in Developing Countries: Promise and Peril.*

17. See Philip G. Altbach, ed., *The International Academic Profession: Portraits from 14 Countries* (Princeton, N.J.: Carnegie Foundation for the Advancement of Teaching, 1996), for a recent example of a comparative study.

18. Examples of this research trend include Guy Neave and Frans van Vught, eds., *Government and Higher Education Relationships Across Three Continents: The Winds of Change* (Oxford: Pergamon, 1994) and Philip G. Altbach, ed., *Private Prometheus: Private Higher Education and Development in the 21ˢᵗ Century* (Westport, Conn.: Greenwood, 2000).

19. In 1981, a directory of research institutes in higher education was published by UNESCO. See Jan Sadlak, ed., *Directory of Institutes and Organiza-*

tions in Research on Higher Education (Geneva: International Bureau of Education, 1981).

20. Institutional researchers have organized themselves into several national and regional groups. The Association for Institutional Research in the United States is one of the largest research-oriented organizations in the world. In Europe, the European Association for Institutional Research has recently expanded its focus beyond institutional research to broader higher education issues.

21. In China, for example, there are some 400 higher education centers and institutes attached to universities. Many of these provide institutional research data and analysis to their sponsoring institutions.

22. In the United States, the Association for Institutional Research has been active for several decades, while the European Association for Institutional Research is newer and reflects a growing interest in the topic.

23. Examples of national organizations focused on higher education research and information are, among many others, the Hochschul-Information-System (HIS) in Germany, the Research Institute on Higher Education in Russia, and the National Center for Educational Statistics in the United States.

24. For a detailed discussion of this topic, see Jan Kluczynski, "Research on Higher Education in European Socialist Countries."

25. The National Center for Higher Education, located at 1 Dupont Circle in Washington, D.C. is well known as the headquarters of many of the Washington-based associations representing the higher education community. The American Council on Education, representing the presidents of a large number of American universities, is the leading organization at 1 Dupont Circle.

26. The International Association of Universities (IAU) has been active recently in sponsoring publications on higher education issues, restoring a tradition established earlier. IAU sponsors an influential book series, published by Pergamon Publishers as well as the journal *Higher Education Policy*.

27. For example, see William S. Saint, *Universities in Africa: Strategies for Stabilization and Revitalization* (Washington, D.C.: World Bank, 1992). This is one of many valuable data-based studies on higher education issues.

28. Most recently, see *Reviews of National Policies for Education: Tertiary Education and Research in the Russian Federation* (Paris: OECD, 1999). See also *The Response of Higher Education Institutions to Regional Needs* (Paris: OECD, 1999).

29. The Regional Institute for Higher Education and Development (RIHED) was at one time active in providing a research base for higher education in

Southeast Asia. In the past decade, however, there is no research or policy institution active in the region.

30. Burton Clark and Guy Neave, eds., *The Encyclopedia of Higher Education,* 4 vols. (Oxford: Pergamon, 1992); Philip G. Altbach, ed., *International Higher Education: An Encyclopedia,* 2 vols. (New York: Garland, 1991). The Clark and Neave encyclopedia was updated and published in a CD-ROM version, combined with Pergamon's 10-volume education encyclopedia, in 1999.

31. Asa Knowles, ed., *Encyclopedia of Higher Education,* 10 vols. (San Francisco: Jossey-Bass, 1976).

32. Carfax Publishing Ltd. in England, now part of the Taylor and Francis group, has established new quarterly journals on teaching, assessment, and technology in higher education.

33. A key bibliographical resource for locating articles in journals in English worldwide is *Contents Pages in Education,* a bimonthly listing of articles in hundreds of educational periodicals.

34. It is also the case that many Chinese higher education journals are officially "restricted" and cannot be circulated outside of China.

35. Hastings Rashdall, *The Universities of Europe in the Middle Ages,* 3 vols. (Oxford: Oxford University Press, 1895).

36. George Makdisi, *The Rise of Colleges: Institutions of Learning in Islam and the West* (Edinburgh: Edinburgh University Press, 1981).

37. John Henry Newman, *The Idea of a University* (London: Longman, Green, 1899).

38. Edward Shils, ed., *Max Weber on Universities: The Power of the State and the Dignity of the Academic Calling in Imperial Germany* (Chicago: University of Chicago Press, 1974).

39. Emile Durkheim, *The Evolution of Educational Thought* (London: Routledge and Kegan Paul, 1977), first published in French in 1938 and originally written by Durkheim in 1904–5.

40. Lester Goodchild, "G. Stanley Hall and the Study of Higher Education," *Review of Higher Education* 20 (fall 1996): 69–100.

41. Abraham Flexner, *Medical Education in the United States and Canada* (New York: Carnegie Foundation for the Advancement of Teaching, 1910).

42. Abraham Flexner, *Universities: American, English, German* (New York: Oxford University Press, 1930).

43. Eric Ashby, *Universities: British, Indian, African: A Study in the Ecology of Higher Education* (Cambridge: Harvard University Press, 1966).

44. See, for example, Joseph Ben-David, *Scientific Growth: Essays on the Social Organization and Ethos of Science* (Berkeley: University of California Press, 1991).

45. The Society for College and University Planning in the United States is probably the largest organization in this area. It publishes its own journal and holds professional meetings.

46. For one of the few contributions by researchers in management studies, see Michael D. Cohen and James D. March, *Leadership and Ambiguity: The American College President* (Boston: Harvard Business School Press, 1986).

47. For an overview of the issues, see Philip G. Altbach, David H. Kelly, and Y. G. M. Lulat, *Research on Foreign Students and International Study: An Overview and Bibliography* (New York: Praeger, 1985).

48. Similar organizations exist in Japan and in several other countries.

49. The Institute of International Education is an American organization with branch offices in many countries. Its main responsibilities include the administration of exchange programs between the United States and other countries. It also sponsored research on international exchanges and related topics. See, for example Craufurd D. Goodwin and Michael Nacht, *Missing the Boat: The Failure to Internationalize American Higher Education* (New York: Cambridge University Press, 1991).

50. The Institute for the Study of the University at the National Autonomous University of Mexico (UNAM) as well as a research group at the Autonomous Metropolitan University and as the Association of Mexican Universities (ANUIES), all in Mexico City, now constitute an impressive research community.

51. Public higher education governing boards in about 15 states in the United States have developed and implemented accountability and performance measurement schemes, and information is collected and published concerning funding, productivity, quality, standards, and related issues.

52. The Association for the Study of Higher Education (ASHE) is the professional organization representing faculty members working in the field of higher education. The American College Personnel Association (ACPA) represents professionals who focus on student services.

53. In the United States as well as other countries there has been considerable criticism of the output of the higher education research community for its lack of relevance to the needs of administrators and policymakers.

CHAPTER 2

Inventory Usage Guide

Philip G. Altbach and David Engberg

This inventory provides details on 187 higher education centers, institutes, and programs. The entries are organized alphabetically, first by country, then by the name of the center, institute, or program. (See the "Country Index" for country-specific page numbers.) U.S. entries, the inventory's largest subgroup, are alphabetized first by state, then by center, institute, or program name.

Every effort has been made to make the inventory user friendly, clear, and complete. Nevertheless, certain entries are more thorough than others. For instance, since most higher education centers do not include a teaching function, they are listed here without entries for courses, and student enrollments. Occasionally, the information received was incomplete. In such cases we have tried to obtain the missing data. As a rule, we have kept the editing of entries to a minimum.

Below are some comments about categories of information in the entries:

• *Name*. Formal center, institute, and program names are listed either alone or after their parent or sponsoring institutions. If available, national language and organizational acronyms are also included.
• *Address*. Addresses are listed in the format in which they were received.

• *Telephone/fax number*. Non-U.S. phone and fax numbers are listed as received. U.S. telephone and fax numbers have been standardized, with dashes separating area code.

• *Website*. All website URLs are complete.

• *Date of establishment*. There exist inconsistencies in date of establishment information. While some entries indicate when a particular higher education program or center was established, others refer to the establishment of the parent organization—a university, for instance.

• Funding source. Most of the places listed in the inventory receive their operational funding from state or federal government sources. For programs and centers affiliated with universities, we have simply listed the university as the funding source.

• *Staff*. Staff members in Asian countries are listed by last name first.

• *Current publications*. We received bibliographic information on textbooks, readings, and journals in a variety of formats. We have attempted to standardize these items.

CHAPTER 3

Inventory of Higher Education Programs, Institutes, and Centers

Philip G. Altbach and David Engberg

Australia

Australian National University, Policy Research Unit in Higher Education, Centre for Continuing Education

Address: ACT, 0221, Australia

Telephone: 61 6249 4623; 61 6249 3256
Fax: 61 6249 4959
E-mail: don.anderson@anu.edu.au; richard.johnson@anu.edu.au

Date established: 1992
Major source of funding: University

Organizational focus:
> Our focus is higher education policy. We undertake two or three projects a year on questions of national (and occasionally international) interest; almost all in response to requests from government agencies. Recent projects (with publications actual or pending) have been: Performance-based Funding of Universities; University Autonomy in Twenty Countries; Qualifications of Australian Academics; The Equity Impli-

cations of Tuition Fees for Participation in Postgraduate Courses; and The Practice of Strategic Planning. A current interest is "how can anyone know what a university's degree standards really are?" We also run a seminar series for senior academics and policy advisers, and provide a point of reference for visitors to ANU who share our professional interests. All members of the Unit are visiting fellows, having been granted the designation by ANU following retirement from salaried posts in university or government.

Staff (name • rank/title):
1. Richard Johnson • professor
2. Don Anderson • professor
3. Bruce Milligan
4. Colin Plowman
5. Geoff Caldwell
6. Larry Saha

Griffith University, Griffith Institute for Higher Education

Address: Mt. Gravatt Campus, Griffith University, Queensland, 4111, Australia

Phone: (+ 61 7) 3875 5982
Fax: (+ 61 7) 3875 5998
Website: http://www.gu.edu.au/centre/gihe/home.html

Date established: 1993
Major source of funding: University

Organizational focus:
The Griffith Institute for Higher Education is Griffith University's center for academic staff development and the study of higher education. GIHE is recognized nationally and internationally for its contributions to the practice of academic staff development and its research. We offer an integrated range of postgraduate programs in higher education, including an internationally accredited qualification in university teaching. We provide practical support to help academic staff improve the quality of their students' learning, enhance their teaching effectiveness, convene their courses, and develop their research performance. We help staff respond to the challenge of flexible learning, providing realistic

advice and sharing expertise. We help Griffith's academic managers to develop needed leadership skills. We provide institutional research and policy advice on issues related to higher education policy and performance. We contribute to the international body of knowledge in the field of higher education through our various research and publication programs. We stimulate public debate about policy and practice and sponsor symposia of national importance on critical issues in higher education. We provide a range of income-generating services, such as programs on academic leadership, to other universities and agencies.

Current Publications:
- *A Guide to Higher Degree Supervision.*
- Martin Bridgstock. *Teaching Without Lecturing: A Description and Analysis of an Educational Experiment.*
- *Developing as Researchers,* 2d. ed.
- *Fourth Manual for Conducting Workshops on Postgraduate Supervision of Non-English-Speaking Background Students.* 1996.
- George Lafferty. *Equity, Access and IndependentLlearning: Maximising the Outcomes for Mature Age Students.*
- Diana Laurillard and Don Margetson. *Introducing a Flexible Learning Methodology: Discussion Paper.*
- Paul Ramsden. *Current Educational Reform and the Significance of Problem-based Learning: Using Research on Student Learning to Enhance Educational Quality.*
- Paul Ramsden and Kylie Rixon. *The Course Experience Questionnaire: A Guide to Use, Structure, and Interpretation.*
- *Reaching More Students.* 1995.
- *Subject Evaluation Resource Book.*
- *Teaching Portfolios: Guidelines for Academic Staff.*
- *Third Manual for Conducting Workshops on Postgraduate Supervision.* 1995.
- Ortrun Zuber-Skerritt. *Academic Staff Development in Australia in the 1990s: A Government-driven Quality Agenda.*

Staff (name • rank/title • specialization):
1. Linda Conrad • Acting Director • evaluation of subjects and teaching; documentation of evaluation (teaching portfolios) and research development
2. Margaret Buckridge • Lecturer
3. Gay Crebert • Senior Lecturer • target program for schools and groups; leadership programs

4. Peter Taylor • Senior Lecturer • flexible learning and the design and assessment of courses and subjects
5. Craig Zimitat • Lecturer • staff development for flexible learning
6. John Bain • Professor • universitywide course evaluation
7. Janet Chaseling • Associate Professor
8. Simon Marginson • Adjunct Professor • higher education policy and management
9. Eva Lietzow • Manager • analysis of the Graduate Careers Council of Australia

Student enrollments: Graduate Certificate (20 part-time); M.A. (7 part-time); Ph.D. (1 part-time)

Melbourne, University of, Centre for the Study of Higher Education

Address: Parkville, 3052, Australia

Telephone: 61-3-93-448060
Fax: 61-3-93-447576
E-mail: c.mcinnis@cshe.unimelb.edu.au
Website: http://www.cshe.unimelb.edu.au

Date established: 1967
Major source of funding: University (50%); external consultancies and research grants (50%)

Organizational focus:
The Centre for the Study of Higher Education (CSHE) has four interrelated functions. It provides:
• academic development services to the University of Melbourne, including workshop programs for academics on teaching and learning;
• independent research-based advice on higher education matters within the University;
• national and international consultancies and research on higher education policy; and
• a research-only graduate student program at the master's and doctoral level.

Staff: (name • rank/title • specialization)
1. Craig McInnis • Director, Associate Professor, Chair of Centre for the Study of Higher Education • the student experience of higher education; the academic profession and academic work; quality assurance processes; disciplinary reviews; policy implementation
2. Margaret Powles • Associate Professor • participation and access; postgraduate education; the professoriate; higher education and industry; interface between higher, technical, and further education
3. Richard James • Senior Lecturer • student experience of higher education; evaluation and quality assurance; higher education administration; integration of new technologies into higher education
4. Gabrielle Baldwin • Senior Research Fellow • disciplinary differences in conceptions of teaching and learning and pedagogical practices; core curriculum programs in general arts degrees; the significance of the total university experience in student learning and personal development; the commodification of education and its implications; socioeconomic disadvantage in Australian higher education

Student enrollments: M.Ed. (9 part-time); Ph.D. (10 part-time); D.Ed. (4 part-time)

New England, University of, Centre for Higher Education Management and Policy

Address: Armidale, 2351 NSW, Australia

Telephone: 02-67-732042
Fax: 02-67-733363

Date established: 1996
Major source of funding: University; external research funding

Organizational focus:
The Centre is located in the university's School of Administration and Training. It provides a research function and is associated with the Education, Health, and Professional Studies Faculty.

Staff: (name • rank/title)
1. Grant Harman • Professor
2. Kay Harman • Senior Lecturer

3. V. Lynn Meck • Associate Professor
4. Fiona Wood • Research Fellow
5. Rene Woodward • Project Officer

Key journals:
- *Higher Education*
- *Higher Education Research and Development*
- *Journal of Educational Administration*
- *Journal of Higher Education Policy and Management*

New England, University of, School of Administration and Training

Address: Armidale, 2351 NSW, Australia

Telephone: 02-67-732581
Fax: 02-67-733363

Date established: 1974
Major source of funding: University

Organizational focus:
    The school is an academic unit in the Faculty of Education, Health and
    Professional Studies.

Staff: (name • rank/title)
1. Grant Harman • Professor
2. David Tether • Professor
3. V. Lynn Meck • Associate Professor
4. Susan Davie • Senior Lecturer
5. Kay Harman • Senior Lecturer
6. Ross Harrold • Senior Lecturer

Courses:
- Teacher Education: Foundations and Organization
- Teacher Education: Administration and Management
- Teacher Education: Course Development and Learning Arrangement
- Human Action in Organizations
- Education: Foundations and Theoretical Perspectives

Student enrollments: M.A.(full-time 40, part-time 6); Ph.D. (full-time 14, part-time 2)

Key journals:
- *Higher Education*
- *Higher Education Research and Development*
- *Journal of Educational Administration*
- *Journal of Higher Education Policy and Management*

Southern Cross University, Teaching and Learning Centre

Address: P.O. Box 157, Lismore NSW, 2480, Australia

Telephone: 61 2 66 203160 or 61 2 66 203177
Fax: 61 2 66 203426
E-mail: mhayden@scu.edu.au
Website: http://staff.scu.edu.au/tl/

Date established: 1993
Major source of funding: University; external research and development funds

Organizational focus:
> To enhance the quality of teaching and learning at the University through the implementation of institutional initiatives, the delivery of programs, the conduct of evaluations, and the provision of research (including policy research) services.

Current publications:
- *Communique* (newsletter)

Staff: (name • rank/title)
1. Martin Hayden • Director and Professor
2. Graeme Speedy • Adjunct Professor
3. Sharon Parry • Lecturer
4. Chris Morgan • Lecturer
5. Meg O'Reilly • Lecturer
6. Jenny Pittman • Lecturer

7. Brian Gaffney • Lecturer
8. Jan Regan • Lecturer
9. Lee Dunn • Lecturer
10. Graham Broadhead • Administrator
11. Susan Coleman • Administrator

Student enrollments: M.Ed. 2(2 part-time); Ph.D. (1 full-time)

Key journals:
• *British Journal of Higher Education Studies*
• *Higher Education*
• *Higher Education Research and Development*

Belarus

Belarusian State University, Institute of Higher Education (Respublikanskii Institut Vysshei Shkoly pri Belorusskom Gosudarstvennom Universitete)

Address: Moskovskaya Str. 15, Minsk, 220001, Belarus

Phone: (+375-172) 228315
Fax: (+375-172) 228315
E-mail: gancher@study.minsk.by
Website: http://www.nihe.nibel.by

Date established: 1994
Major source of funding: University; government
Organizational focus:
    The Institute is affiliated with the largest Belarusian University (17,000 students). The institute has defined its mission as enhancing the attainability, effectiveness, and quality of higher education in Belarus. The Institute approaches the task by improving educational management, increasing the professional knowledge and skills of educational staff and administrators; surveying, developing, and disseminating new ideas in the field of higher education; and preparing professionals in the educational field.

The departments and units carry out research in the field of higher education management. The research program topics are systems and social systems theory, qualitative and quantitative methods and procedures for evaluation, forecasting and strategic planning in education, synergetic and evolutionary approaches to social systems, survey of higher education, and new educational technologies.

Staff (name • rank/title • specialization)
1. Igor I. Gancheryonok • Head Professor • higher education management; internationalization of higher education
2. Lyubov I. Shumskaya • Professor • professional pedagogical education
3. Aleksand N. Sizanov • Professor • practical psychology
4. Vladimir F. Klemyato • Lecturer • student affairs

Student enrollments: M.A. (20 full-time, 10 part-time); Ph.D. (5 full-time, 15 part-time)

Key textbooks/readings:
- *Alma Mater* (Russian journal)
- *Higher Education* (Belarusian journal)
- *International Higher Education* (newsletter, USA)
- *Management in Education* (Belarusian journal)
- Russian-language readings (no textbooks are available on higher education management)
- teaching materials prepared by department staff

Brazil

Sao Paulo, University of, Higher Education Research Center (Nucleo de pesquisas sobre ensino superior da Universidade de Sao Paulo) (NUPES)

Address: Rua do Anfiteatro, 181 - Favo 9, Ciadade Universitaria, Sao Paulo, SP Brasil, 05508–900, Brazil

Phone: (00 55) (011) 815-4134; 818-3272
Fax: (00 55) (011) 818-3157
E-mail: nupes@org.usp.br
Website: http://www.usp.br/nupes

Date established: 1989
Major source of funding: Ford Foundation; Ministry of Education

Organizational focus:
NUPES has always pursued the dual objective of promoting higher education research and policy. Ongoing organizational objectives include:
• macro analysis of the main features and evolution of the Brazilian higher education system; and
• research on the history of Brazilian higher education, its private and public sectors, and regional differentiation.

Current publications: (working papers):
• *Brazilian Higher Education Private Sector: The Last Decade*
• *Curriculum of Undergraduate Courses in Odontology*
• *Higher Education Policies Analysis and Proposal*
• *The Private Sector of Higher Education in Latin America: A Comparative Analysis*
• *The Public Universities and Research in Brazil*

Staff (name • rank/title • specialization)
1. Eunice Ribeiro Durham • Professor • higher education policies
2. Helena Sampaio • Researcher • higher education systems
3. Elizabeth Balbachevsky • Researcher • academic profession
4. Veronica Penaloza • Researcher • public higher education and costs and financing
5. Antonio Cesar Perrio de Carvalho • Associate Researcher
6. Carolina M. Bori • Research Director • learning and graduate teaching

Canada

British Columbia, University of, Higher Education Program

Address: 2125 Main Mall, Vancouver, V6J 1Z4, British Columbia, Canada

Phone: 604-822-5374
Fax: 604-822-4244

Website: http://www.edst.educ.ubc.ca/hied.shtml

Major source of funding: University

Organizational focus:
The Higher Education Program focuses on the study of institutions of higher education and their members, activities, and policies. The Program addresses five central themes:
• the historical, philosophical, social, cultural, and economic foundations of higher education;
• the social, cultural, political, and economic contexts in which institutions of higher education operate;
• international and comparative higher education;
• transitions and access in relation to schooling, postsecondary education, and work; and
• policies and practices in contemporary postsecondary educations systems in Canada and abroad, including workplace-oriented education and training.

Staff (name • specialization)
1. Lesley Andres • sociology of education, foundations of higher education, access to postsecondary participation, quantitative and qualitative research methods
2. William Bruneau • foundations, history, and politics of higher education
3. John Chase • institutional research and planning
4. John Dennison • development of community colleges, current problems and issues in higher education
5. Donald Fisher • public policy analysis, academic industry and culture of universities, philanthropy, historical sociology and privatization
6. Daniel Pratt • adult education, instruction and learning in higher education settings, and cultural diversity
7. Kjell Rubenson • public policy analysis, postsecondary education and the labor market
8. Hans G. Schuetze • human resources and economic development, higher education research, educational organization and finance, adult training and retraining, technology policies, higher education-business cooperation, continuing higher education
9. Thomas J. Sork • program planning and evaluation, continuing professional education, planning in educational organizations, community adult education, professional ethics
10. Allison R. Tom • women, education, and employment; gender and the meaning of work

Courses:
- Foundations of Higher Education
- Organization and Administration of Postsecondary Education and Training
- Current issues in Higher Education
- Comparative and International Higher Education

Student enrollments: M.A. (full-time 15–20, part-time 5); Ph.D. 5; other (full-time 8–10, part-time 6–7)

Manitoba, University of, Centre for Higher Education Research and Development

Address: 220 Sinnott Building, 70 Dysart Road, The University of Manitoba, Winnipeg MB, R3T 2N2, Canada

Phone: 204-474-8309
Fax: 204-474-7607
E-mail: cherd@ccm.umanitoba.ca
Website: http://www.umanitoba.ca/centres/cherd

Date established: 1987
Major source of funding: University; development program income

Organizational focus:
The Centre for Higher Education Research and Development (CHERD) is dedicated to research and the professional development of faculty and administrators in postsecondary education. CHERD aims to:
- foster the preparation of scholars and practitioners through the provision of graduate programs;
- further the professional development of teaching, administrative, and mangerial staff; and
- stimulate, nurture, and champion research, particularly in the areas of teaching and learning, and administration and management; and assist and encourage the dissemination of scholarship.

Organization publications:
Research Monographs in Higher Education:
- Gilles G. Nadeau. *Critères et indicateurs de qualité et d'excellence dans les collèges et les universités du Canada: Bilan des trois phases du projet.* 1995.

• Lance Roberts and Rodney A. Clifton. *Measuring the Quality of Life of University Students.* 1991.
• *Criteria and Indicators of Quality and Excellence in Colleges and Universities in Canada: Summary of the Three Phases of the Project*
• Rodney Clifton, Alexander D. Gregor, and Lance Roberts, eds. *The Canadian University in the Twenty-First Century.* 1995.

Occasional Papers in Higher Education:
• Raymond P. Perry, et al. *A Review of Achievement Motivation and Performance in College Students from an Attributional Retraining Perspective.* 1992.
• Gilles G. Nadeau. *Bibliography on Quality and Excellence in Colleges and Universities.* 1993.
• John D. Dennison and Alexander D. Gregor, eds. *Bibliography on Higher Education in Canada and Index to the Canadian Journal of Higher Education, 1971–1995.* 1996.
• Raymond P. Perry, et al. *Faculty in Transition: The Adjustment of New Hires to Postsecondary Institutions.* 1996.
• Alexander D. Gregor. *Higher Education in Manitoba.* 1995.
• Susan Wilcox. *Learning from Our past: The History of Educational Development in Canadian Universities.* 1997.

CHERD/CSSHE Reader Series:
• John D. Dennison, ed. *Community Colleges in Canada.* 1996.
• Alexander D. Gregor, ed. *Graduate Education in Canada.* 1997.
• Rodney A Clifton and Lance Roberts. *Gender Equity in Postsecondary Educational Institutions.* 1998.
• Lesley Andres, ed. *Revisiting the Issue of Access to Higher Education in Canada.* 1998.
• Glen Jones. *The University and the State: Reflections on the Canadian Experience.* 1998.

Other Publications:
• Alexander D. Gregor and Alexander Darling. *Higher Education in Canada: A Changing Scene.*
• Beverly J. Cameron. *Teaching at the University of Manitoba: A Handbook.* 1993.

Staff (name • rank/title • specialization):
   1. Alexander D. Gregor • Professor and Director • history of higher education, public policy
   2. Rodney A. Clifton • Professor • sociology

3. Frank Hechter • Assistant Professor • professional education, learning and teaching
4. David R. Morphy • Professor • student services
5. Raymond P. Perry • Professor • psychology
6. Lance W. Roberts • Professor • sociology
7. Derek Hum • Professor • economics
8. Lynn Taylor • Assistant Professor • faculty development, curriculum, learning and teaching

Student enrollments: M.Ed. (full-time 2, part-time 15); Ph.D. (full-time 1, part-time 3)

Toronto, University of, the Higher Education Group at the University of Toronto/Ontario Institute for Studies in Education

Address: 252 Bloor Street West, Toronto, Ontario, M5S 1V6, Canada

Phone: 416-923-6641, ext. 2308
Fax: 416-926-4741
Website: http://www.oise.utoronto.ca/Bulletin/tps.html#HigherEd

Date established: 1965
Major source of funding: University

Organizational focus:
  To provide postgraduate education for scholars, researchers, and practitioners, and to conduct research in the field of higher education.
  The Institute offers master's and doctoral programs in higher education designed to prepare graduates for, or enhance their, careers in scholarship, research, or practice in the field of higher education. While the focus is on the broad field of higher education, the Institute has particular strengths in the following: higher education policy; governance; professional education, especially in the health sciences; community college leadership; and women and higher education.

Current publications:
  • *Higher Education Perspectives* (annual journal)
  • occasional books

Staff (name • rank/title • specialization):

1. Ruth E. S. Hayhoe • Professor • comparative higher education, international academic relations, higher education in Asia
2. Angela Hildyard • Associate Professor • cognitive psychology, learning and learning systems in higher education
3. Glen A. Jones • Associate Professor • systems and politics of higher education in Canada
4. Daniel W. Lang • Professor • administration, management, planning
5. Jamie-Lynn Magnusson • Associate Professor • teaching and learning, critical pedagogy, inquiry methods, cognition, motivation, assessement
6. Linda Muzzin • Associate Professor • professional education, sociology of the professions
7. Julia Pan • Research Officer • comparative higher education, higher education in Asia
8. Saeed Quazi • Associate Professor Emeritus • strategic and long-range planning, administration, human resource planning and administration
9. Michael L. Skolnik • Professor • higher education systems and policy
10. Cicely Watson • Professor Emeritus • professional education, planning, forecasting, and policy studies for higher education systems

Student enrollments: M.A. (part-time 3, full-time 3); M.Ed. (part-time 32, full-time 8); Ed.D. (part-time 24, full-time 6); Ph.D. (part-time 22, full-time 18)

Courses:
- The History of Higher Education in Canada
- Recurring Issues in Postsecondary Education
- Issues in Medical/Health Professional Education
- The Community College
- Systems of Higher Education
- Strategic and Long-Range Planning for Postsecondary Systems
- Research in Health Professional Education
- Administration of Colleges and Universities
- Evaluation of Knowledge, Clinical Competence, and Professional Behavior in Health Professions
- Institutional Research and Planning
- Education and the Professions
- Curriculum in Instiutions of Higher Education
- Teaching in Institutions of Higher Education
- Conceptions of Learning in Higher Education

- Educational Development: Examination of Strategies for Improving Teaching and Learning in Postsecondary Institutions
- Governance in Higher Education
- Diversity and Differentiation in Postsecondary Education
- The Idea of the University and the College
- The Planning of Facilities in Higher Education
- Comparative Higher Education (Parts I and II)
- The Politics of Higher Education
- Research Methods in Higher Education
- The University under Communism
- International Academic Relations
- Evaulation in Higher Education
- Planning Instruction and Curriculum: Perspectives and Approaches
- Economics of Higher Education
- Public Finance and Higher Education
- Higher Education and the Labor Market
- Higher Education and the Law

Key journals:
- all leading journals in the field of higher education

Chile

Saint Thomas Unviersity, Center for Research and Development of Teaching (Centro de mejoramiento e innovación académica de la Universidad Santo Tomás)

Address: 146 Ejército Street, Santiago, Chile

Phone: (562) 362 4821
Fax: (562) 360 1376
E-mail: rectoria@ust.cl
Website: http://www.ust.cl

Date established: 1997
Major source of funding: University

Organizational focus:
The Center's main focus is to change current teaching practices by defining what students should read before each class session. This change

implies that the professor must define the topic of each session during the semester, plus writing the relevant questions for each document that should be read beforehand, and evaluating the reading (a one-question quiz) at the beginning of each session. The Center helps professors willing to experiment with this approach and carries out impact evaluations in classes delivered by professors experimenting with this approach.

Current Publications:
- Report on the impact of private universities in the last two decades (available on the web site)
- Report on the implementation of a Pre-lecture Syllabus

Staff (Name):
1. Ernesto Schiefelbein • Rector • class management and cost effectiveness
2. Padre José García Patiño • Pro Rector • ethics and teaching of values
3. Eduardo Morales • Vice Rector • evaluation of academic activities
4. Jorge Crossley • Vice Rector • academic development and project design
5. Francisco Javier Recabarren • Secretary General • student affairs

Key Journals:
- American Education Research Journal
- Review of Educational Research

China

Beijing Forestry University, Institute for Studies on Higher Education under the National Forestry Administration

Address: P.O. Box 82, Beijing Forestry University, Beijing, 100083, China

Phone: 0086-010-62338399

Date established: 1984
Major source of funding: University; National Forestry Administration

Organizational focus:

The Institute, housed at Beijing Forestry University (BFU), is mainly concerned with research on higher education—with an emphasis on forestry education in China—and is under the direct administration of the National Forestry Administration (NFA) and the BFU. The Institute conducts work in three major activity areas:

• micro and macro research on the key issues in the field of forestry;

• courses (e.g., pedagogy, psychology, education law, and professional ethics) for new BFU educators; and

• academic exchanges with related organizations such as the Ministry of Education, Chinese Academy of Forestry Sciences, Beijing Forestry Administration, and the Chinese Society of Higher Education.

Current publications:

• *A Guide to World Higher Education.*
• *Forestry Education: New Trends and Prospects.*
• *Forestry Education in China in the 21st Century.*
• *Learning to Study.*
• *Management of School Funding and Improvement of Efficiency for Forestry Universities in China*

Staff (name • rank/title • specialization)

1. He Qingtang • Director, Professor and President of BFU • ecology, higher education
2. Li Baozheng • Director, Deputy Director for Personnel and Education under the NFA • economics, higher education
3. Ying Weilong • Deputy Director, Professor and Vice President of BFU • biology, higher education
4. Wang Jianzhi • Deputy Director, Section Chief for Forestry Education under the NFA • forestry education
5. Li Yong • Executive Deputy Director, Lecturer and Master of Education • comparative education
6. Wu Ye • Dean of the School of Basic Sciences • mathematics
7. Liu Jia • Associate Professor
8. Tao Jianjun • Administrator

Key Journals:

• *China Higher Education* (Chinese Ministry of Education)
• *China Higher Education Evaluation* (Chinese Society of Higher Education Evaluation)

• *Journal of Higher Education*
• *Studies on China Higher Education* (Chinese Society of Higher Education)

East China Normal University, Educational Information and Testing Center

Address: 3663 Nt. Zhongshan Road, Shanghai, 200062, China

Phone: 0086-21-62233615; 0086-21-62232654
Fax: 0086-21-62232469
E-mail: ECNUEITC@online.sh.cn

Date established: 1998
Major source of funding: University

Organizational focus:
The Educational Information and Testing Center provides education information services, and assistance with foreign tests (TOEFL, GRE, IELTS).

Staff (name • title/rank • specialization)
1. Zhu Zhiting • Professor and Director • educational technology
2. Wang Xinyuan • Lecturer and Vice Director • computer applications
3. Qian Shuyuan • Associate Researcher • education
4. Lu Minfu • Associate Researcher • education
5. Zhang Zhijie • Lecturer • educational management
6. Zhu Lamei • Librarian • psychology
7. Liu Liling • Assistant Researcher • educational management
8. Fu Jinming • Librarian
9. Li Jun • Librarian • information research
10. Yu Guilin • Librarian • Russian language
11. Hu Guoqing • Engineer • media technology
12. Yan Wei • Assitant • media technology
13. Shen Yaping • Assistant Librarian
14. Chen Changqin • Assistant Librarian
15. Chen Min • Assistant • accounting

Fudan University, Higher Education Institute

Address: 220 Handan Road, Shanghai, 200433, China

Phone: 86-21-65642276; 86-21-65642245
Fax: 86-21-65646816
E-mail: rrlin@fudan.edu.cn

Date established: 1986
Major source of funding: University

Organizational focus:
   The Higher Education Institute focuses on both teaching and research. It is an independent research center under the Office of the President of the University.

Current publications:
   • *A Survey of Famous Universities in the World.*
   • *An Introduction to Educational Economics.*
   • *Comparative Research about American and Soviet Degree Systems and Discussion about the Chinese Degree System.*
   • *Private Higher Education in China.*
   • *Reforms at Fudan University*

Staff (name • title/rank • specialization):
   1. Qiang Lianqing • Professor • higher education and socioeconomic development
   2. Sun Laixiang • Professor and Director • higher education administration
   3. Du Zuorun • Professor and Vice Director • higher education administration
   4. Zhang Xiaopeng • Associate Professor • comparative higher education
   5. Wang Liushuan • Associate Professor • internationalization of higher education
   6. Zhou Honglin • Associate Professor • history of Chinese education
   7. Lin Rongri • Lecturer • educational economics
   8. Xiong Qinglian • Lecturer • history of education

Courses:
   • Higher Education
   • Philosophy of Education
   • Educational Economics
   • Comparative Higher Education

Student enrollments: M.A. (6)

Key textbooks/readings:
- *Higher Education.*
- *History of Chinese Higher Education.*
- *History of Education.*
- *The History of Chinese Education.*
- *The Philosophy of Higher Education.*

Key Journals:
- *Chinese Higher Education*
- *Chinese Higher Education Research*
- *Education Research*
- *Higher Education Abroad*
- *Harvard Education Review*
- *International Education*
- *Journal of Higher Education*

Hangzhou University, Institute of Higher Education

Address: Hangzhou University, Tianmushan Road, Hangzhou, Zhejiang Province, 310028, China

Phone: (0086) 0571-8273658; 8273005
E-mail: ye_lin@telekbird.com.cn

Date established: 1982
Major source of funding: University

Organizational focus:
    Our Institute conducts academic research work on:
- comparative studies in higher education;
- consultation in higher education;
- management and planning in higher education;
- information studies in higher education; and
- higher vocational and technological education.

Staff (name • title/rank • specialization):
    1. Xia Yuejiong •Director, Professor •higher education

2. Fang Zhanhua •Executive Director and Professor • basic theory of higher education
3. Guo Yaobang • Associate Professor • consultation in higher education
4. Wang Aiguo •Associate Professor • basic theory of higher education
5. Ye Lin •Lecturer • comparative studies in higher education and evaluation
6. Li Xueping •Lecturer • comparative studies in higher education and history of higher education
7. Liu Jun •Lecturer • information analysis of higher education
8. Lu Yang •Lecturer • higher vocational and technological education
9. Zhang Li •Lecturer • higher vocational and technological education

Key textbooks/readings:
• Pan Maoyuan. *Basic Principles in Higher Education: On Higher Education.* (in Chinese)
• John S. Brubacher. *Philosophy of Higher Education.* (Chinese edition)
• John H. Van de Graaff, Burton R. Clark, et al. *Comparative Studies in Higher Education: Patterns of Authority in Seven National Systems of Higher Education.* (Chinese edition)
• Burton R. Clark. *Perspectives on Higher Education.* (Chinese edition)
• Burton R. Clark. *The Higher Education System.* (Chinese edition)

Huazhong University of Science and Technology, Institute of Higher Education

Address: Huazhong University of Science and Technology, Wuhan, Hubei Province, 430074, China
Phone: 86-27-8754-3347
Fax: 86-27-8754-5438
E-mail: hedu@blue.hust.edu.cn

Date established: 1980
Major source of funding: University

Organizational focus:
The Institute of Higher Education offers programs of study in higher education administration, education administration, and higher education philosophy, moral education in higher education institutes, degree and graduate education, and teaching theory.

Current publications:
- *Journal of Higher Education* (bimonthly, Wuhan)
- *Higher Education Research in China*
- *Higher Education Research Newsletter* (biweekly)
- Zhu Jiusi. *Proceedings of Higher Education*. HUST Press, 1990.
- Wen Fuxiang. *On the Goals of China's Higher Education*. HUST Press, 1995.
- Liu Xianjun. *On the Moral Education of Universities*. HUST Press, 1996.
- Tu Youguang. *On the History of Chinese Higher Education*. 1997.
- Chen Changqui. *Brain Drain and Return*. 1996.
- Chen Min and Yao Qihe. *Higher Education Administration*. HUST Press, 1995.
- Yao Qihe and Shen Hong. *A Study on the Goals of High-Level Universities of Science and Technology*. Hainan Press, 1996.
- Shen Hong. *Formation and Development of the American Research University*. HUST Press, 1999.

Staff (name • title/rank • specialization):
1. Zhu Jiusi • Professor • higher education administration
2. Tu Youguang • Professor • higher education philosophy and higher education history
3. Yao Qihe • Professor • higher education administration
4. Wen Fuxiang • Director and Professor • philosophy of higher education; higher education administration
5. Liu Xianjun • Vice President and Professor • moral education in the university
6. Chen Changgui • Vice Director and Professor • higher education administration
7. Zhang Shunzhu • Vice Director and Associate Professor • higher education administration
8. Shen Hong • Associate Professor • higher education administration and comparative higher education
9. Bie Dunrong • Associate Professor • higher education administration
10. Zhang Yingqiang • Associate Professor • higher education administration
11. Zhang Xiaoming • Associate Professor • education psychology
12. Chen Min • Associate Professor • higher education administration
13. Jia Yongtang • Associate Professor • higher education administration and history of higher education

Courses:
- Higher Education
- Higher Education Administration
- Chinese Higher Education History
- Western Higher Education History
- Education Psychology
- Comparative Higher Education
- Moral Education in the University
- Education Economy
- Education Statistics
- Education Research Methodology
- Education Sociology
- Education Culture
- Higher Education Development and Reformation
- SPSS in Education Research
- Higher Education Philosophy
- Theory and Method of Higher Education Administration
- Seminar on Chinese Higher Education Issues
- Education Ethics
- Foreign Language (first and second)

Student enrollments: M.A. (full-time 12, part-time 150); Ph.D. (full-time 10, part-time 30)

Key textbooks/readings:
- Burton R. Clark. *The Encyclopedia of Higher Education*. 1992. (in English)
- Burton R. Clark. *Places of Inquiry: Research and Advanced Education in Modern Universities*. University of California Press, 1995. (in English)
- Burton R. Clark. *The Research Foundations of Graduate Education: Germany, Britain, France, United States, Japan*. University of California Press, 1993. (in English)
- Burton R. Clark. *The Higher Education System: Academic Organization in Cross-National Perspective*. University of California Press, 1983. (in English and Chinese)
- John H. Van de Graaff and Burton R. Clark. *Academic Power, Patterns of Authority in Seven National Systems of Higher Education*. Praeger, 1978. (in English and Chinese)
- Philip G. Altbach. *Comparative Higher Education: Knowledge, the University, and Development*. 1997. (in English).
- D. Bruce Johnstone. *Sharing the Costs of Higher Education: Student Financial Assistance in the United Kingdom, the Federal Republic of Germany,*

*France, Sweden, and the United State*s. College Entrance Examination Board. (English).
• Ernest L. Boyer. *Scholarship Reconsidered: Priorities of the Professoriate.* Princeton University Press , 1991. (in English and Chinese)
• Fu Juanming. *Comparative Higher Education.* Beijing Normal University Press, 1987. (in Chinese)
• Zhang Ruifan and Wang Chenxu. *Short History of Comparative Studies of Chinese and Foreign Education.* Shangdong Education Press, 1997. (in Chinese)
• *Comparative Education Review* (U.S. journal)
• *International Higher Education* (newsletter of the Boston College Center for International Higher Education)
• *Comparative Education Study* (Beijing Normal University) (in Chinese)
• Yao Qihe and Chen Min. *Higher Education Administration.* 1995. (in Chinese)
• *Education Research* (Institute of Education Science) (in Chinese)
• *Science and Technology Review* (Association of Science and Technology of China) (in Chinese)

Institute of Higher Education

Address: Daxue Road, Shantou, Guangdong, 515063, China

Telephone: 0754-2903301; 0754-2902974
Fax: 0754-2903167

Date established: 1986
Major source of funding: University

Organizational focus:
   The focus of the Institute is on higher education theories and development in China and abroad. Its main purposes are developing the fields of higher education and adolescent psychology, cultivating scholars and practitioners, and promoting all aspects of higher education development.

Current publications:
   • *Theories on Modern Educational Innovation.* 1995.
   • *The Main Goals of Contemporary Higher Education in China.* 1995.

- *Research on the Background of Higher Education Development in China.* 1996.
- *The Founding of New Universities in China.* 1997.

Staff (Name • title/rank):

1. Huang Yuzhi • Professor, Director
2. Qin Guozhu • Associate Professor
3. Yuan Zhuwang • Associate Professor
4. Chen Bing • Associate Professor
5. Huang Jiehua • Lecturer
6. Ma FengQi • Lecturer

Courses:
- Higher Education Theory
- Adolescent Psychology
- Higher Education Management and Administration
- History of Higher Education
- Comparative Higher Education
- Educational Psychology

Student enrollments: M.A. (5 full-time)

Key journals: all the major journals on higher education in China

Nanjing University, Institute of Higher Education Research

Address: 22 Hankou Road, Nanjing, Jiangsu, 210093, China

Phone: (86-25)-3592869
Fax: (86-25)-3302728

Date established: 1982
Major source of funding: University

Organizational focus:
Key research areas of the Institute include:
- principles of higher education;
- administration of institutions of higher learning;
- evaluation of university education; and
- strategies and decisions on the reform and development of Nanjing University.

The Institute also trains advanced personnel in higher education administration or research.

Current publications:
- *Research on Higher Education* (quarterly)
- *Higher Education Research in China* (in English—an annual publication produced jointly with the Higher Education Research Institute of Huazhong and the University of Science and Engineering)
- *Reflections and Prospects of the New Century.* Nanjing University Press, 1995.
- Fang Gong. *A New Look at Higher Education Theory.* Jiangsu Education Press, 1995.
- Rong Mao. *Administration of Institutions of Higher Education.* Nanjing University Press, 1997.

Staff (name • title/rank • specialization):
1. Fang Gong • Director and Professor • principles of higher education, higher education administration, research on higher education in Hong Kong and Taiwan
2. Rong Mao • Deputy Director and Professor • higher education administration, economics of educational, human resources administration in institutions of higher learning
3. Shaozhu Li• Associate Professor • educational psychology, educational evaluation and measurement
4. Yunlai Wang • Associate Professor • history of higher education
5. Xiulan Yu • Lecturer • educational sociology, principles of moral education

Courses:
- Higher Education
- Higher Education Administration
- Educational Psychology
- History of Higher Education
- Economics of Education
- Sociology of Education
- Educational Evaluation and Measurement
- Research Methodology in Higher Education
- Comparative Higher Education
- Reform and Development of Higher Education in China
- Administration of Institutions of Higher Learning
- Computer Applications in Higher Education Administration

Student enrollments: M.A. (full-time 8, part-time 70)

Key textbooks/readings:
- Pan Maoyuan, ed. *A New Course in Higher Education*.
- J. S. Brubacher. *Philosophy of Higher Education*. 1978.
- P. G. Altbach. *Comparative Higher Education*. 1979.
- Mao Rong et al. *Higher Education Administration*.
- Burton R. Clark. *The Higher Education System*. 1983.
- *Education Research*. Beijing.
- *Research on Higher Education*. Wuhan.
- *Higher Education in China*. Beijing.

Nanjing University of Science and Technology, Institute of Higher Education

Address: No. 200 XiaoLing Wei, Nanjing, 210094 China

Telephone: 0086-25-4315236, 0086-25-4315747
Fax: 0086-25-4433146
E-mail: hei@mail.njust.edu.cn
Website: http://www.njust.edu.cn/univ.gaojiao/index.htm

Date established: 1984
Major source of funding: University

Organizational focus:
    Research on higher engineering education, science of learning

Staff: (name • title/rank • specialization)
    1. Zohaomin • Director and Assistant Editor, *Journal of Science and Technology* • social science
    2. Ma Qianli • Chief Editor, *Higher Education Digest*
    3. Zhou Bangxian • Chief Editor for research

Key textbooks/readings:
- *Higher Education Digest* (monthly journal)
- *Journal of Science and Technology* (bimonthly journal)
- *Research in Higher Education* (quarterly journal)

Nankai University, Higher Education Research Institute (HERI)

Address: Weijtl Road, 94 Tranjin, Tianjin, 300071, China
Phone: 022-23501467
Fax: 022-23501732
Website: http://www.nankai.edu.cn

Date established: 1998
Major sources of funding: University

Organizational focus:
> The Higher Education Research Institute (HERI) mainly focuses on the modernization of higher education in developed countries and the current situation of higher education in developing countries. Through the ongoing work in this academic field, a theory of higher education that combines Nankai ideals with foreign educational philosophies will be attained.

> Besides carrying out research on higher education theory, HERI issues timely reports and news about higher education reform here at home and abroad, with reference to higher education reform and development. The Institute is currently undertaking four national and municipal scientific studies as well as other significant research assignments from Nankai University. At the same time, it has made notable achievements turning reform experiences into pragmatic application.

Current publication:
> • *Forum for Nankai Education.*

Staff (name • title/rank • specialization):
> 1. Yong Gui Hua • Director and Professor • philosophy of higher education
> 2. Yong Song Qiu • Researcher • history of higher education
> 3. Zhou Bing • Professor • economics of higher education
> 4. Yong Gao Le • Professor • economics of higher education
> 5. Son Ly Jian • Professor • philosophy of higher education
> 6. Wong Zhong Tian • Professor • philosophy of higher education

Northwestern Polytechinical University, Higher Education Institute

Address: Northwestern Polytecnical University, Xian, Shanxi Province 710072, China

Telephone: 029-8493140
Fax: 029-8493700

Date established: 1985
Major source of funding: University

Organizational Focus:
    The focus of the Institute revolves around study of the following:
    • higher education theory;
    • applied studies of higher education;
    • university management research;
    • university evaluation; and
    • the exchange of higher education research
Current Publications:
    • The Study of The Higher Education (Chinese journal)

Staff: (Name • Title • Specialization)
    1. Boa Guohua • Vice-director, Professor • management in higher education
    2. Qi Suiyuan • Vice-director, Associate Professor • management in higher education
    3. Liu Jun • Associate Professor • management in higher education
    4. Song Shiqi • Editor
    5. Xun Ling • Librarian

Peking University, Institute of Higher Education

Address: Peking University, Beijing 100871, China

Telephone: 0086-10-62751402
Fax: 0086-10-62751409
E-mail: xinw@hedu.pku.edu.cn
Website: http://www.hedu.pku.edu.cn

Date established: 1984
Major source of funding: government; research councils; international funding agencies (World Bank and UNDP)

Organizational focus:
The mission of the Institute is to:
• provide graduate programs in the fields of higher education, philosophy of education, economics of education, educational administration, Chinese higher education, international and comparative higher education, and educational technology;
• conduct theoretical and applied research on higher education;
• provide consultation and policy recommendations to educational institutions and policymaking agencies in education; and
• carry on collaborative research and educational programs with international and domestic institutions and agencies in higher education.

Staff: (name • title/rank • specialization)
1. Min Weifang • Professor, Director, Executive Vice President of the University, Vice Director of the Higher Education Association, Higher Education Editor• organizational theories and higher education administration, educational policy, economics of education, educational finance
2. Wang Yongquan • Professor, Vice Chairman of the China Higher Education Association • theories of education, Chinese higher education, international and comparative education, higher education administration
3. Yu Yueqing • Professor, Vice Secretary General of the Higher Education Research Division of the China Higher Education Association, Executive Director of the Beijing Higher Education Association • theories of higher education, Chinese higher education, higher education administration, education law
4. Wei Xin • Associate Professor, Executive Vice Director of the institute, Executive Director of the Beijing Institution Research Council, Vice Secretary General of the China Economics of Education Association • economics of education, educational finance, higher education administration
5. Chen Xuefei • Professor, Vice Director of the institute, Executive Director of the Comparative Education Division of the Chinese Education Association • American higher education, comparative higher education, philosophy of higher education
6. Ding Xiahao • Associate Professor • economics of education, educational administration, educational research methodology

7. Chen Xiangming • Associate Professor • sociology of education, education and culture, comparative education, educational research methodology, curriculum

8. Ma Wanhua • Lecturer • educational psychology, womens' studies, higher education administration

9. Chen Xiaoyu • Lecturer, Assistant to the Director • economics of education, educational finance, technology of education

10. Li Wenli • Lecturer • economics of education, educational administration, educational psychology

11. Xie Yaling • Lecturer • economics of education, educational finance

12. Yan Fengqiao • Lecturer • higher education administration, educational evaluation and assessment, British higher education

13. Xu Weibin • Lecturer • economics of education, educational methodology

Current publications:
- *Forum of Higher Education* (quarterly journal)
- *International Higher Education Express* (monthly journal)
- *Research on Modern Higher Education Ideas in America, Germany, France, and Japan* (monograph)
- *Sojourners and Foreigners: A Study of Chinese Students' Intercultural and Interpersonal Relationships in the United States* (monograph)
- *The Economic and Social Effects of Education Investment* (monograph)

Courses:
- Advanced Studies in the Economics of Education
- Theory of Teaching and Course Design in Higher Education Institutions
- Educational Statistics
- Principles of Higher Education
- Chinese Higher Education System
- Qualitative Research in Education
- History of Chinese Higher Education
- Computer Application in Educational Research
- History of Foreign Higher Education
- International Comparative Higher Education
- Higher Education Administration
- Organization Theory and Management of Higher Education
- Economics of Education
- Methodology of Educational Research
- Organizational Behavior and Management Psychology

- Basic Education Administration
- Educational Psychology: A Cognitive-Development Perspective
- Introduction of Technology of Education
- Psychological Issues in College Education
- SAS Software and Its application in Educational Research

Student enrollments: M.A. (13 full-time, 9 part-time); Ph.D. (3 full-time, 18 part-time)

Key textbooks/readings:
- *Academy of Management Journal*
- *Administrative Science Quarterly*
- Frederick Rudolph. *A History of Western Education*. 3 vols. New York, 1962.
- *An Introduction to the Economics of Education*. Penguin Books.
- *Compare: A Journal of Comparative Education*
- G. Psacharopoulos and M. Woodhall. *Economics of Education Course: Key Readings in English*. 1985.
- *Economics of Education Review*
- G. Psacharopoulos. *Education for Development*. Oxford University Press, 1987.
- M. Blaug. *Economics of Education Research and Studies*. Pergamon Press, 1976.
- *Educational Economics*
- Educational Research
- *Higher Education*
- *Higher Education Policy*
- *International Journal of Qualitative Studies in Education*
- *Journal of Higher Education*
- *Journal of Human Resources*
- *Studies in Higher Education*
- *The American College and University: A History*. Vintage Books.

Shanghai Institute of Human Resource Development

Address: 21 Cha Ling North Road, Shanghai 200032, China

Telephone: 86-21-64033756
Fax: 86-21-6403367
E-mail: saesihrd@public.sta.net.cn

Date established: 1985
Major source of funding: government, self-generated consultation and training revenues

Organizational focus:
An independent research institution, the Shanghai Institute of Human Resource Development undertakes research, policy consultation, and training activities in the following areas: manpower demand forecasting and educational planning, human resource development and educational policy studies, the financing of education, education administration and evaluation, and information management system development.
In-house publications: *Educational Research Information* (monthly journal)

Staff: (name • title/rank • specialization):
1. Jiang Minghe • Director and Professor • educational administration, economics of education, advanced educational technology
2. Zhang Chunshu • Deputy Director and Associate Professor • educational planning, economics of education, mathematical modeling
3. Mao Hongxiang • Professor • human resource development and educational planning, science and technology and professional development
4. Tang Xiaojie • Associate Professor • education and society, comparative education, curriculum and instruction
5. Zhu Yiming • Associate Professor • measurement and evaluation, comparative education, instruction theory

Key textbooks/readings:
- *Comparative Education Review*
- *Education and Economics* (Chinese)
- *Educational Research* (Chinese)
- *Educational Research Information* (Chinese)
- *Journal of Higher Education*
- *Studies in Higher Education*
- *Shanghai Higher Education Research* (Chinese)

South China Normal University, Higher Education Center

Address: South China Normal University, Guangzhou 510631, China

Telephone: 020-85211413
Fax: 020-85213411

E-mail: giyjs@scnu.edu.cn
Website: http://www.scnu.edu.cn

Date of establishment: 1985
Major source of funding: University
Organizational focus:
> The Center focuses on the following areas:
> * the study of reform policies of national education;
> * research on international educational reform, especially that of the developed countries and of Southeast Asia;
> * providing advice to the president of South China Normal University; and
> * giving lectures concerning higher education to other departments in the University.

Current publications:
> * *A Survey of Higher Educational Reform and Development in China.*
> * *Research on Higher Education* (journal)
> * *Development in Higher Education* (journal)

Staff: (name • title/rank • specialization):
> 1. Ma Zaomin • Lecturer • compartive higher education, professional and technological higher education
> 2. Zhou Lihua • Lecturer • higher and comparative education research
> 3. Yang Huiming • Associate Professor, Vice-chief Editor of *Research on Higher Education* • higher education research and management

Key textbooks/readings:
> * *Educational Research*. Beijing: Education and Research Publishing House.
> * *Comparative Education Review*. Beijing: Beijing Normal University Publishing House.
> * *Teacher Education Research*. Beijing: Beiing Normal University Publishing House.
> * *China Higher Education*. Beijing: Chinese Education Publishing House.
> * *China Higher Education Research*. Beijing: China Higher Education Research Group.
> * *Journal of Higher Education*. (Wuhan Higher Education Research Group)

• *Higher Education Exploration*. Guangzhou: Higher Education Exploration Group.
• *Education Management Research*. Beijing: Education Management Group.

Southwest Jiaotong University, Higher Education Institute

Address: Higher Education Institute, Southwest Jiaotong University, Chengdu, Sichuan, 610031, China

Telephone: 028-7600845
Fax: 028-7600846

Date established: 1986
Major source of funding: University

Institutional funding:
The Institute focuses on both scientific research and journal editing. Its multiple purposes include: educational theory and reform research; philosophy, humanities, and social science research; and university reform and development activities. All Institute activities are connected firmly with issues of educational reform and the practice of engineering higher education.

Current publications:
• *Engineering Higher Education*

Staff (name • title/rank • specialization):
1. Xu Wenlong • Professor • engineering geology
2. Yuan Guanglyn • Assistant Researcher • chemical engineering
3. Chen Yuqi • Lecturer • engineering
4. Yang Shan • Lecturer • Chinese literature
5. Shu Lixia • Library Assistant • higher education administration

Tianjin University, Study Center on Development Strategy

Address: 42 Weijin Road, Tianjin 300072, China

Telephone: 022-27404458
Fax: 022-27401796

Date of establishment: 1998
Major source of funding: University

Organizational focus:
The mission of the Center is to study the direction and functions of universities.

Tsinghua University, Institute of Education Research

Address: Tsinghua University, Beijing 100084, China

Telephone: (086) 62783326; 62771475
Fax: (086) 62784663
E-mail: sunyu-eri@tsinghua.edu.cn

Date established: 1979
Major source of funding: University

Organizational focus:
The Institute's focus is on engineering research in China and abroad. There are two master's degree teaching programs and a program to train education management and research personnel.

Current publications:
• *Education Research*

Staff: (name • title/rank • specialization)
1. Wang Sunyu • Director, Vice Professor • education management
2. Li Yue • Vice Director, Vice Professor • psychology
3. Wang Xiaoyang • Assistant Director, Lecturer • comparative education
4. Lan Jinsong • Assistant Director, Lecturer • higher education
5. Ye Fugui • Lecturer • history of education
6. Li Manli • Lecturer • higher education
7. Liu jun • Assistant Lecturer • higher education
8. Xue Xiuzhen • Assistant Lecturer • education management
9. Jin Fuyi • Librarian

Courses:
- Higher Education
- History of Education
- Education Research Method
- Education Management
- Comparative Education
- Education Psychology

Student enrollments: M.A. (20 full-time, 10 part-time)

Key textbooks/readings:
- Pan, Maoyuan. *Higher Education*.
- Philip G. Altbach. *Comparative Education*.
- *Tsinghua University Education Research*. Institute of Education Research, Tsinghua University.
- *Higher Education Research*. Higher Education Research Institute, Central China Science and Technology University.

Unit of Higher Education Research

Address: 3 Feixi Road, Hefei, Anhui Province, 230039, China

Phone: 86-551-5106234
Fax: 86-551-5107999
Website: http://www.ahu.edu.cn

Date established: 1983
Major source of funding: University

Organizational focus:
    The Unit of Higher Education Research examines the development of Chinese and international higher education.

Current publications:
- *Discussion of Educational Ideology and Concepts*. Anhui University Press, 1998.
- *The Latest Higher Education Research Activities*. University of Science and Technology Press, 1995.
- *Studies on Higher Education* (newsletter)

Staff (name • title/rank • specialization):
1. Shen Huiqing • Director, Associate Research Fellow • comprehensive educational quality
2. Zhang Haihua • Associate Research Fellow • teaching and research of arts courses
3. Dou Hong • Associate Research Fellow • teaching and research of science courses
4. Chen Xin • Research Fellow • educational psychology
5. Zhang Mulian • Research Fellow • educational problems of delinquency

Courses:
- Science of Higher Education
- Educational Psychology
- Administration of Education for Undergraduates

Xiamen University, Institute of Higher Education Science

Address: P. O. Box C, Xiamen University, Xiamen City, Fujian Province, 361005, China

Telephone: (0592) 2180536
Fax: (0592) 2186413
E-mail: gjs@jingxian.xmu.edu.cn
Website: http://www.xmu.edu.cn/ihes/

Date established: 1978
Major source of funding: University

Organizational focus:
The Institute of Higher Education Science focuses on research on higher education theories and trends in China and abroad, issues concerning management of higher education in China, adolescent psychology, developing the fields of higher education and adolescent psychology, cultivating researchers and practitioners in such fields, promoting domestic and international exchanges in the fields of higher education and psychology, and organizing higher education research.

Current publications (all in Chinese):
- Maoyuan Pan. *Higher Education*. 1995.
- Qiuheng Shi. *Enterpreneurs and Higher Education*. 1995.

• Jinhui Lin. *The Development and Education of Creativity in College Students*. 1995.
• Maoyuan Pan. *Teaching Disciplines and Methods of Secondary Schools*. 1995.
• Maoyuan Pan. *New Higher Education*. 1996.
• Futao Huang. *Modernization of Higher Education in Europe*. 1998.
• *Journal of Higher Education Abroad* (quarterly, since 1978)

Staff: (name • title/rank • specialization):
1. Pan Maoyuan • Professor, Tutor for doctoral candidates, Director, Academic Committee Honorary Director • higher education theory, history of modern education of China
2. Liu Haifeng • Professor; Tutor for doctoral candidates, Director • history of higher education of China, imperial examination and entrance exam for higher education institutions
3. Wang Weilian • Professor, Tutor for doctoral candidates • higher education theory, curricula and teaching in higher education institutions
4. Wu Daguang • Professor • higher education theory
5. Li Zeyu • Associate Professor • management of higher education, higher education theory
6. Huang Jianru • Associate Professor • comparative higher education, higher education in South Asia
7. Xie Zuoxu • Associate Professor • comparative higher education, history of higher education abroad
8. Shi Qiuheng • Associate Professor • system engineering of higher education
9. Wu Yiying • Associate Professor • economics of higher education
10. Lin Jinhui • Associate Professor • creativity of college students, study and thinking of college students
11. Huang Futao • Associate Professor • higher education theory, history of higher education abroad
12. Yang Guangyun • Associate Professor • higher education theory
13. Chen Wuyuan • Lecturer • higher education in Japan
14. Zhao Yezhu • Lecturer • higher education theory, women's higher education
15. Qian Lanying • Lecturer • psychology of college students
16. Zheng Ruoling • Lecturer • higher education theory
17. Wen Xinlan • Lecturer • library management
18. Huang Yaming • Teaching Assistant • experimental psychology
19. Wang Tingfang • Senior Researcher • psychology of college students

20. Lin Zhongmin • Professor • psychology of college students, thinking and motives
21. Zhang Xie • Professor • psychology of higher education management
Wang Zengbing • Professor • management of higher education
22. Luo Qixiu • Associate Professor • learning psychology of college students, counseling for college students
23. Chen Ruhui • Associate Professor • higher education theory
24. Wu Liqing • Associate Professor • higher education theory

Courses:
- Marxist-Leninist Theory and Scientific Socialist Theory
- English
- Higher Education
- Adolescent Psychology
- Management of Higher Education
- History of Chinese Higher Education
- History of Higher Education Abroad
- Evaluation of Higher Education
- Economics of Higher Education
- Psychology of Higher Education Management
- Human Motivation Theory
- Psychology of College Students' Thinking
- Selected Works from the History of Higher Education
- Issues in Chinese Education History
- Practice Teaching or Administration
- System Engineering of Higher Education
- Higher Education in South Asia
- Research Methods in Higher Education
- Research on Policy and Law of Chinese Higher Education
- Research on Ideas of Western Higher Education
- Mental Health and Counseling for College Students
- Theory and Teaching of Modern Psychology
- Sociology of Education
- Cultural Studies of Education
- Research on Curricula in Higher Educational Institutions
- Higher Education in Taiwan and Hong Kong

Student enrollments: M.A. (full-time 9, part-time 1); Ph.D. (full-time 6, part-time 8)

Key textbooks/readings:
- Pan Maoyuan, ed. *New Higher Education.* (in Chinese)
- Mu Guoguang. *Management of Higher Education.* (in Chinese)
- Luo Qixiu. *Youth Psychology.* (in Chinese)
- *Educational Research.* China National Institute for Educational Research. (in Chinese)
- *Journal of Higher Education* (in Chinese and English)
- *Higher Education*: The International Journal of Higher Education (imported journal)
- *Comparative Education Review* (imported journal)

Zhejiang University, Institute of Higher Education

Address: Zheda Road 20, Hangzhou, Zhejiang Province, 310027, China

Phone: 0086-(571) 795-1487
Fax: 0086-(571) 795-1358

Date established: 1984
Major source of funding: University

Organizational focus:
The Institute of Higher Education focuses on the following research activities:
- the principles of higher education, especially professional education, Third World culture, and the reform of higher education;
- higher education planning and methods;
- comparative higher education; and
- higher education administration and management, as relates specifically to teaching, research, student affairs, and human resources at the university.

Current publications:
- Jianmin Gu and Peimin Wang. *Basics of Engineering Education: Research on the Ideals and Practice of Engineering Education.* Zhejiang University Press, 1994.
- Jianmin Gu. *Theory and Method of Comparative Education.* People's Education Press, 1994.
- Weimin Zu. *Natural Dialectic.* Zhejiang University Press, 1998.
- Xiaodong Zou. *Knowledge Economy and Innovation.* Zhejiang University Press, 1998.
- *Education Research* (journal, Zhejiang University)

Staff (name • title/rank • specialization):
1. Wang Peimin • Professor and Director • higher education principles
2. Jiang Shaozhong • Professor • higher education planning
3. Yang Shufeng • Professor • higher education administration and management
4. Gu Jianmin • Associate Professor • comparative research in higher education
5. Xu Weimin • Associate Professor • higher education administration and management
6. Wang Yuzhi • Associate Professor • higher education planning
7. Zou Xiaodong • Associate Professor • higher education planning
8. Ye Min • Associate Professor • higher education principles
9. Chen Gugang • Associate Professor • comparative research in higher education
10. Liu Jirong • Associate Professor • higher education administration and management
11. Wang Suwen • Lecturer • comparative research in higher education
12. Kong Hanbin • Lecturer • comparative research in higher education
13. Sun Xiuli • Lecturer • higher education planning

Courses:
- Natural Dialectic
- Foreign Language
- Comparative Research in Higher Education
- Planning in Higher Education
- Principles of Professional Education
- History of Higher Education
- Evaluation and decision of education
- Education Reform Practice
- Management Theory
- Sociology of Education
- University Psychology
- Curriculum and Its Planning
- Education Evaluation and Measurement
- Computer-aided Management

Student enrollments: M.A. (10)

Zhongshan University, Higher Education Institute

Address: Zhongshan University, Guangzhou, China

Phone: 020-84186300-6890
Fax: 020-84186300-6890
E-mail: puherc@zsu.edu.cn; niuduan@163.net

Date established: 1982
Major source of funding: University

Organizational focus:
   The Institute devotes itself to teaching and education research. The Institute now has the right to grant master's degrees in education management and higher education. It now has the following research orientations: comparative education evaluation and measurement of education, research methods of higher education, management of higher education, psychology of university students.

Current publications:
   • *Information of Higher Education.*
   • *Research of Higher Education at Zhongshan University.*

Staff (name • title/rank • specialization):
   1. Wu Fuguang • Professor • comparative studies in education in Hong Kong, Guangzhou, Macao, and Taiwan
   2. Zhang Mingiang • Professor and Director • research methods of education

Courses:
   • Higher Education
   • Principles of Educational Administration
   • Methods of Education Research
   • History of Ideas on Higher Education in China and Foreign Countries
   • Psychology of Educational Administration

Student enrollments: M.A. (part-time 10, full-time 9)

Key journals:
   • *Higher Education* (Xiamen University)
   • *Principles of Modern Education*

- *Psychology*
- *Research of Higher Education*
- *Research of Education*

Cuba

Advanced Education Reference Center (CREA)

Address: calle 127 s/n, Marianao, Ciudad de La Habana, 19390, Cuba

Phone: (537) 20-6336
Fax: (537) 27-2964 ; (537)27-7129
Website: http://www.ispjae.cu/centros/crea/crea.htm

Date established: 1998
Major source of funding: government

Organizational focus:
The Advanced Education Reference Center's focus is to develop and promote advanced studies and research in the field of educational sciences, applied mainly to the teaching of technical sciences, engineering, and architecture, and focusing on the application of the latest developments in informatics, telematics, and educational technology as they relate to higher education.

Staff (name • title/rank • specialization):
1. Angel Emilio Castañeda Hevia • Director of CREA, Professor • curriculum design
2. Elsa M.Herrero Tunis • Assistant Professor • didactics
3. Ana María Fernandez Gonzalez • Interinstitutional Relations Director, Assistant Profesor • psychology, educational communication
4. Orestes D.Castro Pimienta • Assistant Professor, Research Projects Director • educational assessment
5. María Niurka Valdés Montalvo • Assistant Professor, Information Management Director • social sciences
6. Ramón Collazo Delgado • Assistant Profesor, Director of the Virtual University Project • educational technology
7. Héctor Villafranca Cabrera • informatics

8. Osier Joo Hitchman • network administrator
9. Manuela Vargas Villafuerte • scientific information

Courses:
   • Contemporary Higher Education Problems and Curriculum Design at the Threshold of the 21st Century
   • University Didactics and Its Implementation in the New Information Comunications Technologies
   • Communication in the University Teaching Process
   • Institutional and Learning Assessment

Key textbooks/readings:
   • *Prospects* (quarterly review of education, UNESCO)
   • *Mundo escolar*
   • *Actas pedagógicas*
   • *Educación superior contemporánea*
   • *Educación*
   • *El Correo de la UNESCO*
   • *Universitas 2000*
   • *Educación y sociedad*
   • *IEEE Transaction on Education*
   • *Zona Educativa*
   • *Cuadernos de pedagogía*

Havana, University of, Center for Studies in the Improvement of Higher Education at the University of Havana (Centro de estudios para el perfeccionamiento de la educación superior) (CEPES-UH)

Address: Calle 23 No. 453, e/ H e I. Vedado, Ciudad de La Habana. Cuba, Código Postal 10400
Telphone: (53-7) 320344, 324705
Fax: (53-7) 334182
E-mail: cepes@cepes.uh.cu
Webpage: http://www.uh.cu

Date established: 1982
Major source of funding: University

Organizational Focus:
   The Studies Center for the Improvement of Higher Education at the University of Havana (CEPES-UH) is an interdisciplinary center for

research and graduate studies that integrates the perspectives of pedagogical, psychological, sociological, economic, and new information and communications technologies that facilitate the characterization and presentation of solutions for institutional problems in higher education. Our mission is to contribute to the development of scientific thought about higher education by generating, assimilating, adapting, distributing, transferring, and using scientific knowledge and technology—particularly in Cuba, Latin America, and the Caribbean. The fundamental areas of investigation are the development of the theoretical and methodological approaches to study systems and institutions of higher education. Another goal is the improvement of systems and institutions of higher education, their processes and participants.

The Center develops broad academic exchanges with important institutions of higher education in Latin America and other regions of the world with whom it conducts activities such as teaching graduate programs, research, bibliographic exchanges, assessment and consulting, as well as academic and scientific events. In addition, it has collaborative relationships with (among others) the International Institute of Higher Education of Latin America and the Caribbean (IESALC), International Institute of Educational Planning (IIPE), Union of Latin American Universities (UDUAL), InterAmerican Organization of Universities (OUI).

The Center functions as a faculty of UNESCO in University Management and Teaching, the first of its type created in the country. Under its auspices, various projects have been conducted—such as one on teachers as researchers—that have facilitated the possibility of establishing a network of similar faculties in this area in Latin America and the Caribbean and the development—in collaboration with institutions of UNESCO—along these thematic lines of research.

Current publications:
- *World Trends in Higher Education.*
- *Curriculum: Design, Practice, and Evaluation.*
- *The Process of University Teaching-Learning and Didactics.*
- *The Formation of University Teachers.*
- *Group Learning: Value Development in University Students.*
- *Planning, Strategic Management, and Institutional Prospects: Information Systems for Support for University Planning.*
- *Institutional Evaluation and Follow-up with Graduates.*
- *Government, Management Models and Institutional Organization.*

- *Academic Leadership.*
- *Institutional Cultural Change.*
- *Management of Teaching, Research, Extension, and University Resources.*
- *Automated Educational Information Management.*
- *University-Industry and Access to Higher Education.*
- Contempory University Trends. 1998.
- *Participatory Methods: A New Concept in Learning.* Universidad de La Habana, 1998.

The Center publishes the *Review of Cuban Higher Education* quarterly as a mechanism for the academic and scientific distribution for Cuban higher education. It is distributed by exchange or subscription inside and outside Cuba; the *Review* also gathers the experiences of other countries. Articles by scholars from these countries are also published in our journal.

Staff: (name • title/rank):
1. Elvira Martín Sabina • Director
2. Boris Trist Pérez • Assistant Director
3. José Luis Almuiñas Rivero • President of the Scientific Council
4. Ana Margarita Sosa Castillo • Academic Secretary
5. José Luis Almuiñas Rivero • Professor
6. Victoria Ojalvo Mitrany • Professor
7. Benito Romero Sotolongo • Professor
8. Nancy Moreno González • Professor
9. Jesus García del Portal • Professor
10. Miriam González Pérez • Professor
11. Enrique Iñigo Bajos • Professor
12. Verónica Canfux Sanler • Professor
13. Gladys Viñas Pérez • Professor
14. Teresa Sanz Cabrera • Professor
15. Oksana Kratchenko Beoto • Professor
16. Ada Gloria Rodríguez Ortega • Professor
17. Viviana González Maura • Professor
18. Herminia Hernández • Professor
19. Mario Mayor Vázquez • Professor
20. Sinesio Santos Gutiérrez • Professor
21. Jaime López • Professor
22. Thais Marí Díaz • Professor
23. Ana Rosa Rojas Rodríguez • Professor
24. Nora Arrechavaleta Guarton • Researcher
25. Adela Hernandez Díaz • Researcher

26. Ana Victoria Castellanos Noda • Researcher
27. Sonia Martínez Miranda • Researcher
28. Ileana M. Alfonso Cuba • Researcher
29. Ivan Fernández Camino • Researcher
30. Ana Margarita Sosa Castillo • Technician
31. Georgina Estévez Mendoza • Technician
32. Juan Francisco Vega Mederos • Technician
33. Gisela Salazar Jiménez • Technician
34. Maylene Rodríguez Romero • Technician
35. Daniel Folgueira Roque • Technician

Courses:
Doctoral programs are offered in two areas: pedagogical science and science of education. The latter focuses on information and communication in education. In these fields research is oriented toward practical application in higher education. The master's degree programs are offered part time and full time and take two to four years, depending on the course.

Programs are offered in higher education, university management, teaching, and educational research. A certificate program and internships were developed in response to a request from the institution. The Center offers assessment, consulting, and the possibility of engaging in joint research projects. The Center convenes annual and biannual courses and international workshops on diverse topics in higher education. It also offers national workshops in different areas of study.

Student enrollments: M.A. (295); Ph.D. (25); Certificate (105); Intern-ships (402)

Key textbooks/readings:
• *Higher Education and Society*. Regional Center for Higher Education in Latin America and the Caribbean..
• *Prospects* (UNESCO)

Czech Republic

Charles University, Educational Policy Center (Stredisko vzdelavaci politiky)

Address: Myslikova 7, 110 00 Prague 1, Czech Republic

Phone: 420 2 24 91 05 15
Fax: 420 2 24 91 05 15
E-mail: ladislav.cerych@pedf.cuni.cz

Date established: 1984
Major source of funding: government

Organizational focus:
   Work at the Center focuses on:
   • education policy issues in the Czech Republic and other Central and
   Eastern European countries;
   • comparatives studies related to all sectors and levels of education;
   • education issues related to the European integration process; and
   • diversification of higher education; and international exchanges in
   all above areas.

Current publications:
   • *Reviews of National Policies for Education in the Czech Republic*. OECD,
   1996.
   • *Diversification of Tertiary Education in the Czech Republic*. OECD, 1997.
   • *Czech Education and Europe: Pre-Accession Strategy for Human Resource
   Development*. 1999.

Staff (name • title/rank • specialization):
   1. Ladislav Cerych • Director • comparative higher education
   2. Jiri Kotasek • Deputy Director • curriculum and institutional structure, history of education
   3. Jan Koucky • economics of higher education, sociological aspects of
   higher education
   4. Jana Svecova • teacher training

France

Center for Sociology of Organizations (Centre de sociologie des organisations)

Address: 19 rue Amélie, Paris, 75007, France
Phone: 33 (0)1 40 62 65 70
Fax: 33 (0)1 47 35 05 55
E-mail: c.musselin@cso.cnrs.fr OR s.mignot-gerard@cso.cnrs.fr
Website: http://www.cso.edu

Date established: early 1960s
Major source of funding: government, private and public research con-
    tracts

Organizational focus:
    As regards higher education, the Center's main programs relate to:
    • university governance (mainly in France and Germany);
    • academic labor markets (mainly in France, Germany and the United
    States); and
    • higher education policy (mainly in France and Germany).

Current publications:
    • *Brèves* (biannual newsletter)

Staff (name • title/rank):
    1. Christine Musselin • Researcher
    2. Stéphanie Mignot-Gérard

Council of Europe (Conseil de L'Europe)

Address: Strasbourg, 67006, France

Telephone: 33-0-388412643 or 33-0-3884136
Fax: 33-0-388412706 or 33-0-388412788
E-mail: sjur.bergan@coe.fr
Website: http://www/culture.coe.fr/the

Date established: 1949
Major source of funding: governments

Organizational focus:
    The Council of Europe is a political intergovernmental organization that
    encompasses 40 European pluralist democracies, and is distinct from the
    15-nation European Union. One of the Council's primary functions is to
    encourage the mobility of students, research workers, and teaching staff
    in higher education, especially through the new joint Council of Europe/
    UNESCO Convention on the recognition of qualifications concerning
    higher education in the European region (ETS no. 165). The Council is
    focused on a number of themes: building the university of tomorrow,

policies and practice for higher education in Europe, ideas on the renewal of higher education in the new member countries, and higher educaton for a democratic society.

Current publications:
- *Education* (newsletter)

International Association of Universities (IAU) (Association internationale des universites)

Address: 1, rue Miollis, Paris, F 75732 Paris Cedex 15, France

Phone: +331-4568-2545
Fax: +331-4734-7605
Website: http://www.unesco.org/iau

Date established: 1950
Major source of funding: membership fees, contractual services

Organizational focus:
The International Association of Universities (IAU) is an international information and research dissemination center, focusing on institutional leadership at universities worldwide. It organizes international meetings and conferences for university presidents and administrators on issues of mutual and current concern and publishes reference works intended to promote international academic mobility.

The Association makes available the latest research in comparative higher education policy via its quarterly journal, *Higher Education Policy* and through its monograph series, Issues in Higher Education, both of which are associated with UNESCO. The Association has a full-time director of research, who is responsible for the development of both the journal and the monograph series.

Current publications:
- *International Handbook of Universities*. London and White Plains, N.Y.: Macmillan.
- *World List of Universities*. London and White Plains, N.Y.: Macmillan.
- *World Academic Database*.

Key textbooks/readings:
- Sarah Guri Rosenblit. *Distance Teaching and Campus Universities: Tensions and Interactions.* Oxford: Elsevier, 1999.
- Werner Hirsch and Luc Weber. *Challenges Facing Higher Education at Millennium.* Phoenix, Ariz.: Oryx and Oxford:Pergamon, 1999.
- Guy Neave. *The Universities' Responsibilities to Society: Inter-national Perspectives.* Oxford: Pergamon, 1999.
- Burton R Clark. *Creating Entrepreneurial Universities: Organisational Pathways of Transformation.* Oxford,Pergamon, 1998.
- L. B. Bjorkman. *Organising Innovative Research: The Inner Life of University Departments.* Oxford: Pergamon, 1998.

Staff (name • title/rank • specialization):
1. Franz Eberhard • Secretary General • administration
2. Zhang Mai Zheng • Professor, Director of Cooperation
3. Claudine Langlois • Director, IAU/UNESCO Information Centre on Higher Education
4. Guy Neave • Professor, Director of Research • comparative higher education policy
5. Elzbieta Karwat • Head Documentalist

Student enrollments: 1 or 2 interns per year

OECD Programme on Institutional Management in Higher Education (IMHE) (Programme de l'OCDE sur la gestion des établissements d'enseignement superieur)

Address: 2, rue Andre-Pascal, 75775 Paris Cedex 16, France

Telephone: 33 1 45 24 92 24
Fax: 33 1 42 24 02 11
Website: http://www.oecd.org/els/edu/els_imhe.htm

Date established: 1969
Major source of funding: membership fees

Organizational focus:
The IMHE Programme is an international forum serving administrators, researchers, and policymakers in higher education. Its objectives

are to promote exhanges of information and expertise in the management of higher education and to encourage new methods and approaches through: research projects and studies, training opportunities and information exchanges (publications, seminars, and conferences). Topics of interest include: continuing education and lifelong learning, the tertiary education institution as regional actor, diversification of tertiary institutions, management of research, quality in mass tertiary education, internationalization of higher education, and governance.

The IMHE Programme is located at the headquarters of the OECD (Organisation for Economic Cooperation and Development, an intergovernmental organization headquartered in Paris, France)

Current publications:
- *Managing Information Strategies in Higher Education.* 1996.
- *Information Technology and the Future of Higher Education.* 1996.
- *Internationalisation of Higher Education in Asia-Pacific Countries* 1997.
- *Standards and Quality in Higher Education.* 1997.

Journals (triannual)
- *Higher Education Management* (in English)
- *Gestion de l'enseignement supérieur* (in French)
- *Newsletter: IMHE-Info* (in English and French)

Staff (name • title/rank):
1. Richard Yelland • Head of Program
2. Jan Karlsson • expert seconded from the University of Copenhagen
3. Jacqueline Smith • Assistant

Germany

Bavarian State Institute for Research and Planning into Higher Education (Bayerisches Staatsinstitut für Hochschulforschung und Hochschulplanung) (IHF)

Address: Prinzregentenstr. 24, 80538 München, Germany
Phone: (089) 21234-405

Fax: (089) 21234-450
Website: http://www.ihf.bayern.de/index.htm
E-mail: sekretariat@ihf.bayern.de

Date established: 1973
Major source of funding: federal government

Organizational focus:
The Bavarian State Institute for Research and Planning into Higher Education (IHF) assists the ministry with regard to the development of higher education in Bavaria in a national and international context. The Institute's research results are published as monographs. In addition, the Institute edits *Beiträge zur Hochschulforschung*, a quarterly review dealing with all aspects of research into higher education.

The Institute's general fields of research are:
• state and development of the system of higher education in Germany;
• interdependencies between changes in state, society, and the system of higher education;
• special aspects of higher education—its problems and efficiency;
• research activities in universities, in particular coordination and concentration in specific fields;
• support of institutions of higher education in implementing reform concepts;
• assistance to the ministry regarding the master plan for higher education (*Hochschulgesamtplan*);
• systems of higher education abroad; and
• elaboration and implementation of methods for research into higher education.

Current publications:
•The IHF has numerous publications. For a complete list, see website: <http:/www.ihf.bayern. de/ fr_publikationen.htm>.

Staff (name • title/rank):
1. Hans-Ulrich Küpper • Director, Head of Research
2. Siegfried H. Schmidt
3. Brigitte Roth
4. Geneviève Gauvain
5. Carsten Kröger

6. The Institute also employs 15 researchers from various scientific disciplines and 10 technical and clerical staff members.

Center for Higher Education Development (CHE) (Centrum für Hochschulentwicklung)

Address: Carl-Bertelsmann-Str. 256, Gütersloh, 33311, Germany

Telephone: 00 49/(0) 52 41/97 61-22
Fax: 00 49/(0) 52 41/97 61-40
Website: http://www.che.de

Date established: 1994
Major source of funding: private funding

Organizational focus:

The Center for Higher Education Development (CHE) was founded by the Bertelsmann Foundation and the German Rectors' Conference (Hochschulrektorenkonferenz) to initiate and support reform in the German higher education system . The CHE seeks to define politically independent objectives, develop concrete strategies to realize these objectives, and test the extent to which change can be introduced.

As a nonprofit, limited liability company (GmbH), the CHE is in a position to act independently of individual or political interests. Furthermore, the CHE is committed to the common good in both financial and idealistic terms. CHE offices are located in the Bertelsmann Foundation buildings in Gütersloh.

The overarching objective of the CHE is to promote the efficiency of German universities and to strengthen their capacity to evolve. Structural problems in the German postsecondary system, such as increasing numbers of students and underfunding, require revolutionary changes in educational policy—changes that involve the breaking of long-standing taboos. These include, among other things, decreasing state regulation, improving the quality in research and teaching conditions, reorganizing access to postsecondary education, introducing tuition fees, delegating responsibility to all levels of the system and privatizing particular parts, strengthening postsecondary management, and finally bringing alternative principles and models of higher education into consideration.

The CHE regards itself as both a "think tank," and as a consultancy to higher education. Its objectives are to develop models for performance-oriented and competitive management of higher education, and foster acceptance of these new management approaches within institutions of higher education and within society at large. In this context it is imperative to examine the higher education practices and initiatives of other countries and consider their relevance and transferability to the German setting.

Three different approaches characterize CHE's work. They are:
• creating pilot projects involving individual postsecondary institutions and the related state agencies;
• introducing concrete reform proposals into public discussion, such as those concerning higher education access and financing the higher education system, and
• organizing symposia and workshops to ensure the exchange of information between higher education institutions.

Current publications:
• John Brennan, Jutta Fedrowitz, Mary Huber, Peter Maassen, and Tarla Shah, eds. *What Kind of University?* London: Open University Press, 1998.
• Detlef Müller-Böling and Jutta Fedrowitz, eds. *Leitungsstrukturen für autonome Hochschulen.* Gütersloh: Verlag Bertelsmann Stiftung, 1998.
• Evelies Mayer, Detlef Müller-Böling, Anne MacLachlan, and Jutta Fedrowitz, eds. *University in Transition: Research Mission, Interdisciplinarity, Governance.* Gütersloh: Verlag Bertelsmann Stiftung, 1998.
• Detlef Müller-Böling and Lothar Zechlin, et al., eds. *Strategieentwicklung an Hochschulen: Konzepte-Prozesse-Akteure.* Güersloh: Verlag Bertelsmann Stiftung, 1998.
• Hans Joachim Meyer and Detlef Müller-Böling, eds. *Hochschulzugang in Deutschland: Status quo und Perspektiven.* Gütersloh: Verlag Bertelsmann Stiftung, 1996.
• Detlef Müller-Böling, ed. *Qualitätssicherung in Hochschulen: Forschung, Lehre, und Organisation.* Gütersloh: Verlag Bertelsmann Stiftung, 1995.

Staff (name • title/rank • specialization):
1. Detlef Müller-Boeling • Director • higher education management and finance
2. Klaus Neuvians • Deputy Director • organizational development

3. Andreas Barz • program manager • quality management, evaluation
4. Petra Buhr • program manager • evaluation
5. Susanne Dopheide • program manager • public relations
6. Jutta Fedrowitz • program manager • higher education management
7. Petra Giebisch • program manager • evaluation
8. Stefan Hornbostel • program manager • evaluation
9. Olaf Keitzel • program manager • higher education administration
10. Erhard Krasny • program manager • higher education management and strategy
11. Tilman Kuechler • program manager • quality management, organizational development
12. Frank Ziegele • program manager • higher education finance

Higher Education Information System (Hochschul-Informations System) (HIS)

Address: Goseriede G, D-30 59, Hannover, Germany

Phone: 0511-12200
Fax: 0511-220250
E-mail: ederleh@his.de
Website: http://www.his.de

Date established: 1978
Major source of funding: government

Organizational focus:
- social empirical analysis,
- software development, and
- resource utilization analysis

Kassel, University of, Centre for Research on Higher Education and Work (Universität Gesamthochschule Kassel, Wissenschaftliches Zentrum für Berufs- und Hochschulforschung)

Address: Henschelstrasse 4, Kassel, D-34109, Germany
Phone: (+49)561/804 2415; (+49)561/804 2408
Fax: (+49)561/804 7415; (+49)561/804 3301

Website: http://www.uni-kassel.de/wz1/

Date established: 1978
Major source of funding: University

Organizational focus:
The predominant areas of research carried out at the Centre concern the relationship between higher education and work and the system of higher education in general, including its relation to the state and society. The Centre aims to contribute both to the theoretical and methodological advancement of research and to provision of practice-relevant systematic knowledge on higher education. Among the specific topics of research conducted at the Centre are the following: professional careers of graduates from higher education; problems of transition from higher education to the world of work; the academic profession; the situation of women in academia; the development of the higher education system; steering processes and decision making in higher education institutions; higher education in other industrialized countries as well as in developing countries; evaluation of teaching, research, and administrative activities; teaching/learning processes; international mobility of students and academic staff.

The University of Kassel provides the Centre with basic administrative and financial support. Research projects are and were funded among others by: the Carnegie-Foundation for the Advancement of Teaching; Deutsche Forschungsgemeinschaft; the European Commission; German Academic Exchange Service; Federal Ministry of Education, Science, Research, and Technology; Hessian Ministry of Science and Arts; Institute for Employment Research of the Federal Employment Services; Körber Foundation; Ministry of the Interior, North Rhine Westphalia; Schader Foundation; Volkswagen Foundation; Boehringer-Ingelheim Funds; Swiss Science Council.

Current Publications:
The Centre's research consists mainly of the following three series:
• Arbeitspapiere—published by and available at the Centre for Research on Higher Education and Work (34 titles).
• Werkstattberichte—published by the Centre, distributed by Jenior and Prefller Publishers, Lassallestr. 15, D-34119 Kassel (55 titles).
• Hochschule und Beruf. (23 titles). Campus Publishers: Frankfurt a.M., Heerstr. 149, D-60488 Frankfurt am Main.
• *Update* (biannual newsletter)

1998 publications:
- Manuela Schröder, Hans-Dieter Daniel, and Karin Thielecke. *Studienabbruch: Eine annotierte Bibliographie (1975–1997).* Werkstattberichte Band 54. Kassel: Wissenschaftliches Zentrum für Berufs- und Hochschulforschung der Universit at Gesamthochschule Kassel, 1998.
- Andris Barblan, Barbara M. Kehm, Sybille Reichert, and Ulrich Teichler. 1998. *Emerging European Policy Profiles of Higher Education Institutions.* Werkstattberichte 54. Kassel: Wissenschaftliches Zentrums für Berufs- und Hochschulforschung, 1998.
- Ulrich Teichler, Hans-Dieter Daniel, and Jürgen Enders. *Brennpunkt Hochschule: Neuere Analysen zu Hochschule, Beruf, und Gesellschaft.* Frankfurt a.M. and New York: Campus, 1998.
- Hans-Dieter Daniel. "Voraussetzungen für das Studium der Psychologie." In *Studieren heute,* ed. Werner Heldmann. Bad Honnef: Bock, 1998, 186–196.
- Angelika Ernst. *Aufstieg - Anreiz - Auslese: Karrieremuster und Karriereverlaufe von Akademikern in Japans Privatwirtschaft.* Opladen: Leske-Budrich, 1998.
- Max Hübner, Katrin Münch, Jost Reinecke, and Peter Schmidt. *Sexual- und Verhütungsverhalten 16–24 jähriger Jugendlicher und junger Erwachsener.* Köln: Bundeszentrale für Gesundheitliche Aufklärung, 1998.
- Ulrich Teichler, and Akira Takanashi, eds. *Berufliche Kompetenzentwicklung im Bildungs- und Beschäftigungssystem in Japan und Deutschland.* Frankfurter Studien zur Bildungsforschung 13. Baden-Baden: Nomos, 1998.

Staff (name • title/rank):
1. Christiane Bradatsch • head of publication unit
2. Lutz Bornmann • Researcher
3. Hans-Dieter Daniel • Director
4. Jürgen Enders • Executive Director
5. Gabriele Freidank • head of documentation unit
6. Barbara Grünig • Researcher
7. Alexandra Horny • Researcher
8. Friedhelm Maiworm • Researcher
9. Katrin Münch • Researcher
10. Ayl Neusel • Senior Researcher
11. Christoph Oehler • Professor and Senior Researcher
12. Harald Schomburg • Researcher
13. Manuela Schröder • Researcher

14. Stefanie Schwarz • Researcher
15. Martina Schotte-Kmoch • Researcher
16. Christian Solle • Researcher
17. Wolfgang Steube • Researcher
18. Ulrich Teichler • Senior Researcher
19. Helmut Winkler • Senior Researcher

Key journals:
- *Das Hochschulwesen*
- *European Journal of Education*
- *Higher Education*
- *Mitteilungen aus der Arbeitsmarkt- und Berufsforschung*

Wittenberg--Halle, University of, Institute for Higher Education Research

Address: Collegienstrasse 62B, D-06886 Lutherstadt, Wittenberg, Germany

Phone: +49-3491-466254
Fax: +49-3491-46625
E-mail: institut@hof.uni-halle.de
Website: http://www.hof.uni-halle.de

Date established: 1996
Major source of funding: state (two-thirds), federal government (one-third), and third-party/contract funding

Organizational focus:
Work at the Institute revolves around themes related to higher education and social change. Major fields of research include:
- differentiation and flexibility;
- relationships between higher education, the region, and the labor market;
- impacts of internationalization and steering issues;
- efficiency and legitimation;
- governance and steering; and
- quality development

Current publications:
- book series
- Arbeitsberichte (reports)
- *HOF-Berichte* (newsletter)

Staff (name • title/rank • specialization):

1. J. H. Olbertz • Director • education, pedagogics, continuing education, adult education
2. J. Lischka • Managing Director • access, transition to work, continuing education
3. G. Buck-Bechler • Researcher • academic studies, curriculum development, transformation of higher education in East German, institutional profile building, higher education and the region
4. P. Altmiks • doctoral candidate • efficiency, financing higher education, economics
5. H. John • Researcher •reforming academic studies, structures and degrees
6. B.M. Kehm • Researcher • internationalization; steering, quality issues; international comparisons; higher education developments in Europe
7. R. Kohls • Researcher • educational information systems, databases, literature research
8. D. Lewin • Researcher • academic studies, structural data on higher education, multimedia use in higher education
9. P. Pasternak • Researcher • governance; transformation of East German science and higher education systems; profile building; decision making and information structures in higher education institutions; higher education policy

Ghana

Association of African Universities (AAU)

Address: P.O. Box 5744, Accra-North, Ghana

Phone: (233-21) 774495
Fax: (233-21) 774821
E-mail: info@aau.org
Website: http://www.aau.org

Date established: 1967
Major source of funding: membership fees; donors; African governments; OAU

Organizational focus:
The focus of the Association of African Universities is to:
• promote interchange, contact, and cooperation among universities in Africa;
• collect, clarify, and disseminate information on higher education and research;
• study and make known the educational and related needs of African universities; and
• encourage increased contacts between AAU members and the international academic world.

Current Publications:
• *AAU Newsletter* (3 issues annually).
• research reports (2 publications to date).
• *The African experience with Higher Education.*
• various conference papers

Staff (name • title/rank):
1. Alakpa Sawyerr • Director of Research
2. Zoumana Bamba • Head Information and Communication
3. Dominic Tarpeh •Head Administration and Finances
4. G.O.S. Ekhaguere • Head Programs and Cooperation
5. Chris Nwamuo • Senior Program Officer

Hungary

Hungarian Institute for Educational Research (HIER) (Oktatáskutató Intézet)

Address: P.O.Box 427, Budapest, H-1395, Hungary
Phone: (36-1) 329-76-39
Fax: (36-1) 329-76-52
E-mail: H6229IER@ELLA.HU
Website: http://www.hier.iif.hu

Date established: 1981
Major source of funding: government

Organizational focus:

The Hungarian Institute for Educational Research (HIER) carries out empirical, sociological, and statistical economic research on higher education. HIER contributes to the development of the educational system and provides help and scientific background for decision makers in educational policy through comparative, historical, political, legislative, and economic research and analysis. HIER is also a center in postgraduate education, offering an M.A. in pedagogy and a Ph.D. subprogram in higher education research through Kossuth Lajos University (KLTE) in Debrecen.

The main research efforts of the Institute cover the entire system of education. These include:
• higher education;
• public education, including vocational education;
• regional analysis of education;
• minorities in education;
• educational policy;
• nonformal education;
• youth research; and
• financing education.

Current publications:
• *Quarterly Review: Education* (in Hungarian, with English and German summaries)
• *Disadvantaged Position*. 1997.
• *Nonformal Education*. 1997.
• *Balance 1994–98* (periodic analysis of Hungarian education)
• *Mental Health*. 1998.
• *Career Planning*. 1998.
• *National Core Curriculum*.
• Education Papers (series of final reports of research carried out at the Institute)
• Kozma Tamas. *Euroharmonization*. 1998.
• László Tamás Szabó. *Teacher Training in Europe*. 1998.
• newsletter (monthly).

Staff (name • title/rank • specialization):
1. Tamás Kozma • Director • regional analysis of tertiary education
2. Ildikó Hrubos • Group Head, Higher Education Research; Head of the Ph.D. subprogram • comparative research on educational systems

3. Andor Ladányi • Senior Researcher • historical research on higher education, the system and legislation of higher education
4. Peter Tibor Nagy • Group Head • educational policy, religious education, historical research
5. Tamás László Szabó • Senior Researcher • teacher training, comparative research
6. Mariann Szemerszki • Assistant • social position of students, empirical researches
7. Gábor Tomasz • Assistant • social research on higher education
8. Katalin R. Forray • Group Leader • minorities in higher education
9. Gábor Kálmán • Group Leader • social position of students, selection in higher education

Student enrollments: M.A. (part-time 25), Ph.D. 11 (part time 11)

Kossuth University, Doctoral Program for Higher Education Research

Address: Egyetem ter 1, Debrecen, 4010, Hungary

Phone: 36-52-316-666-2223
Fax: 36-52-316-666-2223
Website: http://www.klte.hu/~nevtud/phd/phd.htm

Date established: 1995
Major source of funding: government

Organizational focus:
The main focus of our doctoral program is higher education research. Our dissertation research topics include historical and comparative analyses, the sociology of teaching and the politics of education, and regional and minority issues. Approaches to statistical assessment in higher education, international relations in higher education, policymaking and the analysis of organizational integration are also areas of interest.

Current publications:
• *Regional Cooperation in Higher Education.*
• *Acta Pedagogica Debrecina XCVI.* 1997.
• annual yearbook of the doctoral program
• newsletter of the doctoral progam

Staff (name • title/rank • specialization):
1. Nagy Zoltán Abádi • Professor • international relations in higher education
2. György Bazsa • Professor • science policy
3. Mihály Beck • member of the Hungarian Academy of Sciences, Professor • ethics of science
4. János Csirik • Professor • financing
5. R. Katalin Forray • Associate Professor • regional and minority studies
6. Botond Gaál • Professor • integration in higher education
7. Ildikóhabil Hrubos • Professor • governance of higher education institutions
8. Tamás Kozma • Director, Professor • comparative analysis of education systems
9. Andor Ladányi • Research Professor • history of higher education in the 20th century
10. Péter Lukács • Associate Professor • higher education as a social system
11. László Murakázi • Associate Professor • economics of education
12. András Nábrádi • Associate Professor • institutional management
13. Péter Tibor Nagy • Senior Researcher • higher education policy
14. István Polönyi • Associate Professor • economics of education
15. János Setényi • Senior Researcher • quality assurance
16. Lvszló Tamás Szabó • Associate Professor • teacher training
17. Attila Szentromai • Professor • comparative analysis of higher education systems
18. Jeni Szigeti • Professor • private and denominational higher education

Courses:
• Higher Education and Labor Market
• Evaluation in Higher Education
• Comparative Analysis of Higher Education
• Comparative Perspectives on Higher Education
• Methodology of Higher Education Research

Student enrollments: Ph.D. (full-time 8, part-time 53)

Key textbooks/readings:
• Martin Carnoy, ed. *International Encyclopedia of Economics of Education*. Pergamon, 1995.

• Postlethwaite, ed. *International Encyclopedia of National Systems of Education*. Pergamon, 1995.
• Anderson, ed. *International Encyclopedia of Teaching and Teacher Education*. Pergamon, 1995.
• Tuijman, ed. *International Encyclopedia of Adult and Continuing Education*. Pergamon, 1996.
• Plomp and Ely eds. 1996. International Encyclopedia of Educational Technology, Pergamon.
• DeCorte and Weinert, eds. *International Encyclopedia of Developmental and Instructional Psychology*. Pergamon, 1996.
• Keeves, ed. *International Encyclopedia of Educational Research Methodology and Measurement*. Pergamon, 1997.
• Lawrence J. Saha, ed. *International Encyclopedia of the Sociology of Education*. Pergamon, 1997.

Key journals:
   • *Compare*
   • *Comparative Education*
   • *Higher Education Policy*
   • *Higher Education in Europe*
   • *International Review of Education*

India

Association of Indian Universities

Address: AIU House, 16 Kotla Marg, New Delhi 110002, India

Telephone: 91-011-3230059; 3232429; 3233390; 3232305
Fax: 091-011-3236105
E-mail: aiu@del2.vsnl.net.in
Website: http://www.aiuweb.org
Date established: 1925
Major source of funding: membership fees; government

Organizational focus:
   The Association exists to:
   • serve as an interuniversity organization;

• act as a bureau of information and facilitate communication, coordination, and mutual consultation among universities;

• act as a liaison between the universities and the government;

• act as the representative of Indian universities;

• promote or undertake programs to improve standards of instruction, examination, research, textbooks, scholarly publications, library organization, and other programs that may contribute to the growth and propagation of knowledge;

• help universities to maintain their autonomous character;

• facilitate exchanges of members of the teaching and research staff;

• assist universities in obtaining recognition for their degrees, diplomas, and examinations from other universities, Indian as well as foreign;

• undertake, organize, and facilitate conferences, seminars, workshops, lectures and research in higher learning;

• establish and maintain a sports organization for promoting sports among member universities;

• establish and maintain organizations dealing with youth welfare, student services, cultural programs, adult education, and such other activities conducive to the improvement and welfare of students, teachers and others connected with universities;

• act as a service agency to universities; and

• undertake, facilitate, and provide for the publication of newsletters, research papers, books, and journals.

Staff (name • title/rank):
1. K. B. Powar • Secretary General
2. B. B. Dhar • Director (Research)
3. Sutinder Singh • Jt. Secretary and Editor, *University News*
4. Sampson David • Senior Cultural Officer
5. A. C. Gogia • Accounts Officer
6. Gurdeep Singh • Sports Officer
7. Veena Bhalla • Under Secretary (SIS)
8. B. S. Dahiya • Assistant Sales Officer

Key textbooks/readings:
• *University News* (weekly journal)
Current Publications:
• *Universities Handbook.*
• *Handbook of Computer Education.*
• *Handbook on Library and Information Science.*
• *Handbook of Distance Education.*
• *Handbook of Management Education.*

- *Directory of Distance Education Institution, Part II.*
- *Staff Development in Indian Unviersities.*
- *Higher Education in India: In Search of Quality.*
- *Policies of Higher Education.*
- *Liaison Cells for University-Industry Interaction.*
- *Accountability in Higher Education.*
- *Environmental Challenges and the Universities.*
- *Excellence Achieving Social Relevance in Higher Education.*
- *Higher Education in India: Retrospect and Prospect.*
- *State Funding of Universities.*
- *University Finance: A Statistical Profile II.*

National Institute of Educational Planning and Administration

Address: 17 B Sri Aurobindo Marg, New Delhi 110-016, India

Telephone: (91-11) 696-2120; 696-2335; 696-7780; 696-2126; 696-5305
Fax: (91-11) 685-3041; and 686-5180

Date Established: 1962 (by UNESCO), 1972 (by government)
Major source of funding: government

Organizational focus:
　　To conduct research, provide training, and offer consultancy services in the area of educational planning and development. The main geographical area of focus is India (including various states in India), countries in South Asia, and developing countries in general. The Institute is concerned with all levels and types of education.

Current publications:
　　Journals:
- *Journal of Educational Planning and Administration* (in English)
- *Pariprekshya* (in Hindi)

　　Books:
- *Reforms in School Education: Issues in Policy, Planning and Implementation.* 1996.

- *Modules on District Planning in Education.* 1997.
- *Educational Administration* (in various states in India, 1994-98).
- *Single-teacher Schools in Tribal Areas.* 1994.
- *Costs of Distance Education in India.* 1994.
- *Expenditure on Education.* 1994.

Staff (name • title/rank):
1. Jandhyala B. G. Tilak • Senior Fellow and Head, Educational Finance Unit
2. K. Sudha Rao • Senior Fellow, Higher Education Unit
3. N. V. Varghese • Senior Fellow, Sub-National Systems Unit

Courses:
Only Diploma Courses are offered (not exclusively in higher education). These include: diploma in educational planning and administration (6 months) for Indian nationals; international diploma in educational planning and administration (6 months) for participants outside India. In addition, several short term (1–3 weeks) training programs are offered. They are mostly in-service programs for officers in government education departments.

Key textbooks/readings:
- *Higher Education Reform in India.*
- *International Encyclopedia of Higher Education.*
- *Journal of Educational Planning and Administration*
- *International Journal of Educational Development*
- *Higher Education Review*
- *Comparative Education*
- *Comparative Education Review*
- *Perspectives in Education*
- *Higher Education Quarterly*

Japan

Hiroshima University, Research Institute for Higher Education

Address: 2-2, Kagamiyama 1-chome, Higashi-Hiroshima 739-8512, Japan

Telephone: 0824-24-6240

Fax: 0824-22-7104
E-mail: x920009@ipc.hiroshima-u.ac.jp
Website: http://www.ipc.hiroshima-u.ac.jp/rihe/Japanese/index.html

Date Established: May 1972
Major Source of Funding: University

Organizational focus:
The Institute's first priority is to serve as a national focal point of higher education research activities. Its second priority is to serve Hiroshima University in its effort as an organization of institutional study to improve the quality of university education and management. The third function relates to international activity. Additionally, the Institute takes part in various international joint research activities with UNESCO, OECD, and other university consortia outside Japan.

Current publications:
- a collection of studies of the university (an annual publication featuring academic essays and research reports on higher education)
- a research papers series (a collection of short interim reports, bibliographical notes, translations of important foreign documents, etc.)
- *Colleague* (a newspaper).
- a catalogue of books on higher education
- a book of statistical data on higher education

Staff (ame • title/rank • specialization):
1. Arimoto Akira • Professor and Director • sociology of education
2. Kurimoto Kazuo • Professor • educational administration
3. Yamanoi Atsunori • Professor • sociology of education
4. Imai Shigetaka • Professor • comparative education
5. Otsuka Yutaka • Professor • comparative education
6. Hata Takashi • Associate Professor • history of higher education in Japan
7. Yonezawa Akiyoshi • Assistant Professor • sociology and economics of education
8. Nanbu Hirotaka • Research Associate • comparative education
9. Kanno Fumi • Research Associate • sociology of education
10. Hirata Yuji • Research Associate • history of education
11. Murasawa Masataka • Research Associate • sociology of education

Courses:
- The University and Higher Education

- Comparative Higher Education
- Higher Education Policy
- Comparative University Systems
- University Economics and Budgets
- International Academic Exchanges

Student enrollments: M.A. (2 full-time), Ph.D. (2 full-time), other (1 full-time)

Key textbooks/readings:
- Burton R. Clark. *The Higher Education System: Academic Organization in Cross-National Perspective*. University of California Press. 1983.
- *Japanese Journal of Higher Education Research*

Hokkaido University, Center for Research and Development in Higher Education

Address: Kita 17, Nishi 8, Kita-ku, Sapporo 060-0817, Japan

Telephone: +81-11-706-5247
Fax: +81-11-706-7854
E-mail: kyomu@high.hokudai.ac.jp
Website: http://infosys.hokudai.ac.jp

Date established: 1995
Major source of funding: University

Organizational focus:
The Center was established in the course of a university-wide reorganization in1995, as a cooperative research unit to study education at the undergraduate level and beyond, including adult education and lifelong learning. The three objectives of the center are as follows:
- Planning and adjustment of general education: undergraduate education at the Hokkaido University has two components: specialized education and general education. These two components are intergrated into a coherent curriculum. The Center plans and adjusts the general education component to implement the curriculum smoothly and effectively;
- Research on higher education: the Center researches and studies higher education. This includes the study of teaching evaluation and improvement of teaching technique; and

• Research on adult education and lifelong learning: the Center researches and studies adult education and lifelong learning. This includes the systemization of lifelong learning plans and the organization of community extension programs.

Current publications:
  • *Higher Education and Lifelong Learning* (journal)
  • *Center News* (newsletter)

Staff (name • title/rank):
  Research Division for Higher Education:
  1. Abe Kazuhiro • Director, Professor
  2. Ogasawara Masaaki • Professor
  3. Nishimori Toshiyuki • Professor
  4. Hosokawa Toshiyuki • Professor

  Research Division for Lifelong Learning:
  5. Kobayashi Hajime
  6. Machii Teruhisa
  7. Kimura Makotao
  8. Takeuchi Shinya

Institute for Democratic Education

Address: 2-16-1 Nishi-Shinbashi, Minato-ku, Tokyo 105-0003, Japan

Telephone: 03-3431-6822
Fax: 03-3431-6822

Date established: July 1954
Major source of funding: membership and subscription fees

Organizational focus:
  The Institute for Democratic Education (IDE) is a nonprofit private organization concerned with higher education management, teaching, and research. IDE's main purpose is to discuss and report on problems and issues in the field of higher education. Research questions include: What are the tasks of universal higher education? How should institutions be managed? What are the important issues for students and

teachers? IDE publishes a monthly magazine, *IDE: Current Higher Education*, with a circulation of more than 6,000.

Current publications:
- *IDE: Current Higher Education*
- *Reconsidering Liberal Education.*
- *Articulation between Higher Education and High School Education.*

Institute for Higher Education

Address: 2-16-1 Nishi-Shinbashi 1, Minato-ku, Tokyo 105-0003, Japan

Telephone: 03-3451-6822
Fax: 03-3451-6822

Date established: 1979
Major source of funding: grants; philanthropic organizations

Organizational focus:
The Institute for Higher Education is a private research institute that was established as a sister organization to the Institute for Democratic Education. The Institute's main purpose is to research the problems of higher education, mainly from a research-oriented and policy-oriented standpoint.

Current publications:
- *Bulletin of Higher Education*

Kobe University, Research Institute for Higher Education (Kobe Daigaku Daigakukyouiku Kennkyuu Senta)

Address: 1-2-1 Tsurukabuto, Nada-ku, Kobe, Hyogo-ken 657-8501, Japan
Telephone: +81-78-881-1212 (Operator)
Fax: +81-78-803-7640
Website: http://www.kurihe.kobe-u.ac.jp

Date established: October 1992
Major source of funding: University

Organizational focus:
    The institute has three primary objectives:
    • research undergraduate and graduate education and related issues;
    • conduct institutional assessments of the universitywide general education program; and
    • plan and organize the universitywide general education program.

Current publications:
    • *Kobe Journal of Higher Education* (annual)

Staff (name • title/rank • specialization):
    1. Tsuchiya Motonori • Director and Professor • educational administration
    2. Hada Shigeki • Vice Director, Chief of Research Division and Professor • geology
    3. Kawashima Tatsuo • Professor • sociology of education, comparative higher education
    4. Maiya Kiyoshi • Associate Professor • experimental psychology
    5. Yamanouchi Kenshi • Associate Professor • educational planning, sociology of education

Kyoto University, Research Center for Higher Education

Address: Yoshida-Honmachi, Sakyo-ku, Kyoto 606-8501, Japan

Telephone: +81-75-753-3087
Fax: +81-75-753-3045
E-mail: mishiwat@ip.media.kyoto-u.ac.jp
Website: http://www.adm.kyoto-u.ac.ip/higherdu/indexE.htm

Date established: 1994
Major source of funding: University

Organizational focus:
    The Research Center's areas of focus include:
    • the investigation and research of creative thinking and its development through higher education;
    • reform of university curricula;

• development of evaluation systems for university education;
• practical counseling, seminars, and training courses for academic staff development; and
• international and interdisciplinary research on staff development.

Current publications:
   • *Research in Higher Education* (annual)
   • *The Questionnaire Research on Kyoto University Graduates.*
   • *Fundamental Research on the Higher Education Teaching System.*
   • *The Record of Open Laboratory Class.*
   • *For Research and Development of the Teaching System.*
   • *Toward the Open University Class: One Year of the Open Laboratory Class of Kyoto University.*

Staff (name • title/rank • specialization):
   1. Ogino Fumimaru • Director/Professor
   2. Tanaka Tsunemi • Professor • educational philosophy
   3. Ishimura Masao • Associate Professor • system, policy, and organization in higher education
   4. Oyama Yashuhiro • Associate Professor • clinical psychology, student counseling
   5. Mizokami Shinichi • Instructor • self-identity theory, youth and adolescent psychology
   6. Shinto Takaai • Instructor • educational psychology, developmental psychology

Courses:
   • Studies in Higher Education
   • Advanced Studies: Higher Education I
   • Advanced Studies: Higher Education II
   • Advanced Studies: Higher Education I II
   • Advanced Studies: Higher Education IV
   • Seminar in Higher Education

Student enrollments: M.A. (10 full-time), Ph.D. (1 full-time)

Key textbooks/readings:
   • *Higher Education*
   • *Research in Higher Education*

Nagoya University, Center for the Studies of Higher Education (Nagoya Daigaku Koutoukyouiku Kenkyusenta)

Address: Furo-cho, Chikusa-ku, Nagoya-City, 464-8601 Japan

Telephone: 81-52-789-5385
Fax: 81-52-789-5695
E-mail: j45818a@nucc.cc.nagoya-u.ac.jp
Website: http://www.cshe.nagoya-u.ac.jp/

Date established: 1998
Major source of funding: University

Organizational focus:
Research for improving undergraduate curriculum and teaching methods, and for strengthening graduate programs through joint study projects and seminars in cooperation with Japanese and international researchers in higher education.

Staff (name • title/rank • specialization):
1. Umakoshi Toru • Director • comparative higher education
2. Todayama Kazuhisa • Associate Professor • science philosophy
3. Chikada Masahiro • Assistant Professor • comparative higher education
4. Nakai Toshiki • Research Associate • educational development
5. Two professorships—one for foreigners, the other for Japanese—are also funded every year.

National Institute of Multimedia Education (NIME)

Address: 2 -12 Wakaba, Mihama-ku, Chiba 261-0014, Japan
Telephone: 81-43-298-3000
Fax: 81-43-298-3471
E-mail: sakamoto@nime.ac.jp
Website: http://www.nime.ac.jp/

Date established: 1978
Major source of funding: governmet

Organizational focus:

The National Institute of Multimedia Education (NIME) promotes the use of multimedia in higher education, researches and develops curricula and methods for education using various advanced media, and disseminates the findings of its research and development activities.

The Institute's activities are currently focused on the following areas:
- space collaboration systems,
- database projects,
- multimedia instructional materials, and
- faculty development.

Current publications:
- *Survey of National Institute of Multimedia Education.*
- *Media and Education.*
- Yasuo Fukui. *Instructional Materials for Undergraduate Education: Research and Practice.*
- Keizo Magaoka. *Research and Development of Broad-Band Multimedia Network Systems for Education.*
- Jane M. Bachnik. *A Pedagogy for Cross-cultural Teaching and Learning.*
- Kobayashi Toshio. *An International Symposium: Bringing Today's Education into the Hi-tech World of Tomorrow.*
- Hirro Saga. *Media in Higher Education and Instructional Skill Development.*
- newsletter (monthly)

Staff (name • title/rank • specialization):
1. Jane Bachnik • Professor • media-based learning
2. Itoh Hideko • Professor • media-based learning
3. Kikukawa Takeshi • Professor • digital media distribution
4. Kobayashi Toshio • Professor • networks
5. Mizushima Kazuo • Professor • copyright handling systems
6. Otsuka Yusaku • Professor • media-based learning
7. Saga Hiroo • Professor • media literacy
8. Sugimoto Yuji • Professor • networks
9. Tashiro Kazuhisa • Professor • media literacy
10. Yuki Kiyohiro • Professor • networks

Niigata University, Center for Cooperative Research (CCRNU)

Address: 8050, Ikarashi 2-no-cho, Niigata-shi, Niigata-ken 950-2181, Japan

Telephone: +81-25-262-7554
Fax: +81-25-262-7550
Website: http://www.ccr.niigata-u.ac.jp/

Date established: April 1991
Major source of funding: University

Organizational focus:
   The Center's main purpose is to assist with the arrangement and accomplishment of cooperative research projects between private companies and Niigata University.

Current publications:
   • *News of CCRNU*
   • *Annual Report of CCRNU.*
   • *Professors' Research Subjects for Cooperative Research.*
   • *About CCRNU.*

Staff (name • title/rank • specialization):
   1. Kimura Isao • Associate Professor • chemical and materials engineering

Tohoku University, Research Center for Higher Education

Address: Kawauchi, Aobaku, Sendai 980-8506, Japan

Telephone: +81-22-217-7533 (Professor Hoshimiya); +81-22-217-7540 (Office)
E-mail: nozumu@hoshimiya.ecei.tohoku.ac.jp
Website: http://www.high-edu.tohoku.ac.jp

Date established: 1993
Major source of funding: University

Organizational focus:
    The Research Center for Higher Education (RCHE) is now the organization responsible for institutional planning at Tohoku University.

Current publications:
    • newsletter (semi-annual)
    • annual report

Staff (name • title/rank • specialization):
    1. Hoshimiya Nozomu • Professor • engineering
    2. Saihot Koichi • Professor • chemistry
    3. Sekiguchi Takashi • Western history
    4. Tomita Makoto • Associate Professor • law
    5. Kuzuu Masanoro • economics

Tokyo, University of, Center for Research and Development of Higher Education

Address: University of Tokyo, 7-3-1 Hongo, Bunkyo-ku, Tokyo 113-0033, Japan

Telephone: +81-3-5841-2390
Fax: +81-3-5802-3372
E-mail: <kaneko@educhan.p.u-tokyo.ac.jp>; <masadayo@educhan.p.u-tokyo.ac.jp>;<ymabuchi@educhan.p.u-tokyo.ac.jp>; <otawa@educhan.p.u-tokyo.ac.jp>
Website: <http://www.he.u-tokyo.ac.jp/>

Date established: 1996
Major source of funding: University

Organizational focus:
    The Center provides two primary functions: to carry out research concerning the reform of the university, in particular, in the management and finance; and to support the development of curricula and teaching at the University of Tokyo and other universities. The Center provides basic data and information to assist the university in reforming its academic and administrative arrangements, and engages in academic research into the structure and contents of higher education. Its specific duties concern the following three activities:

• The first mission of the Center is to analyze the current problems and possible ways to improve higher education. In 1997 it conducted a survey of all fourth-year undergraduates to analyze the problems with current classroom teaching. The insights obtained through the survey have been reported to the whole university and to individual faculties. It is planning a follow-up survey on the class of 1997.

• The Center's second mission is to analyze current practices in governance and forms of control, decision making, and finance at the university, while exploring alternative forms. A research project was launched in 1997 for this purpose.

• The third mission of the Center is to help create and participate in the networks linking various initiatives for university reforms both in Japan and overseas. It has been cooperating with similar centers in Japan and has a close relation with international organizations including OECD-IMHE. In 1997, in cooperation with UNESCO it held a round table on "the relationship between research, policy and practice in higher education."

Current publications:
• newsletter (in Japanese)

Staff (name • title/rank • specialization):
1. Kaneko Motohisa • Director, Professor • economics of education
2. Yano Masakazu • Professor • social engineering
3. Kobayashi Masayuki • Associate Professor • educational planning
4. Mabuchi Yasutaka • Research Associate • educational research
5. Ohtawa Naoki • Research Associate • student culture

Key textbooks/readings:
• *Higher Education*
• *Higher Education Review*
• *Economics of Education Review*
• *Journal of Human Resources*
• *European Journal of Education*
• other journals (in Japanese)

Tsukuba University, Research Center for University Studies

Address: Otsuka 3-29-1, Bunkyo-ku, Tokyo 112-0012, Japan

Telephone: +81-3-3942-6304, 6307
Fax: +81-3-3942-6310

Website: http://130.158.176.12/

Date established: 1986
Major source of funding: University

Organizational focus:
   The purpose of the Center is to provide universities and policymakers with various kinds of analysis on higher education systems through problem-oriented research.

Current publications:
   • *University Studies* (journal)

Staff:
   • One, each, of the following: Director; Professor; Associate Professor; Assistant Professor; Research Associate
   • Part-time researchers: 2 within the University of Tsukuba, 13 outside the University of Tsukuba

Key textbooks/readings:
   • *Journal of Higher Education*
   • *Science*
   • *Japanese Journal of Higher Education Research*

Waseda University, Higher Education Program, Graduate School of Letters

Address: Waseda University, Totsuka-cho, Shinjuku-ku, Tokyo Japan

Telephone: 03-3203-4141
Fax: 03-3232-3970
E-mail: kitamura@nier.go.jp

Date established: 1950
Major source of funding: University

Organizational focus:
   Training academics and administrators in higher education

Staff (name • title/rank • specialization):
    1. Kitamura Kazuyuki • Visiting Professor

Courses:
- lectures on higher education
- seminars on higher education
- guidance and tutoring regarding M.A. and Ph.D. dissertations

Student enrollments: M.A. (5 full-time, 3 part-time), Ph.D. (3 full-time, 3 part-time)

Key textbooks/readings:
- Clark Kerr. *The Uses of the University.*
- Clark Kerr. *The Troubled Times of American Higher Education.*
- Kerr, Clark. Higher education cannot escape history.
- Eric Ashby. *Any Person, Any Study.*
- *Higher Education*
- *Chronicle of Higher Education*
- *Times Higher Education Supplement*
- *Change Magazine*

Jordan

The Association of Arab Universities (AARU)

Address: P.O. Box 401, Jubeyha, Amman 11941, Jordan

Telephone: 962-6-5345131; 962-6-5340135
Fax: 962-6-5332994
Website: http://www.aaru.edu.jo

Date established: 1964
Major source of funding: membership fees

Organizational focus:
    The goals of the Association of Arab Universities are:
- to enhance cooperation among Arab universities and to coordinate their efforts with a view to raising the quality of university and higher education;

- to encourage scientific research—especially applied research;
- to exchange knowledge and experience among universities; and
- to hold scientific conferences and symposia (in support of the autonomy of universities).

AARU activities include:

- to hold seminars and conferences;
- to prepare guides that contain data on member universities and their academic staff;
- to issue specialized journals, bulletins, and brochures; and
- to monitor activities of the institutions affiliated with our organization.

Current publications:

- *Journal of the Association of Arab Universities* (semiannual)
- *AARU Bulletin*
- *The Association of Arab Universities: A Brief Account*. (AARU promotional brochure)
- journals issued by other faculty associations at Arab universities—such as, *Journal of the Association of Arab Universities for Medical Studies and Research; Journal of the Association of Arab Universities for Engineering Studies and Research; Journal of the Association of Arab Universities for Agricultural Studies and Research.*
- *The Guidebook of Arab Universities.*
- proceedings of conferences and scientific seminars held by AARU

Korea, Republic of

Korean Council for University Education

Address: 27-2 Youido-dong, Youngdungpo-gu, Seoul 150-749, South Korea

Telephone: 822-783-3065
Fax: 822-780-7941
E-mail: hclee@mail.kosco.or.kr

Date established: 1982
Major source of funding: University

Organizational focus:
    The Council is a nonprofit, nongovernmental, and intermediating
    organization between government and university communities.

Current publications:
    • *Higher Education* (journal)
    • *An Evaluation Report of Institutional Accreditation.* 1998.
    • *University Entrance Examination Information Book.* 1998.

Korean Educational Development Institute (KEDI)

Address: 92-6, Umyeon-dong, Seocho-gu, Seoul 137-791, Korea

Telephone: (882) 572-8393
Fax: (882) 573-2361
E-mail: kwak@ns.kedi.re.kr
Website: http://www.kedi.re.kr

Date established: 1972
Major source of funding: government

Organizational focus:
    KEDI's main purposes are:
    • to undertake research and development activities concerning edu-
    cational ideals, objectives, contents, and methodology;
    • to assist the government in formulating educational policy;
    • to develop modern educational methods, technology, and mate-
    rials; and
    • to publish and disseminate research findings and educational
    information.
    Our main programs include the following areas: schooling research,
    lifelong education research, the Educational Credit Bank System,
    the Air and Correspondence High School, education information
    research, education statistics; and Understanding Korea.

Current publications:
    • *Annual Review of Korean Education.*
    • *Journal of Korean Education—Education Development*
    • *KEDI Newsletter*

• research reports—such as, *Tuition for Private Education Institutes (Hakwon): Problems and Appropriate Measures; Action Research on Curriculum Reconstruction and Teaching: Learning Methods for Implementing Open Education. Korean Education Vision 2020: Recent Developments and Prospects for Korean Education. Korean Education and National Development (1945–1995); A Study of UNESCO Education Policy and Program Analysis.*

Staff (name • title/rank • specialization):
1. Kwak Byong-Sun • Acting President • curriculum and instruction
2. Chung Taek-Hee • Director, Center for Educational Measurement and Schooling Research and Evaluation
3. Kim Young-Chul • Director, Center for Lifelong Education Research • educational administration
4. Park Duk-Kyu • Director, Center for Education Information Research • educational policy
5. Kong Eun-Bae • Director, Office of Planning and Coordination • educational finance
6. Han You-Kyung • Researcher • educational administration
7. Kim Hung-Ju • Researcher • educational administration
8. Lee Jeong-Kyu • Researcher • educational administration
9. Park Jae-Youn • Researcher • educational administration
10. Kim Jeong-Rae • Researcher • educational philosophy
11. Ko Jeon • Researcher • educational policy
12. Paik Sung-Jun • Researcher • educational finance
13. Yu Hyun-Sook • Researcher • educational administration
14. Im Youn-Kee • Researcher • educational administration
15. Kim Hey-Sook • Researcher • educational administration
16. Lee In-Hyo • Researcher • educational policy
17. Choi Don-Min • Researcher • educational sociology
18. Park In-Jong • Researcher • educational sociology
19. Kim Ee-Gyeong • Researcher • educational administration

Lithuania

Lithuanian Center for Quality Assessment in Higher Education (Studiju Kokybes Vertinimo Centras)

Address: Suvalku 1, Vilnius LT-2009, Lithuania

Telephone: (370-2) 23 25 55, 23 25 52
Fax: (370-2) 23 25 53

Website: http://www.skvc.lt

Date established: 1995
Major source of funding: state government

Organizational focus:
The basic goals of Center are as follows:
> • to coordinate the regular self-evaluation process of scientific and pedagogical activity of state and nonstate institutions of research and higher education. The Center also organizes assessment of that self-evaluation, accumulates and publishes information about the process, to offers suggestions for improving it; and
>
> • to provide information, consultation, and recommendations for research and higher education institutions and other juridical persons on all questions connected with the recognition of higher education acquired abroad.

Current publications:
> • information bulletins

Staff (name • title/rank • specialization):
1. Algirdas Cizas • Director, Professor • engineering, education
2. Birute Mockiene • Vice Director • education
3. Irmantas Aleliunas • Head of the Group for Systematization and Information • informatics
4. Silvestra Satkuviene • Program Specialist • education
5. Darius Tamosiunas • Program Specialist • history, education
6. Vytautas Daujotis • Program Specialist • chemistry, education

Mexico

Department of Educational Research (Departamento de investigaciones educativas)

Address: San Borja 938, 03100, Mexico

Telephone: (52-5) 559-4080
Fax: 575-0320
E-mail: kentr@data.net.mx

Date established: Center 1960; Department 1973
Major sources of funding: government, research funds from the National
    Council for Science and Technology, patents, services

Organizational focus:
    The Department of Educational Research is a an educational research
    department belonging to the Higher Education Research Center, a pub-
    lic research and postgraduate science institute. The Center employs
    550 full-time researchers, all PhD's, in Physics, math, neurophysiol-
    ogy, biotechnology, electrical engineering, chemistry, education, and
    various other fields. The Center has its main campus in Mexico D.F.,
    plus departments in five other cities in Mexico.

    Our department does research on all educational topics including
    higher education. We have a master's program in educational research
    (2 years, plus thesis) and a Ph.D. program run on a tutorial basis (3 1/
    2 years including dissertation). We have 22 full-time professors, plus
    17 research assistants.

Current publications:
    • The Department publishes books (mostly selected theses) and work-
    ing papers from on-going research projects.

Staff (name • title/rank • specialization):
    1. Rollin Kent • Full Professor • higher education policy in Mexico and
    Latin America, institutional change in Mexican higher education
    2. Sylvie Didou • Full Professor • higher education policy in North
    America, decentralization of the higher education system in Mexico
    3. Eduardo Remedi • Full Professor • regional history of higher educa-
    tion in Mexico 1950–1980
    4. German Alvarez • Associate Professor • higher education policy in Mexico
Courses:
    • master's program: Educational Policy in Mexico
    • doctoral program: because of the tutorial system, coursework varies, but all
    Ph.D. candidates in higher education take a four-month seminar in compara-
    tive higher education policy.

Student enrollments: M.A. (25 full-time); Ph.D. (15 full-time)

Key textbooks/readings:
    • Jose Joaquin Brunner. *Educación superior en América Latina: Cambios y
    perspectivas*. Mexico: Fondo de Cultura Económica, 1991.•

- Burton R. Clark. *The Higher Education System*. University of California Press.
- Rollin Kent. *Modernización conservadora y crisis académica en la UNAM*. Mexico: Editorial Nueva Imagen, 1990.
- Burton R. Clark and Guy Neave, eds. *Encyclopedia of Higher Education*. Pergamon.
- *Universidad futura*. Mexico: Autonomous Metropolitan University, 1989–1996.
- *Revista mexicana de investigación educativa*. Consejo mexicano de investigación educativa (Mexican Educational Research Association)
- *Higher Education*
- *European Journal of Education*
- *Review of Higher Education*
- *Latin American Research Review*
- *Journal of Latin American Studies*

National Association of Universities and Institutions of Higher Education (ANUIES)

Address: ANUIES, Tenayuca 200. Col. Sta Cruz Atoyac, C.P. 03310, Mexico D.F.

Telephone: 54-20-49-09; 54-20-49-08; 54-20-49-19; 54-20-49-10
Fax: 56-04-42-63; 54-20-49-53
E-mail: dtm@anuies.mx; dsanchez@anuies.mx; etenorio@anuies.mx; mfresan@anuies.mx
Website: http://www.anuies.mx

Date established: 1991
Major source of funding: membership fees; Office of the Secretary of Public Education

Organizational focus:
Our main purpose is:
- to foster a complete and permanent improvement of quality, relevance, and coverage of programs and services offered by the member institutions;
- to analyze higher education in order to foresee changes, design, define and coordinate policies, and provide information to support

decision making;
- to identify common academic and administrative interests of the associated institutions and represent these institutions before the executive, legislative, and judicial powers; and before public and private organizations in the country and overseas;
- to participate with Mexican organizations that coordinate higher education, to strengthen the development of models, methods ,and procedures for planning and evaluation;
- to foster upgrading and updating of higher education faculty, administrators, and leaders, enhance exchanges among members and organize interintitutional activities and projects to achieve better comunication and collaboration; and
- to promote relationships and agreements with national and international organizations and with social and productive sectors having common or complementary goals with the Association.

Current publications:
- Library of Higher Education Collection
- series: Essays and Research Reports, Reports and Documents; Bibliographies, International Experiences, annuals, catalogues, directories
- Contemporary Issues on Higher Education Collection
- Collection of Information and Statistics
- *Higher Educational Journal*
- *Confluencia* (monthly newsletter)
- *Confluencia regional* (bulletin)
- materials providing information on the activities and programs of Association members

Staff (name • title/rank):
1. Julio Rubio Oca • General Executive Secretary
2. Martha Riebeling Solache • Secretary
3. Dolores Sánchez Soler • Academic Secretary
4. David Torres Mejía • Secretary of Analysis and Studies
5. Enrique Tenorio Guillén • Secretary of Planning
6. Rodríguez Santillán • Coordinator of Information and Public Relations
7. Rafael Campos Sánchez • Coordinator of Boards and Regional Programs
8. Ruiz Lugo • Coordinator of Extension Programs
9. Rebeca Ambriz Chávez • Coordinator of Institutional Programs
10. Magdalena Fresín Orozco • Coordinator of Special Projects
11. Huíscar Taborga Torrico • Coordinator of Research

12. Homero E. Pérez Flores • Coordinator
13. José Luis Cuevas Nava • Coordinator of Continuing Education

Courses: ANUIES offers courses in continuing education only.

Universidad autónoma metropolitana, Sociology of the Universities Research Area (Area de investigación en sociología de las universidades)

Address: Av. San Pablo 180, Col. Reynosa-Tamaulipas, Delegación Azcapotzalco, Distrito Federal, Ciudad De Mexico 02200, Mexico
Telephone: 52 (5) 724 4340
Fax: 52 (5) 723 5924

Date established: 1990
Major source of funding: University

Organizational focus:
The main purpose of the Research Area is to conduct research in the higher education field from a sociological perspective. We have three research programs: the academic profession in Mexico, organizational change in Mexican universities (public policies in higher education); and Mexican students. The research programs correspond with our main objective of studying higher education actors, processes, and organizational structures.

Current publications:
• *Los rasgos de la diversidad: Un estudio sobre los académicos mexicanos.* Mexico: UAM-Azcapotzalco, 1994.

Staff (name • title/rank • specialization):
1. Rocío Grediaga-Kuri • Director • academic profession program
2. Manuel Gil-Antún • Researcher • academic profession program
3. María Lilia Pérez-Franco • Researcher • academic profession program
4. Romualdo López-Zarate • Researcher • organizational change in Mexican universities
5. Adrián de Garay-Sanchez • Researcher • Mexican students program
6. León Tomás Ejea-Mendoza • Researcher • organizational change in Mexican universities
7. Miguel Casillas-Alvarado • Researcher • academic profession program

8. Mario González-Rubí • Researcher • organizational change in Mexican universities
9. Mery Hamui-Sutton • Researcher • academic profession program
10. Norma Rondero-López • Lecturer • organizational change in Mexican universities
11. Dinorah Miller-Flores • Lecturer • Mexican students program
12. Claudia Cárdenas-Cabello • Lecturer • academic profession program

Morocco

Research into Higher Education Unit

Address: Faculte des Lettres, Dhar Mehraz, Fez, Morocco
Telephone: (05)600141

Date established: 1998
Major source of funding: government

Organizational focus:
The research program of the unit deals with attrition rates in higher education in Morocco, with special reference to departments of English in arts faculties. Our aim is to assess the potential causes and effects of attrition, as well as organizational, teaching, and assessment strategies that may help attenuate the negative effects of attrition.

Staff (name • title/rank • specialization):
1. Mohamed Ouakrime • Coordinator, Professor, Researcher • applied linguistics and research into higher education
2. Fatima Mouaid • Lecturer, Researcher • sociolinguistics, women's studies, and research into higher education
3. B. Akabouch • Assistant Lecturer, Researcher • assessment and research into higher education
4. A. Hakim • Assistant Lecturer, Researcher • British studies and research into higher education
5. M. Moubtassime • Assistant Lecturer, Researcher • linguistics and research into higher education
6. A. Azennoud • secondary school teacher, Researcher • English language and research into higher education

7. A. El Heggach • Assistant Lecturer, Researcher • applied linguistics and research into higher education

Key textbooks/readings:
- *Journal of College Student Retention: Research, Theory and Practice*
- *SRHE Abstracts*
- various journals on higher education and assessment

The Netherlands

Twente, University of, Center for Higher Education Policy Studies (CHEPS)

Address: P.O. Box 217, Enschede 7500 AE, The Netherlands

Telephone: + 31 53 489 3263
Fax: + 31 53 434 0392
Website: http://www.utwente.nl/cheps

Date established: 1984
Major source of funding: University (25%), Contract research and other services (75%)

Organizational focus:
The Center for Higher Education Policy Studies (CHEPS) is an interdisciplinary research organization that contributes to debates on policymaking, governance, and management in higher education on the basis of its research program. This research program has three broad research themes: higher education governance and management, higher education finance, and quality assurance and quality management in higher education. The Center also supports higher education institutions and organizations through applied research, courses, workshops, and consultancy.

Current publications:
- Ben Jongbloed, Peter Maassen, Guy Neave, eds. *From the Eye of the Storm: Higher Education's Changing Institution.* Dordrecht/Boston/London: Kluwer, 1999.

• Jeroen Bartels. *Concentrating the Minds: The Institutionalisation of the Graduate School Innovation in Dutch and German Higher Education*. Utrecht: Lemma, 1999.

• J. Scheele, P. Maassen, and D. Westerheijden, eds. *To Be Continued ... Follow-up of Quality Assurance in Higher Education*. Maarssen: Elsevier/De Tijdstroom, 1998.

• A. Rip, ed. *Steering and Effectiveness in a Developing Knowledge Society*. Utrecht: Lemma, 1998.

Staff (name • title/rank • specialization):

1. J. Bartelse • Adviser • doctoral education and research training
2. E. Beerkens • Research Associate • globalization and international cooperation in higher education
3. J. Beverwijk • Research Associate • higher education monitor
4. H.F. de Boer • Senior Researcher • governance, management, decision making and policy analysis
5. P. Boezerooy • Researcher • higher education monitor
6. J. File • Associate Director • higher education planning and management
7. L. Goedegebuure • Senior Researcher • higher education management
8. O. van Heffen • Senior Researcher • governance, institutional analysis
9. M. Hoppe • Researcher • quality management
10. J. Huisman • Research Coordinator • curriculum change, diversity, steering
11. I. Jenniskens • Course Coordinator • curriculum change, distance education
12. B. Jongbloed • Senior Researcher • resource allocation, cost analysis, marketization
13. F. Kaiser • Senior Researcher • higher education monitor, use of indicators
14. A. Klemperer • Researcher • higher education monitor, research policy
15. J. Koelman • Senior Researcher • financial management, resource allocation, marketization
16. G. Leibbrandt • Researcher • distance education
17. E. Lugthart • Researcher • effectiveness, comparing diversity
18. P. Maassen • Director • steering, university governance, academic profession, economic role of institutions
19. L. van der Maat • Researcher • higher education monitor
20. P. van der Meer • Postdoctoral Fellow • labor market, marketization, privatization

21. G. Neave • Visiting Professor • European integration, higher education policy in Europe
22. V. Rakic • Postdoctoral Fellow • Europeanization, institutional analysis
23. H. Scholte • Consultant • project acquisition, and tendering; project management and implementation
24. H. Theisens • Research Trainee • policy studies, institutional theory
25. A. Verkleij • Senior Adviser • quality management mechanisms for institutions, research and education
26. H. Vossensteyn • Researcher • student financial support, economics
27. A. van Wageningen • Research Trainee • Dutch public law
28. E. de Weert • Senior Researcher • higher education and employment, human resources management
29. M. van der Wende • Senior Researcher • internationalization of higher education; information technology in higher education
30. D. Westerheijden • Senior Researcher • quality management, transformation in Central and Eastern Europe, buffer organizations

Courses:
   • Institutional Management and Change in Higher Education—a one-year, postgraduate certificate course at the master's level, this course consists of three units: (1) Nature of Academic Organisation; (2) Management and Decision-Making in Higher Education Institutions; and (3) Quality Management in Higher Education Institutions. Each unit has its own course guide and reader.

Student enrollments: (21 part-time)

Key textbooks/readings:
   • *Higher Education Policy*
   • *Comparative Education*
   • *European Journal of Education*
   • *Quality in Higher Education*
   • *Higher Education Quarterly*
   • *Comparative Education Review*
   • *Education Economics*
   • *Higher Education in Europe*
   • *Higher Education*
   • *Higher Education Management*
   • *New Directions for Higher Education*
   • *New Directions for Institutional Research*

Norway

Norweigan Institute for Studies in Research and Higher Education (NIFU)

Address: Heldehaugsveien 31, Oslo N-0352, Norway

Telephone: +47 22 59 51 0083
Fax: +47 22 59 51 01
E-mail: jannecke.wiers-jenssen@nifu.no
Website: http://www.nifu.no

Date established: 1969
Major source of funding: Norwegian Resource Council, contract research

Organizational focus:
   Research and development statistics and resource analysis, science policy studies, institutions of higher education, study conditions, and student flow

Current publications:
   • *Forskinigspolitikk* (Research Policy, quarterly journal)

Oslo, University of, Institute for Educational Research (Universitetet i Oslo Pedagogisk forskningsinstitutt)

Address: Sem Saelands vei 7, Blindern, Oslo N–0317, Norway

Telephone: 47 22 85 5348
Fax: 47 22 85 4250

Date established: 1998
Major source of unding: University

Organizational focus:
   At the Institute for Educational Research, a master's program in comparative and international education and a research project on the service university have produced a group of researchers and research students focusing on higher education. Within the M.Phil. program, and related

to it, there are several courses (of 7–14 weeks per term) on topics related to international higher education policies.

Current publications:
Reports on higher education research are published both within the series published by the Nordic Network of International and Comparative Education and the Institute for Educational Research's series, Studies in Comparative and International Education.

Some recent titles:
• "The Service University in a Service Society: The Oslo Case," Kristine Holtet. *Higher Education*, 1997.
• "The Service University in Service-Societies: The Norwegian Experience. " In *Globalization and the University: Critical Perspectives*, ed. J. Currie and J. Newson. Thousand Oaks, Calif.: Sage, 1997.
• *A Service University in Scandinavia? Studies in Comparative and International Education*. Vol. 1. Oslo: University of Oslo Institute for Educational Research, 1997.

Staff: (name • title/rank):
1. Arild Tjeldvoll • Professor
2. Lise Vislie • Professor, Dean of the Faculty of Education
3. Karen Jensen • Researcher
4. Berit Karseth • Researcher
5. Suzanne Lie • Researcher
6. Gunnar Handal • Researcher
7. Per Lauvås • Researcher
8. Kirsten Lycke • Researcher
9. Sten Ludvigsen • Researcher

Courses:
• Globalization and Higher Education Policies
• The Service University
• Evaluation of Higher Education

Student enrollments: M.A. (7 full-time), Ph.D. (44 full-time)

Key textbooks/readings:
• *Comparative Education Review*
• *Higher Education*

- Maassen, P. M and F. v. Vugt . *Inside Academia: New Challenges for the Academic Profession*. Utrecht: Tijdstroom, 1996.
- R. Arnove, P. G. Altbach, and G. Kelly. *Emergent Issues in Education: Comparative Perspectives*. Albany: SUNY Press, 1992.
- Ivar Bleiklie. *Knowledge and Power: Norwegian Higher Education in Change*. Oslo University Press, 1996.

Poland

Warsaw, University of, Center for Science Policy and Higher Education (Centrum Badan Polityki Naukowej i Szkolnictwa Wyzszego, Uniwersytet Warszawski)

Address: Warsaw University, Nowy Swiat 69, Warsaw PL 00-046, Poland

Telephone: 48 (22) 826 07 46
Fax: 48 (22) 826 07 46
E-mail: bialecki@mercury.ci.uw.edu.pl

Date established: 1992, in the University—replacing the former Institute on Science Policy and Higher Education, established in 1962 and affiliated with the Ministry of Higher Education.
Major source of funding: University

Organizational focus:
The focus of the Center is research on science, innovation policy, and higher education. Our main fields of study are science policy, organization and financing of research, higher education policy, organization and financing reforms and transformation of higher education institutions, financial aid to students, quality assurance in higher education and research, problems of selection and admission to higher education, and higher education and labor market.

Current publications:
- *Science* and *Higher Education* (journals)

Selected books:
- M. Darowa-Szefler, H. Gulczynska, J. Jabtecka, and E. Zwierzbowska-Kowalik, eds. *Mobilnosz pracownikòw naukowych w Polsce* (Mobility of research personnel in Poland). Warsaw, 1998.

• I. Biatecki and J. Sikorska. *Wyksztatcenie i rynek* (Education and the market). Warsaw, 1998.
• I. Biatecki, J. Kosider, E. Wnuk-Lipinska, and M. Pastwa, eds. *Education in Changing Society*. Warsaw, 1995. (background report for OECD review of Polish education)
• E. Wnuk-Lipinska and M. Wojcicka, eds. *Quality Review in Higher Education*. Warsaw, 1995
• *Development of Higher Education in Poland*. Warsaw, 1996.
• I. Biatecki and M. Darowa-Szefler, eds. *Changes in Higher Education in Central European Countries*. Warsaw, 1994.

Staff (name • title/rank • specialization):
1. Jeneusz Biatecki • Professor • problems of selection and admission to higher education, graduates and the labor market, autonomy of higher education institutions
2. Matgorzata Darowa-Szefler • Professor • economics, science education, higher education financing
3. Maria Wojcicka • Professor • quality assurance, innovations in higher education
4. Pawed Sztabinski • Associate Professor • methodology of sociological research
5. Jan Piskurewicz • Associate Professor • history of research institutions scientific societies
6. Elizbieta Drogosz-Zabtocka • Research Fellow • higher education and the labor market
7. Hanna Gulczydska • Research Fellow • transformation of research institutions and higher education
8. Julita Jabtecka • Research Fellow • science policy, research management and evaluation, higher education management
9. Jan Koztowski • Research Fellow • science policy, innovation
10. Elizbieta Soszynska • Research Fellow • higher education and employment statistics, econometrics
11. Ewa Zwierzbowska-Kowalik • Research Fellow • student motivations and aspirations, inancing higher education

Courses: (all M.A.)
• Science Policy and Research Funding
• Sociology of Education
• Statistics Econometrics
• Methodology of Sociological Survey
• Social Structure and the Educational System

Student enrollments: 10

Key textbooks/readings:
Articles from various books, journals, and statistical sources:
- *Nauka i szkolnictwo wysze* (Science and knowledge)
- *Nauka Polska* (Polish science)
- *Zagadnienia naukoznawstwa* (Science studies)
- *European Journal of Education*
- *Higher Education*
- *Higher Education in Europe*

Romania

Unesco, European Center for Higher Education (CEPES)

Address: 39 Stirbei Vodă, Bucharest R-70732, ROMANIA
Telephone: 40-1-313 08 39; 40-1-313 06 98; 40-1-313 99 56 (Director)
fax: 40-1-312 35 67
Website: www: http//www.cepes.ro

Date established: 1972.
Major source of funding: UNESCO regular budget

Organizational focus:
The activities of UNESCO-CEPES are focused on higher education in
the European Region (the countries of Europe, North America, and
Israel), and also on maintaining contacts with relevant organizations
and institutions in other regions. The organization's activities include:
1. undertaking projects relevant to the development and reform of
higher education in the European countries, especially in Central,
Southeastern, and Eastern Europe
2. promoting research on higher education and serving as a forum
for discussing important topics in higher education
3. gathering and disseminating a wide range of information on
higher education
4. serving as secretariat of specialized networks
5. providing consulting services
6. participating in the activities of other governmental and nongovernmental organizations

Current publications:
- *Higher Education in Europe* (quarterly journal)
- Studies on Higher Education, a series that presents studies on issues on higher education. Recent titles include: "Ten Years After and Looking Ahead: A Review of the Transformations of Higher Education in Central and Eastern Europe" (2000).
- Papers on Higher Education, a series that presents shorter studies and occasional papers. Recent titles include: "The Internationalization of Higher Education: An Institutional Perspective (2000).
- Monographs on Higher Education, a series that presents studies on national systems of higher education. Recent titles include: "Higher Education in Bulgaria" (2000), "Higher Education in Germany" (1999).
- Studies on Science and Culture, a series initiated to assist the publication of the research findings, undertaken foremost by the UNESCO Chairs, which are collaborating with UNESCO-CEPES, in subject areas other then higher education. Recent titles: "Sustainable Development: Theory and Practice" (2000).

International staff:
1. Jan Sadlak, Director and Representative of UNESCO in Romania
2. Lazar Vlasceanu, Senior Program Specialist (also acts as a Deputy Director)
3. Leland Conley Barrows, Program Specialist/ Senior Editor
4. Oleg Kouptsov, Program Specialist
5. Alexandrina Cucoanes, Administrative Officer

Russia

Moscow State University, Center for Sociological Studies

Address: 11 Mokhovaya Ulitsa, Moscow 103009, Russia

Telephone: (7–095) 203–2545; 203–6074; 203–2543
Fax: (7–095) 203–6334
Website: http://www.opinio.msu.ru
Date established: 1993 by integration of two organizations within Moscow State University—the Laboratory for Research on Education and Students (founded in 1972) and the Center for Public Opinion (founded in 1987)
Major source of funding: federal government

Organizational focus:
> The primary focus of the Center for Sociological Studies is the study of the sociology of higher education. Oganizational objectives include:
> • research and knowledge dissemination regarding higher education—its state, trends, improvement, and perspectives;
> • contributing to policy analysis and research on students and faculty; and
> • monitoring education practices at Moscow State University.

Current publications:
> • *Education, Culture, Business*. Moscow, 1997.
> • *Education, Society, Business*. Moscow, 1996.
> • *Society—Higher Education—Youth*. Moscow, 1995.
> • V. Dobrynina and T. Kukhtevich. *Formation of the Intellectual Elite in Higher Educational Institutions*. Moscow, 1996.
> • L. Gegel, L. Mockvicheva, E. Schepkina. *Paternalism or Self-dependence*: *Russian Students Choose Their Path*. Moscow, 1998.
> • O. Lapsheva and E. Faustova. *Sociological Portrait of the Economics Faculty Student (Sociologicheskiy portret studenta ekonomicheskogo fakulteta MGU)*. Moscow, 1998 .

Staff (name • title/rank • specialization):
> 1. Sergey Tumanov • Director • new approaches in sociology of higher education
> 2. Tatiana Kukhtevich • Professor, Head of Research • formation of an intellectual elite in higher educational institutions, student value systems
> 3. Valentina Dobrynina • Professor, Senior Researcher • status of higher education in society, educational conceptions, content of education
> 4. Elmira Faustova • Senior Researcher • student subculture, deviant behavior (narcotics, etc.)
> 5. Ludmila Gegel • Senior Researcher • value orientation of students
> 6. Oksana Krukhmaleva • Researcher • commercialization of higher education
> 7. Olga Lapsheva • Senior Researcher • social, academic, and professional issues concerning students and faculty
> 8. Ludmila Moskvicheva • Senior Researcher • student value and culture systems
> 9. Elena Schepkina • Researcher • higher education and the labor market, vocational training, motivation
> 10. Anna Smolentseva • Researcher • higher education in a market economy, higher education and the labor market, conflicts in higher education

11. Nina Sorokina • Senior Researcher • staff (faculty) policy and innovation in higher education, conflicts in higher education
12. Irina Vasenina • Senior Researcher • social and professional issues concerning students and faculty, analysis of new educational system, students lifestyles, comparative analysis

Key textbooks/readings:
Russian journals:
- *Vyssheye obrazovanie v Rossii* (Higher education in Russia)
- *Alma Mater*
- *Magister*
- *SocIs: Sociologicheskie issledovaniya* (Sociological research)
- *Sociologicheskiy zhurnal* (Journal of sociology)
- *Sociologiya 4M: metodologia, metody, matematocheskiye modeli* (Sociology 4M: methodology, methods, mathematical models)
Foreign journals:
- *Higher Education*
- *Journal of Higher Education*

University of the Russian Academy of Education (URAE)

Address: Bolshaya Polyanka 58, Moscow 109180, Russia
Telephone: 7-095-237-31-51
Fax: 7-095-237-45-61
E-mail: diana@urao.edu (Diana Antonova)
Website: http://www.urao.edu

Date established: 1989
Major source of funding: publishing revenues

Organizational focus:
We are concerned with higher and postsecondary education. The University of the Russian Academy of Education (URAE) has 12 departments and is a teaching, as well as research, institution. Its main aim is to train scientists who participate in the elaboration of teaching and learning methodologies. A principal objective of URAE is to combine the process of education with scientific research. We offer courses in the following areas: business and marketing, foreign languages, law, psychology, pedagogy, natural sciences, philosophy, journalism, history, philosophy, geography and regional policy, and plastic arts. The University has evening and correspondence departments.

Current publications:
   • URAE's publishing house issues student training guides, lecture courses, study manuals and methodological materials, programs of training courses, individual works of classic scientific texts, original monographs, collections of research articles, collected works by different authors, promotional materials, and other similar materials.
   • *Tatyana's Day* (anthology, 6 per year)

Staff (name • title/rank):
   1. Boris Bimbad • President, Professor, Academician, Rector
   2. Yury Rudin • Vice-President, Vice-Rector
   3. V.A. Ivannikov • Professor, Vice-Rector
   4. N.N. Nichaev • Professor, Director, Academician
   5. Arthur Petrovsky • Professor, Academician
   6. A. Proskuryakov • Financial Director

Research Institute for Higher Education

Address: 20, 1, Tretya Cabelynaya Street, Moscow 111024, Russia
Telephone: (095) 273-48-19
Fax: (095) 273-48-19
E-mail: postmaster@educ.msc.su; ind@niivo.hetnet.ru
Website: http://www.informika.ru; http://www.mirea.ac.ru/WWWNIIVO/index.htm (in Russian)

South Africa

Cape Town, University of, School of Education

Address: Stanley Road, Rondebosch, Cape Town, Western Cape Province 7701, South Africa

Telephone: +27-21-650-2772; +27-21-650-2768
Fax: +27-21-650-3489
Website: http//uct.ac.za/education

Date established: about 1970
Major source of funding: state government

Organizational focus:
    The School of Education provides preservice teacher training to gradu-
    ate students and has a large postgraduate division. In its postgraduate
    work, the School offers a first academic qualification in Education called
    the Bachelor of Education. This area of work is focused on the upgrad-
    ing of teachers' professional profiles as well as introducing students
    into research in education. A relatively new focus in the School is in
    master's level work, and here a large cohort of students has been de-
    veloped in the areas of educational policy, science education,
    mathematics education, history, teaching, language and literacy, lit-
    eracy, and language studies.

Staff (name • title/rank • specialization):
    1. Johan Muller • Professor, Department Head • sociology of knowl-
    edge and higher education
    2. Crain Soudien • Associate Professor, Deputy Head of Department
    • sociology of education, comparative education, and higher educa-
    tion

Courses:
    • Educational Policy and Implementation
    • Education and Development
Student mrollments: 15 (5 full-time, 10 part-time)

Key textbooks/readings:
    • *Comparative Education*
    • *Journal for Higher Education*

Centre for Higher Education Transformation (CHET)

Address: HSRC Building, 134 Pretorius Street, Pretoria, Gauteng 0001,
South Africa

Telephone: +27-12-324-1024
Fax: +27-12-324-1044
Website: http://chet.hsrc.ac.za

Date established: 1996
Major source of funding: U.S. development agency funding

Organizational focus:
> The Centre for Higher Education Transformation (CHET) is a nongovernmental organization that strives to develop transformation management capacity and skills throughout the higher education system, by integrating skill development training processes with new knowledge production, debates, and information dissemination. CHET pursues its aims within a framework of cooperative governance, the promotion of institutional, regional, national, and international links and the flexible mobilization of expertise.

Current publications:
> • *Diversity and Unity: The Role of Higher Education in Building Democracy.*
> • *Globalisation, Higher Education, High Level Training and National Development.*
> • *The Best in Higher Education.*
> • *Higher Education Qualifications in Relation to the National Qualifications Framework.*
> • *Higher Education in a Global Innovation Economy.*
> • *South African Higher Education Reform: What Comes after Postcolonialism?*
> • *Knowledge, Identity and Curriculum Transformation in Africa.*
> • *Effective Governance: A Guide for Council Members of Universities and Technikons.*
> • *A Proposed European Consortium to Assist South African Higher Education in the Development of Management and Leadership Capacity.*
> • *Reflections on 3-Year Planning at the Historically Disadvantaged Institutions.*

Staff (name • title/rank):
> 1. Nico Cloete • Director
> 2. Jane Kabaki • Finance and Operations Manager
> 3. Tembile Kulati • Project Manager
> 4. Charmaine Johnson • Project Manager
> 5. Bridget Shatkovsky • Project Assistant
> 6. Michelle Nadison • Administrative Assistant

South African Universities Vice-Chancellors' Association (SAUVCA)

Address: P.O. Box 27392, Sunnyside, Pretoria, South Africa

Telephone: +27 12 4293015

Fax: +27 12 429 3071
E-mail: sauvca1@unisa.alpha.ac.az

Date established: 1997
Major source of funding: University

Organizational Focus:
> The South African Universities Vice-Chancellors' Association (AUVCA) is the representative body of chief executive officers of South African universities.

Staff (name • title/rank • specialization):
1. P. Kotecha • Chief Executive Officer
2. N A Ogude • Director • academic affairs

University of the Orange Free State, Unit for Research into Higher Education

Address: Bureau for Academic Support Building, University of the Orange Free State, Bloemfontein, Free State 9301, South Africa

Telephone: +27 51 401 2441; +27 51 401 2862; +27 51 2588
Fax: +27 51 540 6714
Date established: 1989
Major source of funding: Centre for Science Development of the Human Sciences Research Council (a government research agency), University

Organizational focus:
> The Unit is mainly engaged in research, postgraduate teaching and supervision, and development work. The Unit seeks to generate scientific knowledge within the field of higher education. Currently, the Unit focuses on making a contribution to the investigation into a quality assurance system for South African higher education. Attention is paid to the monitoring of the development and implementation of policy at all levels, with particular focus on self-evaluation in both institutional audits and program accreditation. Other research projects include the development of an institutional self-evaluation system, and the monitoring of a resource-based learning and bridging program. In addition to the coursework (M.Ed., higher education studies) offered by the Unit, it also has initiated an interinstitutional master's program in higher education studies. The Unit is involved in the presentation of

workshops, seminars and conferences, at the regional, national, and international level.

Current publications:
- *Quality Assurance in South African Higher Education: National and International Perspectives.*
- *Enhancing Institutional Self-evaluation and Quality in South African Higher Education: National and International Perspectives.*
- *Introducing Community Colleges to South Africa.*
- Essays in Higher Education—a series of occasional research papers.

Staff (name • title/rank • specialization):
1. A.H. Strydom • Chief Director • education, philosophy
2. M. Fourie • Deputy Director • education
3. D. Hay • Senior Researcher • education
4. L. van der Westhuizen • Researcher • history
5. H. Alt • Researcher • philosophy
6. J. Letuka • Researcher • education
7. S. Holtzhausen • Professional Officer • psychology

Courses:
Diploma in Higher Education (postgraduate):
- Qualifications Frameworks
- Curriculum/Program Planning and Development
- Student Development
- Higher Education Management
- Higher Education Practice

M.Ed. (Higher Education):
- Processes and Structures in Higher Education
- Higher Education Systems
- Fields/Disciplines of Knowledge, Teaching and Learning
- Economic Aspects of Higher Education
- Management/Governance of Higher Education
- Quality Management of Higher Education

Ph.D. (Higher Education):
- research project under supervision of senior researcher(s)

Student enrollments: M.Ed. (10–12part-time), Ph.D. (10 part-time)

Key textbooks/readings:
- *Higher Education*
- *Journal of Higher Education*
- *Research in Higher Education*
- *Studies in Higher Education*
- *South African Journal of Higher Education*
- *Review of Higher Education*
- *Quality in Higher Education*

Western Cape, University of, Education Policy Unit

Address: Private Bag X 17, Bellville, Western Cape 7535, South Africa

Telephone: 27-21-9592580/2810
Fax: 27-21-9593278
Date established: 1991
Major source of funding: overseas development agency funding

Organizational focus:
The Education Policy Unit (EPU) specializes in higher education studies and policy research. EPU is committed to the development of a higher education system that is equitable; responsive to the economic, social development, and personpower needs of South Africa; strives towards excellence and quality provision; and is governed democratically.

EPU objectives are to:
- conduct theoretical and policy-relevant research in higher education, including the relations between higher education and other levels of education and strategies for social and economic development;
- contribute to the development of higher education and high-level personpower—through self-initiated research; research identified in consultation with government departments, social movements and higher education organizations and institutions; commissioned projects; and consultancies;
- serve as a research, information and statistical data resource through the development of a specialist library on higher education;
- contribute to the institutionalization of the field of higher education studies through collaboration and cooperation with other academic and research organizations and institutions; and

• train students, particularly from historically disadvantaged social backgrounds, in higher education and education policy research

Current publications:

EPU Research Reports:

• *The Enhancement of Graduate Programmes and Research Capacity at the Historically Black Universities*. 1997.

• *Distance Universities and Technikons in South Africa*. 1998.

• *Beyond the Equality-Development Impasse: Towards Policy Formulation for Equality and Development*.

EPU Occassional Papers:

• *Aid and Education in Africa: A Review of Recent Developments with Particular Relevance to South Africa*.

Books and book chapter:

• *Handbook on Key South African Higher Education Statistics*.

• *Black Student Politics, Higher Education and Apartheid, 1968–1990*.

• M. Breier. "Whose knowledge? Whose learning? Recognition of Prior Learning and the National Qualifications Framework." In
   Whither the University? ed. D. Bensusan. Cape Town: Juta, 1997.

Other EPU materials :

• "Higher Education in South Africa: The Historically Disadvantaged Institutions" (briefing paper, prepared for the Kellog Foundation).

• "Principal Distinguishing Features between Historically White Universities and Historically Black Universities" (fact sheet, produced for the Kellog Foundation).

Staff (name • title/rank • specialization):

1. Saleem Badat • Director • equity, development, governance, research, student politics
2. George Subotzky • Senior Researcher • development, knowledge production, aid
3. Mignonne Brier • Senior Researcher • curriculum, qualifications, access
4. Paul Lundall • Researcher • finance, student funding
5. Colleen Howell • Researcher • staff equity, disability
6. Mahlubi Mabizela • Trainee Researcher • private higher education, student politics
7. Charlton Koen • trainee researcher

8. Andre Burness • data processor • higher education statistics
9. Ian Bunting • Associate Senior Researcher • funding, financing, information systems
10. Dave Cooper • Associate Senior Researcher • regional development, information systems, technikons

Key textbooks/readings:
- *Higher Education*
- *Studies in Higher Education*
- *Journal of Education Policy*
- *Minerva*

Switzerland

Association of European Universities (CRE) (Association des universitées européennes)

Address: 10, rue de Conseil General, CH-1211 Geneve 4, Switzerland
Telephone: + 41 22 329 26 44
Fax: + 41 22 329 28 21
E-mail: cre@uni2a.unige.ch
Website: http://www.unige.ch/cre/

Date established: 1959
Major Source of Funding: member and associate university contributions, governmental agencies

Organizational focus:
The Association of European Universities (CRE) aims to facilitate dialogue and cooperation between its members. It also tries to represent European universities by promoting members' interests in European policymaking concerning higher education and research. In addition, the CRE attempts to enhance contact between the academic community, governments, industry, and the media.

Current publications:
- *CRE info* (newsletter, in French and English)
- *CRE doc* (thematic series, in French and English)
- *CRE guide* (thematic guidelines, in French and English)
- *CRE action* (thematic issues and directory of member universities and associations dealing with higher education)

Staff (name • title/rank):
1. Andris Barblan • Secretary General
2. Mary O'Mahoney • Deputy Secretary General
3. Daniel Samoilovich • Program Officer
4. Sami Kanaan • Program Officer
5. Lewis Purser • Program Officer

UNESCO, International Bureau of Education

Address: P.O. Box 199, 1211 Geneva 20, 15, Route des Morillons, 1218 Grand-Saconnex, Geneva, Switzerland

Telephone: (41-22) 917.78.00
Fax: (41-22) 917.78.01
E-mail: v.adamets ibe.unesco.org
Website: http://www.unicc.org/ibe

Date established: 1925
Major source of funding: UNESCO's regular budget, contributions from
    extra-budgetary sources

Organizational focus:
    • to collect, process, analyze, and disseminate documentation and informa-
    tion concerning education, in particular on innovations concerning curricula,
    teaching methods, and teacher education;
    • to seek to coordnate its work with that of other national, regional, and inter-
    national institutions pursuing similar objectives, surveys, and studies in the
    field of education, particularly comparative education;
    • to maintain and develop an international educational information center;
    • to provide technical assistance for the strengthening of national
    capcities regarding information compilation and comparative research;
    and
    • to conserve the archives and historical collections of the International
    Bureau of Education.

Current publications:
    • *Prospects* (quarterly)
    • *Educational Innovation and Information* (quarterly newsletter)
    • *Study Abroad* (a guide to foreign study programs)
    • *INNODATA* monographs.

• Noor Nkake and Lucie-Mami. *Education for International Understanding: An Idea Gaining Ground.*
• Pamela Baxter. *Mine-awareness Education: A Country Review and Curriculum Guidelines for Bosnia.*

Staff (name • title/rank):
1. Jacques Hallak • Assistant Director-General, Director, International Bureau of Education
2. Victor Adamets • Head, Studies Unit, International Bureau of Education
3. Massimo Amadio • Program Specialist
4. Jeanine Thomas • Study Abroad Specialist
5. Jennifer Fisher
6. Gonzalo Reramal

Courses:
The IBE does not organize regular training courses. However, it does receive fellows, visiting professors, university teachers, and research personnel during their sabbatical leaves, etc.— normally at master's degree and higher levels. A certain number of undergraduate students, as well as documentalists and librarians are trained under UNESCO participation programs or at the request of universities and national documentation centers.

Student enrollments: Up to 15 persons annually. For each of them an individual program is prepared.

Thailand

UNESCO, Principal Regional Office for Asia and the Pacific (PROAP)

Address: 920 Sukhumvit Road, Prakanong, Bangkok 10110, Thailand

Telephone: (66-2) 3910879-80; 3910577; 3910815
Fax: (66-2) 3910866
E-mail: Y.WANG@unesco.org
Website: http://www.education.unesco.org/proap/new/home~1.htm

Date established: UNESCO PROAP, Bangkok 1961; ACEID (Asian Centre of Educational Innovation for Development) 1973

Major source of funding: member-state contributions, extra-budgetary resources from other agencies and governments

Organizational focus:
The Office's focus is to:
• encourage and organize policy debate on higher education in Asia and the Pacific;
• create and manage UNESCO UNITWIN and UNESCO Chairs in the region (at the moment around 30 UNITWIN Networks and UNESCO Chairs have been formulated);
• promote and implement the Regional Convention on Recognition of Studies, Diplomas and Degrees in Higher Education in Asia and the Pacific; and
• implement the project on the Role and Contribution of Women Graduates in the Development Process.

Current publications:
• *Declaration about Higher Education in Asia and the Pacific and Plan of Action.*
• *Proceedings of the Regional Conference on Higher Education: National Strategies and Regional Co-operation for the 21st Century.*
• *Higher Education in Transition Economies in Asia: Proceedings of the First Workshop on Strategies and Policies in Higher Education Reform in Transition Economies in Asia.*
• *Handbook on Diplomas, Degrees and other Certificates in Higher Education in Asia and the Pacific.*

Staff (name • title/rank):
1. Wang, Yibing • Program Specialist in Higher Education

United Kingdom

Bath, University of, International Centre for Higher Education Management

Address: ICHEM, School of Management, University of Bath, Bath BA2 7AY, United Kingdom

Telephone: +44 1225 826213
Fax: +44 1225 826543
E-mail: M.K.Kelly@bath.ac.uk
Website: http://www.bath.ac.uk/Departments/Management/research/
ichem/ichem.htm

Date established: 1994
Major source of funding: self-funding, external contracts and grants (the
   British Council, World Bank, and the Commonwealth Secretariat)

Organizational focus:
   The International Centre for Higher Education Management (ICHEM)
   provides an arena for research, development, training, and liaison for
   the benefit of effective management in higher education institutions in
   the United Kingdom and overseas. ICHEM's research base supports
   comparative studies of costs, structures, and practices in institutions
   of higher education learning. Another area of research is the examination results of secondary school pupils through the associated work of
   the Schools Examination and Results Analysis Project. Professional consultation has been provided around the world, supporting and
   producing higher education development plans. Training opportunities include the British Council International Seminars directed by
   ICHEM and held in Bath and overseas. ICHEM works with higher edu-
   cation institutions, government bodies, and support agencies.
Current publications:
   ICHEM Occasional Papers:
   • *Landscape Development: A Landscape for People.*
   • *Alumni Activities: A Comparative Study of the University of Bath and Uni-
   versities in Eastern Canada.*
   • *Comparison of University Development in the United Kingdom with the United
   States.*
   • *Student Support: An International Outlook.*
   • *Reflections and Perceptions of Higher Education in Southern Africa.*

Staff (name • title/rank • specialization):
   1. Richard Mawditt • Director • higher education management
   2. Melanie Kelly • Administrator • management of the arts in higher
   education
   3. Robert Parfitt • Visiting Professor • higher education management
   4. Ernst Wilmink • Research Associate • knowledge and industry

Courses:
> Weekly methodology classes are taken with the other postgraduates in the School of Management as directed by the School's Research Office. ICHEM supervises the individual theses. Unless the student has already taken a master's degree by research, they must first register as an M.Phil. student. If they successfully complete the M.Phil. transfer, they can then move on to a Ph.D. if they wish. Most of our courses take the form of short training seminars or workshops held at Bath or overseas, for senior higher education managers.

Student enrollments: Ph.D. (2 part-time), M.Phil. (2 part-time)

Central England in Birmingham, University of, Centre for Research into Quality

Address: 90 Aldridge Road, Birmingham, B42 2TP, United Kingdom
Phone: 0044-121-331-5715
Fax: 0044-121-331-6379
E-mail: crq@uce.ac.uk
Fax: http://www.uce.ac.uk/crq

Date established: 1991
Major source of funding: University, various external sources (research grants and consultancy income)

Organizational focus:
> The Centre undertakes research into higher education policy at institutional and system level, including international comparisons. Research areas include: quality and quantity monitoring, stakeholder satisfaction, funding, higher education-employer interface, teaching and learning, the use of information technology in the development of learning access, and the construction of knowledge in higher education discipline and its relation to policy implementation.

Current publications:
- *Work Experience: Expanding Opportunities for Undergraduates.*
- *Graduate's Work: Organisational Change and Student Attributes.*
- *Employer Satisfaction.*
- *The Role of Professional Bodies in Higher Education Quality Monitoring.*
- *Funding Higher Education: Student Perspectives.*

- *TQM and New Collegialism.*
- *Criteria of Quality.*
- *Journal of Quality in Higher Education*

Staff (Name • title/rank):
1. Lee Harvey • Professor, Director of Centre
2. Sue Moon • Senior Researcher
3. Vicki Geall • Senior Researcher
4. Alison Blackwell • Researcher
5. Lindsey Bowes • Researcher
6. Adele Williams • Researcher
7. Emma Williamson • Researcher
8. Lesley Plimmer • Centre Administrator
9. Sunita Dewitt • Administrator

London, University of, Centre for Higher Education Studies (CHES), Institute of Education

Address: Bedford Way, London WC1H OAL, United Kingdom

Telephone: 44 (0)171 612 6363
Fax: 44 (0) 171 612 6366
Website: http://www.ioe.ac.ac.uk

Date established: 1985
Major source of funding: research and teaching contracts

Organizational focus:
The Centre for Higher Education Studies (CHES) focuses on teaching and research as relates to higher education practice. CHES offers Ph.D., Ed.D., and M.A. programs in higher education policy and management, and also in teaching and student learning in higher education. All academic members of the Centre's staff are also active researchers.

Staff (name • title/rank • specialization):
1. Gareth L Williams • Professor, Head of CHES • economics, finance and policy
2. Ronald A Barnett • Professor • philosophy and sociology of higher education

3. Louise M Morley • Senior Lecturer • sociology of higher education, gender issues in higher education
4. Greg Light • Lecturer • teaching and learning in higher education
5. Michael Shattock • Visiting Professor • higher education policy and management
6. Kelley Coate • Research Officer • gender and higher education, policy and sociology

Courses:

M.A. in higher and professional education; Ed.D. in postcompulsory education: students are registered on the basis of individual supervision by a named supervisor and undertake a general research training program for all students working in postcompulsory education.

Student enrollments: M.A. (60 part-time), Ph.D. (30 part-time)

Key textbooks/readings:
- *Higher Education*
- *Studies in Higher Education*
- *Higher Education Quarterly*
- *European Journal of Education*

Middlesex University, Centre for Higher Education Research

Address: Middlesex University, Trent Park, London N14 4YZ, United Kingdom
Telephone: (44) 0208 362 5345
Fax: (44) 0208 362 5345
E-mail: P.Newby@mdx.ac.uk
Website: http://www.lle.mdx.ac.uk/research/cher/index.html

Date established: 1994
Major source of funding: University, contracts

Organizational focus:
The Centre is concerned with policy and practice in higher education. Its current research concerns:
- the nature of the student experience;
- the development and accreditation of skills;
- partnership in higher education;

- universities as agents of social and economic development; and
- the globalization of higher education.

Staff (name • title/rank • specialization):
1. Peter Newby • Head of Centre
2. John Whomsley • Centre Member
3. Chris Osborne • Centre Member
4. Derek Grant • Centre Member
5. Mike Riddle • Centre Member
6. Gillian Hilton • Centre Member

Student enrollments: Ph.D. (4 part-time)

Quality Support Centre (QSC), Centre for Higher Education Research and Information

Address: 344-354 Gray's Inn Road, London WC1X 8BP, United Kingdom

Telephone: + 44 171 447 2506
Fax: + 44 171 837 0290
Website: http://www.open.ac.uk/OU/Admin/QSC

Date established: 1992
Major Source of Funding: projects/consultancies from national and international funding councils; private organizations, agencies, and universities

Organizational focus:
The Quality Support Centre (QSC) provides research, development, and information services to support the maintenance and improvement of quality in higher education in the United Kingdom and internationally. Its development and information services cover a broader spectrum of interests through the provision and analysis of information on higher education policies and developments at both national and institutional levels. Its principal research focuses are:
- systems and methods of quality assessment, assurance, and evaluation; and
- issues for quality arising from the relationship between higher education and the world of work.
   A connecting theme in all of QSC's work is the rapidly changing external context for higher education, its implications for the internal

structures and cultures of higher education institutions, for the work of their staff and the experiences of their students. Rapid—if not revolutionary—change is an international phenomenon in higher education and QSC works in close collaboration with international research groups and policy bodies.

QSC operates as a free-standing and self-financing unit within the Open University. The Centre is able to draw on the expertise of the OU and has full access to its resources, technology, and facilities.

Current publications:
- *Higher Education Digest* (journal)

Staff (name • title/rank • specialization):
1. John Brennen • Director
2. Brenda Johnston • Research Fellow
3. Richard Lewis • Co-Director
4. Brenda Little • Projects and Development Officer
5. Jonathan Mills • Research Assistant
6. Anna Scesa • Administrative Assistant
7. Tarla Shah • Administrative Head
8. Malcolm Frazer • Visiting Professor
9. Harold Silver • Visiting Professor
10. Naomi Sargant • Visiting Professor

Society for Research into Higher Education (SRHE)

Address: 3 Devonshire Street, London W1N 2BA, United Kingdom

Telephone: 00 44 171 637 2766
Fax: 00 44 171 637 2781
E-mail: srheoffice@srhe.ac.uk
Website: http://www.srhe.ac.uk/

Date established: 1965
Major source of funding: subscription revenue

Organizational focus:
The Society, an international body, exists to stimulate research into all aspects of higher education and disseminate the findings by publications, conferences, networks, and seminars.

Current publications:
- *Studies in Higher Education* (journal)
- *Research into Higher Education Abstracts* (journal)
- Higher Education Quarterly (journal)
- *International Newsletter* (journal)
- *SRHE News*
- SRHE Open University Press books (approximately 12 per year)
- *SRHE Register of Members' Research Interests*

University College London, Higher Education Research and Development Unit

Address: University College London, 1-19 Torrington Place, London WC1E 6BT, United Kingdom

Telephone: + 171 504 5992
Fax: + 171 813 0277
E-mail: a.mcgee@ucl.ac.uk; l.elton@ucl.ac.uk
Website: http://www.ucl.ac.uk/herdu

Date established: 1994
Major source of funding: University

Organizational focus:
    Research and development and institutional support in:
- teaching and learning in higher education;
- work-based learning;
- the use of information technology in higher education;
- skills development in higher education;
- postgraduate education;
- institutional management in higher education; and
- management of change.

Current publications:
- articles in refereed journals (e.g., *Studies in Higher Education*)

Staff (name • title/rank • specialization):
    1. Robert J Audley • Professor and Consultant • literacy and numeracy
    2. Lesley Black • Skills Development Coordinator • development of generic and transferable skills, and providing training in them for both undergraduates and postgraduates

3. Pat Cryer • Senior Visiting Fellow • support of postgraduate students undertaking research and support of their supervisors
4. Maureen Donelan • Lecturer • higher education learning, peer- assisted learning, year abroad preparation, mentoring, network support for teaching and learning innovations
5. Lewis Elton • Professor • teaching, learning, and assessment innovations; curriculum design; quality enhancement; institutional management; management of change
6. Toni Griffiths • Director of Education and Professional Development and Head (interim) of HERDU • work-based learning, education business partnerships
7. Jane Hughes • Lecturer • educational technology, computer supported co-operative learning, technology-mediated communication and other aspects of human-computer interaction
8. Kim Issroff • Lecturer • educational technology, motivation in relation to computer-assisted learning, evaluation, time-based analyses
9. Judith MacBean • Researcher and Financial Administrator • maths education, specifically numeracy and "service" maths in higher education; peer-assisted learning
10. Anne McGee • Administrator
11. Paul Walker • Senior Lecturer • teaching and learning strategies (especially in physical sciences, engineering, and mathematics); open and distance learning (including IT); generic and transferable skills development; conceptions of learning and teaching

Courses:
  • Higher Education Research and Development
  • Skills Training

Student enrollments: M.A. (6 part-time), Ph.D. (6 part-time), MREs (70 full-time)

Key textbooks/readings:
  • L. Elton. *Teaching in Higher Educatioin: Appraisal and Training.* London: Kogan Page.
  • P. Cryer, ed. *Effective Learning and Teaching in Higher Education.* CVCP, 1992.
  • P. Cryer and L. Elton. *Conducting Small Scale Research into Teaching and Learning in Higher Education.* HERDU, 1995.
  • P. Cryer. *The Research Student's Guide to Success.* Open University Press, 1996.

- *Effective Learning and Teaching in Higher Education.* 12 vols. Universities and Colleges Staff Development Agency of the Committee of Vice-Chancellors and Principals.
- *Action Learning*
- *American Educational Research Journal*
- *Assessment and Evaluation in Higher Education*
- *Competency*
- *European Journal of Education*
- *Higher Education Review*
- *Higher Education Quarterly*
- *Higher Education*
- *Higher Education Digest*
- *Higher Education Research and Development*
- *Innovative Higher Education*
- *Innovations in Education and Training International*
- *International Journal for Academic Development*
- *Journal of Further and Higher Education*
- *Journal of Higher Education Policy and Management*
- *Journal for Education and Work*
- *Quality and Assessment in Education*
- *Quality Assurance in Higher Education*
- *SEDA Papers*
- *Studies in Higher Education*
- *Teaching in Higher Education*
- *Tertiary Education and Management*
- *Zeitschrift für Hochschuldidaktik*

United States

Alabama

Alabama, University of, Higher Education Administration Program/Institute for Higher Education Research and Service

Address: University of Alabama, College of Education, Box 870302, 206 Wilson Hall, Tuscaloosa, AL 35487, United States

Telephone: (205) 348-1170
Fax: (205) 348-2161

E-mail: mmiller@bamaed.ua.edu
Website: www.bamaed.ua.edu/ahe/ahe_home.htm

Date established: 1972
Major source of funding: University, external contracts and grants, some
    consultative fee-based funding

Organizational focus:
    The Program is designed to provide professional development and academic
    preparation to those who currently or will in the future pursue a career in
    college management. Particular emphasis is placed on college student affairs
    administration and general college management. The Institute's focus is on
    providing action research to institutions and agencies in the Southeastern
    United States. The Institute also operates the National Data Base on Faculty
    Involvement in Governance.

Current publications:
    • The Institute publishes a biannual directory of higher education pro-
    grams in the Southeastern United States.
    • The Higher Education Administration Program publishes a biannual
    monograph. The 1996 monograph was titled *Delivery of Postsecondary
    Education by Community Colleges in Rural Alabama.*

Staff (name • title/rank • specialization):
    1. Lynn G. Beck • Professor • organizational behavior
    2. Albert S. Miles • Professor • college law
    3. Charles Brown • Associate Professor • student affairs, diversity
    4. Michael T. Miller • Associate Professor • faculty governance, student
    affairs
    5. Kathleen Randall • Assistant Clinical Professor • student affairs
    6. Daniel Nadler • Assistant Clinical Professor • student affairs
    7. Myron Pope • Assistant Clinical Professor • faculty governance, com-
    munity colleges
    8. Lisa D. Brister • Assistant Clinincal Professor • student affairs

Courses:
    The Higher Education Administration Program offers 17 graduate-level
    courses per academic year, including 9 M.A.-level courses and 8 doc-
    toral courses. Course titles include:
    • Organization and Administration of Higher Education
    • College Law
    • Finance and Business Affairs in Higher Education

- The Student in Higher Education
- Grant Writing and Contract Management
- Personnel and Human Resource Management in Higher Education
- Seminar in Academic Program Development and Evaluation
- Power, Politicals, and Change in Higher Education Systems
- Academic Cultures and Learning in Academe
- Civil Rights Law
- Seminar in Adult and Continuing Education

Student enrollments: M.A.(35 full-time, 15 part-time), Ed.D. (6 full-time, 24 part-time)

Key textbooks/readings:

The introductory course for doctoral students is "Professional Seminar in Higher Education," where the key texts are *Administration as a Profession* and the APA manual (as well as supplementary introductory material, such as the *Chronicle of Higher Education, Change* magazine, etc.). The introductory course for the M.A. program is "Perspectives on Higher Education," which makes use of a variety of materials printed by NASPA and other professional associations.

Ed.D.: *Research in Higher Education, Journal of Higher Education, Community College Review* and *Journal of Research and Practice*, etc.

M.A.: *NASPA Journal, Journal of College Student Development, ACUHO Journal, NODA Journal*, etc.

Arizona

Arizona, University of, Program/Center for the Study of Higher Education

Address: College of Education, University of Arizona, Tucson, Arizona 85721, United States

Telephone: 520-621-7951 (administrative assistant); 520-621-0947 (Gary Rhoades)
Fax: 520-621-1875
E-mail: GRhoades@mail.ed.arizona.edu

Date established: 1977

Major source of funding: University, fee-based consulting, and research, and development activities

Organizational focus:

We are a graduate program (M.A., Ph.D.) that prepares professionals for positions in postsecondary education, on campuses and in policy settings. Our faculty conduct scholarship on policy issues in various substantive areas regarding postsecondary education. Our faculty also provide some service to the university and the state, although that has decreased considerably in recent years.

Staff (name • title/rank • specialization):

1. Larry Leslie • Professor and Vice-Dean College of Education • finance
2. John Levin • Associate Professor • community college, organizational change
3. Gary Rhoades • Professor and Director • sociology of higher education, professional labor, restructuring policy
4. Sheila Slaughter • Professor • science policy, women and higher education
5. Doug Woodard • Professor • student affairs, especially retention; the profession of student affairs
6. Scott Thomas • Assistant Professor • finance

Note: Like most higher education programs, we have many adjunct professors as well, largely administrators, who teach courses for us and sit on committees.

Courses:

- Introduction to Higher Education
- Organization and Administration
- Finance
- College Student
- Student Personnel Administration
- College Teaching

Seminars:

- How College Affects Students
- Higher Education Law
- Counseling

Note: other seminar offerings vary by semester

Student enrollments: M.A .(17 full-time), Ph.D. (73 part-time)

Key textbooks/readings:
- *Journal of Higher Education*
- *Review of Higher Education*
- *Research in Higher Education*
- *Higher Education*
- *Journal of College Student Development*
- *Sociology of Education*
- *Economics of Education*
- *Community College Review*

Arizona State University, Higher and Postsecondary Education Program

Address: Division of Educational Leadership and Policy Studies, P.O. Box 872411, Tempe AZ, United States

Telephone: 602-965-6248; 602-965-6357; 602-965-0841
Fax: 602-965-1880
E-mail: hlsimmons@asu.edu; simmonshoward@netscape.net
Website: http://asu.edu

Major source of funding: University

Organizational focus:
Our program, with strong theoretical and applied components, prepares doctoral graduates for positions in policy studies research and administration at all levels of postsecondary education. The division of educational leadership and policy studies offers the M.Ed., Ed.D. and Ph.D. degrees, as well as a M.A. in social and philosophical foundations.

Current publications:
- Internet newsletter
- Internet *Journal of Education Policy and Practice*

Staff (name • title/rank):
1. Mary Lee Smith • Professor and Division Director
2. Howard L. Simmons • Professor and Program Coordinator
3. Robert Fenske • Professor
4. Kay Hartwell Honeycutt • Associate Professor
5. Laura I. Rendon • Professor
6. Richard C. Richardson • Professor

7. Christine Wilkinson • Associate Professor
8. Leonard A. Valverede • Professor

Courses:
- Introduction to Higher Education
- The Community/Junior College
- Curriculum, and Instruction in Higher Education
- Higher Education Financing and Budgeting
- Law of Higher Education
- The American College Student
- Organizational Theory
- Leadership in Higher Education
- omnibus courses on special topics in higher education

Student enrollments: M.A. (3 full-time, 7 part-time), Ph.D. (30 full-time, 10 part-time), Ed.D. (2 full-time, 23 part-time)

Key textbooks/readings:
- *Journal of Higher Education*
- *Change*
- *Liberal Education*
- *Journal of Educational Policy*

Northern Arizona University, Educational Leadership Program

Address: Northern Arizona University, Center for Excellence in Education, P.O. Box 5774, Flagstaff, AZ 86004, United States

Telephone: 520-523-5098
Fax: 520-523-1929
E-mail: gaye.luna@nau.edu

Date established: 1984
Major source of funding: University

Current publications:
- *The Meaning of Intelligence.*
- *International Education and the Search for Human Understanding.*

- *Dimensions of Diversity.*
- *Technology, Integration, and Learning Environments.*

Staff (name • title/rank • specialization):
1. Gaye Luna • Professor • community college and higher education administrations, adult learners
2 .Ronda Beaman • Associate Professor • college teaching and students, student services

Courses:
- Higher Education in the United States
- Adults Learners
- The Community College
- College Teaching
- Education Technology in the College Classroom
- Programs for At-Risk College Students
- Curriculum Construction in Community Colleges
- internships

Student enrollments: M.Ed. (25 part-time), Ed.D. (15 full-time, 10 part-time)

Arkansas

Arkansas, University of, Higher Education Leadership Program

Address: University of Arkansas, 251 Graduate Education Building, Fayetteville, Arkansas 72701, United States

Telephone: (501) 575-2207
Fax: (50910 575-2492
E-mail: jhammons@comp.uark.edu

Major source of funding: University

Organizational focus:
Our mission is to graduate doctoral, educational specialists, and master's degree students, from diverse backgrounds.

Courses:
First Year:
- Management

- Design/Evaluation of College Teaching
- The Professoriate
- Curriculum Design
- Overview of American Higher Education
- Student Personnel Services
- Seminar: Introduction to Study of Higher Education

Second Year:

- Legal Aspects
- History andPhilosopy of Higher Education
- The Student in Higher Education
- Curriculum Design
- Applied Management
- Governance
- Higher Education Problems, Issues, and Trends

Student enrollments: M.A .(11 full-time, 4 part-time), Ed.D. (2–3 full-time, 38 part-time)

Arkansas at Little Rock, University of, Higher Education Program

Address: University of Arkansas at Little Rock, College of Education, 2810 South University Avenue, Little Rock, AR 72204, United States

Telephone: (501) 569-3446; (501) 569-3113
Fax: (501) 569-8694
E-mail: gdchamberlin@ualr.edu

Date established: 1992
Major source of funding: University

Organizational focus:
   The program is designed to prepare students for administrative or faculty positions in higher education institutions.

Staff (name • title/rank • specialization):
   1. Gary Chamberlin • University Professor, Program Coordinator • governance, finance, research
   2. Pat Somers • Associate Professor • law, management, qualitative research
   3. Rob Kennedy • Professor • statistics, research methods

4. Kathy Franklin • Assistant Professor • history and philosophy, college teaching, qualitative research
5. Nim Vander Putten • Assistant Professor • history and philosophy

Courses:
- College Instruction
- Curriculum Development
- The American College Student
- The Community Junior College

Student enrollments: Ed.D. (5 full-time, 95 part-time)
Key textbooks/readings:
- *ASHE Reader on the History of Higher Education*
- F. Rudolph. *The American College and University*
- *Journal of Higher Education*
- *Research in Higher Education*
- *Review of Higher Education*

California

California at Los Angeles, University of, Higher Education and Organizational Change Division (HEOC)

Address: 405 Hilgard Avenue, Los Angeles, California 90290, United States

Telephone: (310) 206-1980
Fax: (310) 206-6293
Website: http://www.gseis.ucla.edu/division/heoc/heoc.html

Date established: 1960
Major source of funding: University

Organizational focus:
The Higher Education and Organizational Change (HEOC) Division of the Graduate School of Education and Information Studies of UCLA is committed to advancing the scholarship, research, and practice of higher education and organizational transformation in the United States and abroad.

The structure and content of the Division reflects the faculty's commitment to research and a scholarly approach to the study and practice of higher education. Because research and scholarly inquiry are the acknowledged foundation for the study and practice of higher education, they are emphasized throughout the course work, seminars, research projects, and other HEOC activities. In order to provide Ph.D. students with the highest-quality research and scholarly training, our students must participate in a minimum "year of engagement," where, as full-time students, they fully participate in courses, seminars, and research training activities in a way not possible on a part-time basis.

HEOC courses and seminars are often interdisciplinary in approach and responsive to current issues and changes in the policies, practices, and impact of higher education. Students are encouraged to develop, as much as possible, an individualized program of study that reflects their personal and professional interests and goals and satisfies the degree requirements of the Division, the Graduate School of Education and Information Studies, and UCLA.

Staff (name • title/rank • specialization):

1. Alexander W. Astin • Professor and Director, Higher Education Research Institute (HERI) • higher education policy in the United States, educational reform, values in education, impact of different types of institutions on student development, assessment and evaluation research in higher education

2. Helen S. Astin • Professor and Associate Director, HERI • education and career development of women, faculty performance and rewards, leadership

3. Arthur M. Cohen • Professor and Director, ERIC Clearinghouse • history and issues in higher education, college curriculum and instruction, community colleges

4. Patricia M. McDonough • Associate Professor and Education Department Chair • access, equity, and the stratification of individuals and institutions in education; organizational theory and analysis; sociology of education; higher education policy analysis; links between K–12 and higher education; and qualitative research

5. Linda J. Sax • Lecturer, Associate Director, HERI, and Director, CIRP Project • gender differences in college student development, science and engineering talent development, volunteerism and service-learning, gender and racial differences in self-concept development

6. James W. Trent • Associate Professor and Undergraduate Program Division Head • student subcultures; educational movements, such

as student activism; differentiation of collegiate institutions; the sociology and psychology of religion among young adults
7. Wellford W. Wilms • Professor • work systems, organizations, their cultures and ideas

Student enrollments: M.A (8–10); Ph.D. (75); Ed.D. (20)

Key textbooks/readings:
- *Research in Higher Education*
- *Review of Higher Education*
- *Journal of Higher Education*

California at Los Angeles, University of, Higher Education Research Institute (HERI)

Address: 3005 Moore Hall, UCLA, Los Angeles, CA 90095-1521, United States

Telephone: (310) 825-1925
Fax: (310) 206-2228
E-mail: http://www.gseis.ucla.edu/heri/heri.html

Date established: 1973
Major source of funding: Cooperative Institutional Research Program; Grants and contracts; University

Organizational focus:
The Higher Education Research Institute is based in the Graduate School of Education at the University of California, Los Angeles. The Institute serves as an interdisciplinary center for research, evaluation, information, policy studies, and research training in postsecondary education. HERI's research program covers a variety of topics including the outcomes of postsecondary education, leadership development, faculty performance, federal and state policy, and educational equity. Visiting scholars, faculty, and graduate students have made use of HERI facilities and research resources since its affiliation with UCLA in 1973. The Institute's holdings include more than a hundred datasets that are regularly maintained for analysis of postsecondary education.
The Cooperative Institutional Research Program (CIRP) is a national longitudinal study of the American higher education system. Established in 1966 at the American Council on Education, the CIRP is

now the nation's largest and longest empirical study of higher education, involving data on some 1,500 institutions, over 9 million students, and more than 250,000 faculty.

Current publications:
• L. J. Sax, A. W. Astin, W. S. Korn, and S. K. Gilmartin. 1999. *The American College Teacher: National Norms for the 1998–99 HERI Faculty Survey*. Los Angeles: Higher Education Research Institute, UCLA.
• L. J. Sax, A. W. Astin, W. S. Korn, and K. Mahoney. 1998. *The American Freshman: National Norms for Fall 1998*. Los Angeles: Higher Education Research Institute, UCLA.
• L. J. Sax, A. W. Astin, W. S. Korn, and K. Mahoney. 1997. *The American Freshman: National Norms for Fall 1997*. Los Angeles: Higher Education Research Institute, UCLA.
• A. W. Astin, S. A. Parrott, W. S. Korn, and L. J. Sax. 1997. *The American Freshman: Thirty Year Trends*. Los Angeles: Higher Education Research Institute, UCLA.
• H. S. Astin, A. L. Antonio, C. M. Cress, and A. W. Astin. 1997. *Race and Ethnicity in the American Professoriate, 1995–96*. Los Angeles: Higher Education Research Institute.

Staff (name • title/rank • specialization):
1. Alexander W. Astin • Director • student development, assessment of higher education, citizenship development
2. Helen S. Astin • Associate Director • gender equity, faculty, leadership, social change
3. Linda J. Sax • Associate Director • women in science, faculty, student development
4. William S. Korn • Associate Director for Operations • computer programming, data analysis
5. Kathryn Mahoney • Business Manager

Key textbooks/readings:
• *Journal of Higher Education*
• *Research in Higher Education*
• *Review of Higher Education*
• *Journal of College Student Development*
• *Change*

Claremont Graduate University, Center for Educational Studies/Higher Education Program

Address: 150 E. Tenth Street, Claremont CA 91711, United States

Telephone: 909-621-8075
Fax: 909-621-8734
E-mail: Ethel.Rogers@cgu.edu
Website: http://www.cgu.edu
Date established: 1925
Major source of funding: University; research grants and contracts
Organizational focus:
  Ours is primarily a doctorate granting program (with some master's students) aimed at developing scholarly and policy skills for experienced persons in higher education. Our students pursue senior- level administrative positions or faculty positions.

Current publications:
  • *Higher Education Abstracts*

Staff (name • title/rank • specialization):
  1. Jack Schuster • Professor of Education and Public Policy • faculty, accreditation
  2. Daryl G. Smith • Professor of Education and Psychology • diversity, student affairs, governance, planning, human development
  3. Philip Dreyer • Professor, Education and Psychology • college student development, adult education, human development
  4. Antonia Darder • Professor, Education and Cultural Studies • bicultural theory, critical theory
  5. Lourdes Arguelles • Professor • Immigration issues, sexuality, community learning
  6. David Drew • Professor and Center Director • research methods, sciences policy, science education
  7. Ethel Rogers • Associate Director

Courses:
  • College Student Development
  • College Student Experience
  • Politics and Governance of Higher Education
  • History and Philosophy of Higher Education

- The Professoriate
- Policy Seminar in Higher Education
- Issues in Higher Education
- Planning and Assessment
- Leadership in Higher Education
- Financing of Higher Education

Student enrollments: M.A. (4 full-time, 3 part-time), Ph.D. (7 full-time, 47 part-time)

Key textbooks/readings:
- ASHE readers and original source material
- *Journal of Higher Education*
- *Review of Higher Education*
- *Journal of Educational Psychology*

Southern California, University of, Center for Higher Education Policy Analysis (CHEPA)

Address: University of Southern California; Waite Phillips Hall 701, Los Angeles, California 90089-0031, United States

Telephone: (213) 740-7218
Fax: (213) 740-3889
Website: http://www.usc.edu/dept/chepa/

Date established: 1993

Major source of funding: external grant and funding agencies (Lilly Endowment, Pew Charitable Trusts, James Irvine Foundation, TIAA-CREF, Ford Foundation, U.S. Department of Education, and the University of Southern California)

Organizational focus:
The Center for Higher Education Policy Analysis (CHEPA) is an interdisciplinary research unit. The Center was established to actively engage the postsecondary education community. The Center's mission is to improve urban higher education, strengthen school-university relationships, and to focus on international higher education, emphasizing Latin America and the Pacific Rim. Programs include: 1) a master's degree in postsecondary administration and student affairs, 2) an Ed.D. in educa-

tional leadership, with an emphasis in higher education, and 3) a Ph.D. in educational policy and organization, with an emphasis on higher education.

Current Publications:
Occasional Papers from the Center for Higher Education Policy Analysis:
• William Plater. *Using Tenure: Citizenship within the New Academic Workforce.* Spring 1997.
• David W. Leslie. *Redefining Tenure: Tradition vs. the New Political Economy of Higher Education.* Spring 1997.
• Erwin Chemerinsky. *Is Tenure Necessary to Protect Academic Freedom.* Spring 1997.

Staff (name • title/rank • specialization):
1. Estela Mara Bensimon • Professor • academic leadership, organizational change, feminist analyses of traditional organization and management theories
2. Linda S. Hagedorn • Assistant Professor • low-income and minority youths' success in college, community colleges
3. Melora Sundt • Assistant Dean, Academic Outreach, Adjunct Associate Professor • student development theory, campus interventions, paraprofessional counseling, student affairs
4. William G. Tierney • Wilbur-Kieffer Professor of Higher Education, Director, Center for Higher Education Policy Analysis • faculty productivity, organizational reengineering, curricular theory, administration; policy; organizational behavior, qualitative methodology
5. William Maxwell • Associate Professor • higher education, educational research and evaluation, the sociology and politics of education, students in community colleges; student equity in higher education; the international expansion of higher education

Courses:
• Foundations of Higher, Adult, and Professional Education
• Applied Educational Ethnography
• Management of Student Services in Higher Education
• Introduction to Student Affairs
• The Community College
• Educational Leadership
• International Higher Education in Postindustrial Societies

- Administration of Higher, Adult, and Professional Education
- Curriculum, Teaching, and Learning
- The Politics of Difference

Student enrollments: M.A. (20), Ph.D. (10)

Key textbooks/readings:
- Alexander Astin. *Four Critical Years*. San Francisco: Jossey-Bass, 1977.
- Estela M. Bensimon and Anna Neumann. *Redesigning Collegiate Leadership: Teams and Teamwork in Higher Education*. Baltimore: Johns Hopkins University Press, 1994.
- Derek C. Bok and William G. Bowen. *The Shape of the River: Long- term Consequences of Considering Race in College and University Admissions*. Princeton, N.J. Princeton University Press, 1998.
- Michael D. Cohen and James G. March. *Leadership and Ambiguity: The American College President*. New York: McGraw-Hill, 1974.
- Ernest T. Pascarella and Patrick T. Terenzini. *How College Affects Students: Findings and Insights from Twenty Years of Research*. San Francisco: Jossey-Bass, 1991.
- William G. Tierney. Building Communities of Difference: Higher Education in the Twenty-first Century. Westport, Conn.: Bergin & Garvey, 1993.
- William G. Tierney. *Building the Responsive Campus: Creating -High-Performance Colleges and Universities*. Thousand Oaks, Calif.: Sage, 1999.
- Laurence R. Veysey. *The Emergence of the American University*. Chicago: University of Chicago Press, 1965.
- *Academe* (AAUP Journal)
- *American Educational Research Journal*
- *Black Issues in Higher Education*
- *Community College Journal*
- *Educational Researcher*
- *Harvard Educational Review*
- *Higher Education Management*
- *Higher Education Review*
- *Journal of Blacks in Higher Education*
- *Journal of College Student Development*
- *Journal of Higher Education*
- *Research in Higher Education*
- *Review of Educational Research*
- *Review of Higher Education*
- *Studies in Higher Education*

- *Teachers College Record*
- *Thought and Action*

Stanford University, National Center for Postsecondary Improvement

Address: Stanford School of Education, 520 Galvez Mall, 508 CERAS, Stanford, CA 94305-3084, United States
Telephone: 650-723-7724
Fax: 650-725-3936
Website: http://www.ncpi.stanford.edu

Date established: 1996
Major source of funding: federal government

Organizational focus:
  NCPI's research, dissemination, and outreach efforts are creating a national forum for examining and improving teaching, learning, and reorganization efforts across a wide range of postsecondary settings—from community colleges to research universities. The Center's research is organized into six interconnected areas of study: postsecondary organizational improvement, transitions from initial education to working life, postsecondary markets and student outcomes, professional development to enhance teaching and learning, student learning and assessment, and improving quality, productivity, and efficiency.

Current publications:
  • Michael S. McPherson and Morton O. Schapiro. *Reinforcing Stratification in American Higher Education: Some Disturbing Trends.* NCPI Technical Report #3–02, 1999.
  • Robert Zemsky, Daniel Shapiro, Maria Iannozzi, Peter Cappelli, and Thomas Bailey. *The Transition from Initial Education to Working Life in the United States of America.* NCPI Project Paper #1, 1998.
  • Patricia J. Gumport and Barbara Sporn. "Adaptation to Changing Environments: Prescriptions for Management Reform." In *Higher Education: Handbook of Teaching and Research,* ed. John Smart. New York: Agathon Press. NCPI TechnicalReport #1–07, 1999.
  • Michael T. Nettles and John J. K. Cole. *State Higher Education Assessment Policy: Research Findings from Second and Third Years.* NCPI Technical Report #5–05, 1999.
  • Eric Dey et al. *Long-term Effects of College Quality on Occupational Status of Students.* NCPI Technical Report #5–06. Executive Committee, 1998.

Staff (name • title/rank • specialization):
1. Patricia J. Gumport • Professor, Director • postsecondary organizational improvement project area
2. Peter Cappelli • Professor • transitions from initial education to working
3. Robert Zemsky • Professor, University of Pennsylvania; Project Area Director, Institute for Research on Higher Education, • postsecondary markets and students
4. Richard Shavelson • Professor • student learning and assessment
5. Michael Nettles • Professor, Center for the Study of Higher and Postsecondary Education, University of Michigan • improving quality, productivity and efficiency
6. William Massy • Professor, Jackson Hole Higher Education Group
Note: There are also over 60 other researchers at institutions across the country.

Stanford University, Stanford Institute for Higher Education Research

Address: Stanford University School of Education, 520 Galvez Mall, 508 CERAS, Stanford, CA 94305-3084, United States

Telephone: (650) 723-7724
Fax: (650) 725-3936
Website: www.stanford.edu/group/SUSE/research/siher.html

Date established: 1989
Major source of funding: federal government; private funders

Organizational focus:
The Stanford Institute for Higher Education Research (SIHER) is home to sponsored research projects that examine contemporary higher education planning and policy issues from a wide range of analytical perspectives, including those of social scientists and policy audiences in the United States and abroad.

Staff (name • title/rank • specialization):
1. Patricia J. Gumport • Director • academic planning and curricular change, reform of graduate education, management of knowledge production, academic restructuring
2. Christopher D. Roe • Managing Director

3. Michael Kirst • Associate Director • policy nexus between higher education and K-12 education, signaling effects between higher education and secondary school practices
4. Anthony Lising Antonio • Assistant Director • access and equity issues, the college choice process, diverse college campuses and student outcomes, college student friendship groups
5. John Jennings • Research Associate • trend analyses of revenues and expenditures, academic profession and faculty productivity; graduate student/graduate student employee relationships; student outcomes assessment
6. Andrea Venezia • Research Associate • education policy research, the transition from K-12 to postsecondary education, issues of access, equity, and policy coherence
7. William F. Massy • Professor Emeritus (recalled status) • academic productivity; quantitative methods for setting teaching loads, institutional strategic visions
8. Susan Christopher • Visiting Research Fellow • gender studies in the higher education curricula, cross-national comparisons of women's studies; the political discourse surrounding multicultural curricular reforms
9. Lori S. White • Visiting Research Fellow • the experiences and identity development of black students, higher education and school reform

Colorado

Colorado State University, Student Affairs Program

Address: Palmer Center, 1005 West Laurel Avenue, Fort Collins, Colorado 80521, United States
Telephone: 970-491-7243
Fax: 970-491-7427
E-mail: sherwood@sacc.colostate.edu
Website: http://www.colostate.edu/Depts/SOE/SAHE/index.html

Date established: 1969

Organizational focus:
   Students seeking careers in students affairs on college campuses.

Current publications:
   • *Journal of Student Affairs*

Denver, University of, Higher Education and Adult Studies Program

Address: College of Education, University of Denver, 2450 S. Vine Street, Denver, Colorado 80208, United States
Telephone: 303-870-2491
Fax: 303-871-4456
E-mail: lgoodchi@du.edu
Website: http://www/du/edu/education/higher_ed/programs.html
Date established: 1966
Major source of funding: University

Current publications:
* *College of Education Newsletter*

Staff (name • title/rank):
1. James R. Davis • Professor
2. Lester F. Goodchild • Associate Professor and Coordinator of the Higher Education and Adult Studies Program
3. Cheryl D. Lovell • Assistant Professor and Coordinator of the M.A. program
4. Sheila P. Wright • Vice Provost for Undergraduate Studies, Associate Professor
5. Maggie Miller • Instructor
6. Richard Gonzales • Instructor
7. Kerry McCaig • Adjunct Faculty
8. James F. Weber • Adjunct Faculty

Courses:
* College and Student Personnel Administration
* Current Issues in Higher Education
* College Organization and Administration
* Sports and Higher Education
* Students and the Law
* Student Affairs Practicum
* The American College Student
* Teaching Strategies for College Students and Adult Learners
* Ethical Issues in Higher Education
* History of American Higher Education
* Curriculum Development in Higher Education

Student enrollments: M.A. (13 full-time, 9 part-time), Ph.D. (6 full-time, 43 part-time)

Key textbooks/readings:
- Altbach, Berdahl, Gumport. *American Higher Education in the 21st Century*.
- Fife and Goodchild. *Administration as a Profession*.
- Boyer. *The College: The Undergraduate Experience in America*.
- Komives, Woodard, and Associates. Student Services: *A Handbook for the Profession*.
- Barr and Associates. *The Handbook of Student Affairs Administration*.
- Rentz. *Student Affairs: A Profession's Heritage*.
- Whitt. *College Student Affairs Administration, ASHE Reader*.
- *Journal of Higher Education*
- *Review of Higher Education*
- *Research in Higher Education*
- *History of Higher Education Annual*
- *History of Education Quarterly*
- *Journal of College Student Development*
- *NASPA Journal*
- *Higher Education*
- *Change*

Northern Colorado, University of, College Student Personnel Administration Program

Address: 418 McKee Hall, University of Northern Colorado, Greeley, Colorado 80639, United States

Telephone: 970-351-1682
Fax: 970-351-3334
E-mail: spooner@edtech.unco.edu

Date established: 1963
Major source of funding: University

Organizational focus:
To prepare top-level administrators in students affairs (student services) for higher education institutions

Staff (name • title/rank • specialization):
1. Sue Spooner • Professor and Program Coordinator • student development, counseling, and administration of student affairs.

2. Flo Guido-DiBrito • Associate Professor • student development, diversity, social change, and qualitative research in student affairs

Student enrollments: Ph.D. (20 full-time, 10 part-time)

Courses:
- Drama of Leadership
- Teaching to Transgress
- Teamwork
- Ethics and Leadership
- Ethics for Today's Campus
- Research Design
- Leading Change

Key textbooks/readings:
- Machiavelli. *The Prince*.
- *Journal of College Student Personnel*
- *NASPA Journal*
- *Initiatives*
- *AAHE Bulletin*
- *About Campus*
- *ASHE - ERIC Higher Education Reports*
- *Change*
- *Journal of Higher Education*
- *New Directions for Student Services*

Florida

Florida State University, Higher Education Program

Address: 113 Stone Building, Florida State University, Tallahassee, Florida 32306-4452, United States

Telephone: (850) 644-6777 or (850) 644-5553
Fax: (850) 644-1258
E-mail: beckham@coe.fsu.edu
Website: http://www.fsu.edu/~coe

Date established: 1957
Major source of funding: University

Organizational focus:

> The mission of the Program is to prepare individuals for positions of leadership in colleges and universities and related agencies whose activities impact higher education.

Staff (name • title/rank • specialization):

> 1. Joseph Beckham • Professor and Program Coordinator • law, policy, finance
> 2. Beverly Bower • Assistant Professor • academic leadership, community colleges
> 3. Jon Dalton • Associate Professor and Vice-President for Academic Affairs • student development theory
> 4. Lee Jones • Associate Professor and Assistant Dean of the College • organizational theory
> 5. Dale Lick • University Professor • administration, learning systems, change theory
> 6. Barbara Mann • Associate Professor • student affairs, ethics, inquiry
> 7. Robert Schwartz • Associate Professor • student affairs, outcomes of the college experience

Courses:

> - Graduate Inquiry Resources
> - Basic Understandings: Higher Education
> - American College Student
> - Legal Aspects of College Administration
> - Ethics and Inquiry
> - Postsecondary Survey
> - Higher Education Finance
> - Organization and Administration
> - Research Design
> - Literature Review and Prospectus
> - Organizational Theory
> - State Education Policy
> - Student Development Theory
> - Academic Leadership
> - College Teaching I
> - College Teaching II
> - Institutional Advancement
> - Program Financial Management

- Outcomes of Undergraduate Education
- Student Personnel Work
- History of Higher Education
- Current Problems in Higher Education
- Institutional Research
- Interventions in Student Personnel

Student enrollments: M.A. (30 full-time), Ph.D. (30 full-time)

South Florida, University of, Higher Education Program

Address: 4202 E. Fowler Avenue, FAO 207, Tampa, Florida 33620-5650, United States

Telephone: 813-974-9196
Fax: 813-974-3366
E-mail: parnell@tempest.coedu.usf.edu

Date established: 1998
Major source of funding: University

Organizational focus:
   Five degree programs and one certificate program in college teaching.

Staff (name • title/rank • specialization):
   1. Lynn Taber • Associate Professor • teaching and learning
   2. Steve Dermuth • Professor • ethics
   3. Arthur Shapiro • Professor • curriculum and instruction
   4. Bill Blank • Professor • occupations education
   5. Laurie Stryker • Professor • finance
   6. Bob Sullins • Professor • organization and administration
   7. Dale Parnell • Visiting Professor • organization and administration

Courses:
   - Adult Learner
   - Community Colleges in Higher Education
   - Ethical Dimensions of Higher Education
   - Strategic Planning in Higher Education
   - Analysis of Curriculum and Instruction
   - College Teaching Seminar
   - Higher Education Seminar

- Organizational Theory and Processes
- Legal and Policy Dimensions
- Vocational Education Program Planning
- Higer Education Finance

Student enrollments: M.A. (3 full-time, 22 part-time), Ph.D. (4 full-time, 26 part-time), D.Ed. (27 part-time); Ed.S. (10 part-time)

Key textbooks/readings:
- Cohen and Brawer. *The American Community College.*
- Darnell. *Dateline 2000.*
- *Chronicle of Higher Education*
- *Community College Times*
- *Community College Journal*

Georgia

Georgia, University of, Institute of Higher Education

Address: Meigs Hall, Athens, Georgia 30602-1772, United States

Telephone: 706-542-3464
Fax: 706-542-7588
Website: http://service.uga.edu/ihe/

Date established: 1964
Major source of funding: University

Organizational focus:
- to develop instructional resources for the continuing professional education of administrative leaders in higher education;
- to provide inservice developmental and training opportunities for academic administrators, faculty members, and professional staff;
- to analyze and interpret—through seminars, conferences, workshops, and publications—significant events, policy decisions, and public policy issues affecting higher education; and
- to cooperate with other institutions and agencies in serving the various constituencies of colleges and universities.

Current publications:
- *IHE Perspectives* (newsletter)
- *Cultural Change and Continuity.* June 1998

- *The Changing Future of Academic Leadership.* August 1998.
- *Quality and Diversity: The Mystique of Process.* October 1998.
- *Teaching and Technological Innovation.* December 1998.
- *Planning Imperatives for the Next Century.* January 1999.
- *Investments in the Future.* March 1999.
- *The Consolation of Scholarship.* May 1999.
- Cameron Fincher, ed. *Planning Imperatives for the 1990s.* 1989.
- Cameron Fincher. *Assessment, Improvement, and Cooperation: The Challenge of Reform in Higher Education.* Athens: University of Georgia, Institute of Higher Education, 1991.
- Cameron Fincher. *The Historical Development of the University System of Georgia: 1932–1990.* Athens: University of Georgia, Institute of Higher Education, 1991.
- Libby V. Morris and Catherine J. Little. *Georgia's Health Professions: A Decade of Change 1985–1995.* Athens: University of Georgia, Institute of Higher Education, 1996.

Staff (name • title/rank • specialization):
1. Thomas G. Dyer • University Professor • history of higher education
2. Cameron Fincher• Regents Professor • administrative development
3. Melvin B. Hill Jr. • Robert G. Stephens, Jr. Senior Fellow in Law and Government • administrative law
4. Sylvia Hutchinson • higher education and reading education
5. Larry G. Jones • Public Service Associate and Associate Professor • institutional research
6. Patricia Kalivoda • Adjunct Assistant Professor of Higher Education • instructional and faculty development
7. Zell B. Miller • Distinguished Professor of Higher Education • southern politics and history
8. Libby V. Morris • Associate Professor of Higher Education • assessment and program development
9. Edward G. Simpson, Jr. • Distinguished Public Service Fellow • public policy analysis and outreach
10. Ronald D. Simpson • Professor of Higher Education and Science Education • instructional and faculty development
11. D. Parker Young • Professor Emeritus of Higher Education • legal issues and implications

Courses:
- History of American Higher Education

- The Law and Higher Education
- Finance of Higher Education
- Academic Programs in Higher Education
- Instructional Processes in Higher Education
- Organization and Governance in Higher Education
- Adminstrative Leadership in Higher Education
- Institutional Research
- Assessment in Higher Education
- Research Seminar in Higher Education
- Applied Project in Higher Education
- The Two-Year College
- Critical Issues in Higher Education
- Using Technology in the College Classroom
- The American Professoriate
- Comparative Education
- Policy Studies in Higher Education
- Critique of Education Literature in Higher Education
- Internship in Higher Education

Georgia State University, Higher Education Program

Address: Educational Policy Studies, Georgia State University, Atlanta, Georgia 30303, United States

Telephone: (404) 651-2582
Fax: (404) 651-1009
Website: http//www.coeweb1.gsu.edu/eps/

Major source of funding: University

Organizational focus:
    The examination of theory and practice in higher education, and the relationships between the two.

Staff (name • title/rank • specialization):
    1. Philo Hutcheson • Assistant Professor • faculty and governance issues, the history of higher education
    2. Benjamin Baez • Assistant Professor • diversity, faculty issues, qualitative research

3. Wayne Urban • Professor • desegregation, history of education
4. Susan Talburt • Assistant Professor • curriculum, postmodern studies
5. James Scott • Associate Professor • student personnel

Courses:
- Advanced Study of the College Student
- History of Higher Education
- Organization, Governance, and Policy in Higher Education
- elective courses (one or two per semester)

Student enrollments: Ph.D. (2 full-time, 48 part-time)

Key textbooks/readings:
- assigned readings consist mostly of books, monographs, and chapters. Students use a variety of journals for their research, as do professors.

Hawaii

Hawaii at Manoa, University of, Educational Administration Program

Address: Department of Educational Administration, College of Education—Wist Hall 220, 1776, University Avenue, Honolulu, Hawaii 96822, United States

Telephone: 808-956-7843
Fax: 808-956-4120
E-mail: rheck@hawaii.edu
Website: http://www2.hawaii.edu/edea/

Date established: 1963
Major source of funding: University

Organizational focus:
The Educational Administration program at UHM is designed to prepare educational administrators and supervisors for a broad range of education-related administrative and faculty positions. The department's focus in both higher and lower education degrees provides students the opportunity to explore issues of national and

international importance to education and to specialize in their area of interest.

Staff (name • title/rank • specialization):

1. J. E. Cooper • Associate Professor • qualitative research and organizational change
2. L. K. Johnsund • Professor • faculty and administrative worklife, academic governance and leadership, women and minorities
3. S. L. Thomas • Assistant Professor • higher education finance, research methods, policy, and student culture

Courses:
- Introduction to Higher Education
- The American College Student
- Human Factors in Organizations
- Curriculum in Higher Education
- Higher Education Finance
- Management and Higher Education Leadership
- Seminars: Ethics; Advanced Statistics; Governance

Student enrollments: M.Ed. (3 full-time, 32 part-time), Ph.D. (2 full-time, 18 part-time)

Key textbooks/readings:
- *Foundations of American Higher Education, 1999 ASHE Reader.* Bess and Webster.
- Moore and Twombly. *Administrative Careers and the Marketplace.* Jossey-Bass, 1991.
- Bohman and Deal. *Reframing Organizations: Artistry, Choice, and Leadership.* Jossey-Bass, 1991.
- *Journal of Higher Education*
- *Review of Higher Education*
- *Research in Higher Education*
- *Higher Education*

Illinois

Eastern Illinois University, Counseling and Student Development Program

Address: 600 Lincoln Avenue, Charleston, Illinois 61920-3099, United States
Telephone: 217-581-2400
Fax: 217-581-7147
E-mail: cfrlr@eiu.edu
Website: http://www.eiu.edu/eiucssd

Date established: 1952
Major source of funding: University

Organizational focus:
   This is a department of counselor education with emphasis in school counseling, community counseling, and student affairs in higher education.

Staff (name • title/rank • specialization):
   1. Charles G. Eberly • Professor of counseling and student development • enrollment management, student life and activities, the American college fraternity
   2. French Fraker • Associate Professor of counseling and student development • legal and ethical issues, internet counseling
   3. Barbara Powell • Assistant Professor of counseling and student development • motivation
Courses:
   • Student Affairs in Higher Education
   • Leadership and Administration in Higher Education
   • Student Development Theory
   • Assessing Collegiate Environments
   • Consultation Skills and Organizational Development
   • Governenace and Finance in Higher Education
   • Practicum in Student Affairs
   • Practicum in Student Affairs

Student enrollments: M.A. (30 full-time, 10 part-time)

Illinois at Urbana-Champaign, University of, Higher Education Program

Address: University of Illinois at Urbana-Champaign, 1310 South Sixth Street, Champaign, Illinois 61820, United States

Telephone: (217) 333-2155
Fax: (217) 244-3378
E-mail: falexndr@uiuc.edu

Date established: 1965
Major source of funding: University

Organizational focus:
    Located in the the Department of Education Organization and Leadership, the Program is designed to train graduate students to become policy researchers, college and university administrators, and faculty in higher education.

Staff (name • title/rank):
    1. F. King Alexander • Assistant Professor, Director
    2. Chris Brown • Assistant Professor
    3. Debra Bragg • Associate Professor
    4. Howard Schien • Adjunct Professor
    5. Bill Riley • Adjunct Professor
    6. Dick Wilson • Adjunct Professor
    7. Lawrence Mann • Adjunct Professor

Student enrollments: M.A. (10 full-time, 25 part-time,; PhD (3 full-time, 7 part-time), Ed.D. (3 full-time, 7 part-time)

Key textbooks/readings:
    • *The American College and University*
    • Birnbaum. *How Colleges Work.*
    • Lucas. *Higher Education: A History.*
    • *Journal of Higher Education*
    • *Higher Education*

Illinois State University, Educational Administration and Foundations Program

Address: Campus Box 5900, Illinois State University, Normal, Illinois, 61790-5900, United States

Phone: 309-438-2043
Address: 309-438-8683
Website: http://www.ilstu.edu/depts/coe/eafdept/

Date established: 1965
Major source of funding: University
Organizational focus:

> The Department of Educational Administration and Foundations prepares people of diverse backgrounds for leadership roles in education. The Department offers programs leading to the master's degree and doctorate (Ed.D. and Ph.D.) in educational administration. The master's degree includes concentrations in student personnel administration (higher education) and the principalship (K–12). Doctoral concentrations are available in K–12 school administration, higher education administration, research and evaluation, and educational policy studies.

Current publications:

- *Planning and Changing* (a quarterly journal on educational administration)
- *Grapevine* (an annual report of state subsidies to higher education; available at: http://coe.ilstu.edu/grapevine/)
- *Illinois School Law Quarterly*

Staff (name • title/rank):

1. Vic Boschini • Assistant Professor of Higher Education and Vice President for Student Affairs
2. Edward Hines • Distinguished Professor of Higher Education
3. Anita Lupo • Professor of Higher Education
4. James C. Palmer • Associate Professor of Higher Education

Courses:

- Student Personnel Administration in Higher Education: Evolution and Development
- The Organization and Administration of Student Personnel Functions
- The American College Student
- Practicum in Student Personnel Administration

- Organization and Administration of Community Colleges
- Administration of Continuing Education and Public Service
- Organizational Patterns in Higher Education
- Decision Making in Higher Education
- Crucial Issues in American Higher Education
- Planning in Higher Education
- Public Finance of Higher Education
- College Administration
- Legal Bases of Higher Education

Student enrollments: M.A. (54), Ph.D. (107)

Loyola University Chicago, Higher Education Program
ddress: School of Education, 1041 Ridge Road, Wilmette, Illinois 60091, United States

Telephone: 847-853-3354
Fax: 847-853-3375
E-mail: twillia@luc.edu
Website: http://www.luc.edu/depts/edleader/elps.htm

Date Eestablished: 1982
Major source of funding: University

Organizational focus:
Located in the Department of Educational Leadership and Policy Studies, the Program prepares, at the doctoral level, professionals for work in postsecondary institutions, in administrative and teaching capacities.

Staff (name • title/rank • specialization):
1. Terry E. Williams • Associate Professor • student affairs administration, higher education law, enrollment management
2. Jennifer Grant Haworth • Assistant Professor • curriculum education, organization/governance, the college student
3. Lisa Lattuca • Visiting Assistant Professor • curriculum, qualitative research, student development theories, assessment
4. F. Michael Puko, S.J. • Professor • history of higher education, church-affiliated higher education

Courses:
- American Higher Education
- Curriculum in Higher Education
- Organization and Governance in Higher Education
- Proseminar: Introduction to Higher Education as a Field of Study
- Student Affairs Profession in Higher Education
- Student Affairs Administration in Higher Education
- Junior and Community College
- Selected Topics: Student Development
- Selected Topics: American College Student
- Selected Topics: Enrollment Management in Higher Education
- Selected Topics: Teaching and Learning in Colleges Universities
- Selected Topics: Women in Higher Education
- Selected Topics: Student Affairs and the Law
- Evaluation in Higher Education
- American Schooling and Social Policy
- Legal Aspects of Higher Education
- Budgeting and Finance in Higher Education
- Indepedent Study
- Internship in Higher Education
- Seminar: Religiously Affiliated Colleges and Universities
- Inquiry into Educational Policy
- Documentary Research
- Comparartive Methodology
- Qualitative Research Methods
- Computers in Education Research
- Survey Research Methods
- Research Methods
- Advanced Educational Statistics

Student enrollments: M.Ed. (20 full-time, 20 part-time), Ph.D. (4 full-time, 66 part-time), other (10 part-time)
Key textbooks/readings:
- *Review of Higher Education*
- *Journal of Higher Education*
- *Journal of College Student Development*
- *Change*

Indiana

Indiana University, Higher Education and Student Affairs Program

Address: 201 N. Rose, Bloomington, IN, 47405-1006, United States

Phone: 812-856-8364
Fax: 812-856-8394
E-mail: HESA@Indiana.edu
Website: http://www.education.indiana.edu

Date established: 1947
Major source of funding: University

Organizational focus:
   The Program offers coursework leading to an M.S. in higher education
   and student affairs. Ph.D. and Ed.D. students may focus on one of several areas—such as, administration, research, students, college teaching,
   and policy.

Staff (name • title/rank • specialization):
   1. John P. Bean • Associate Professor • student retention, the professoriate, strategic planning, student outcomes
   2. Deborah Carter • Assistant Professor • diversity issues concerning
   African American and Latino students, academic climate issues related
   to minorities and females
   3. Don Hossler • Professor • enrollment management, college choice,
   student affairs, higher education finance
   4. George D. Kuh • Professor • academic and student affairs administration, assessment of student learning and campus environment, student
   learning outside the classroom, institutional culture
   5. Michael D. Parsons • Associate Professor • federal and state higher
   education policymaking, organizational change, leadership and administration
   6. Frances K. Stage • Associate Professor • college student satisfaction
   and retention, multicultural issues, research methods, learning and
   teaching at the college level

Student enrollments: M.A.(56 full-time, 9 part-time), Ph.D. (70 full-time, 30
part-time)

Iowa

Iowa State Uniuversity, Higher Education Program

Address: Iowa State University, N243 Lagomarcino Hall, Ames, Iowa 50011, United States

Telephone: 515-294-6393
Fax: 515-294-4942
E-mail: jschuh@iastate.edu
Website: http://www.educ.iastate.edu/elps/hged/homepage.htm
Major source of funding: University

Organizational focus:
   The program, a subset of the Department of Educational Leadership and Policy Studies, prepares individuals to serve as administrators and faculty in postsecondary institutions.

Staff (name):
   1. Robert J. Barak
   2. Larry H. Ebbers
   3. Nancy J. Evans
   4. Florence A. Hamrick
   5. George A. Jackson
   6. Beverly J. Kruempel
   7. Daniel C. Robinson
   8. John H. Schuh
   9. Elizabeth C. Stanley
   10. Thomas B. Thielen

Student Enrollments: MA (73); PhD (52)

Key Textbooks/Readings:
   • Lucas, C. J. (1994). American Higher Education: A History
   • Rudolph, F. (1965). The American College and University: A History
   • Komives, S. R., and Woodard, D. B., Jr. Student Services (3rd Edition)
   • Journal of Higher Education
   • Journal of College Student Development
   • NASPA Journal
   • Review of Higher Education
   • AER Journal
   • Change

- *Review of Higher Education Research*
- *Journal of Community College Research and Practice*
- *AACC Journal*
- *Anthropology and Education Quarterly*

Iowa, University of, Higher Education Program

Address: University of Iowa, 491 Lindquist Center North, Iowa City, Iowa 52242-1529, United States

Telephone: 319-355-5302
Fax: 319-384-0587
E-mail: ppls@uiowa.edu
Website: http//www.uiowa.edu/ppls

Major source of funding: University

Organizational focus:
   The Program provides preparation of professionals at the master's and doctoral level across both applied and technical areas of higher education (administration, policy studies, academic planning and program development, and community college administration). Students enter administrative fields in many postsecondary areas— including positions in business, human resources, institutional advancement, instructional research, financial aid, student services, technology, and faculty/teaching. The Program is designed to provide basic interdisciplinary knowledge, research skills and applied training as well as specialized knoweldge in areas of student interest. It is associated with the Division of Planning, Policy, and Leadership Studies.

Staff (name):
   1. Joyce A. Brandt • Adjunct Assistant Professor
   2. Jerald Dallams • Adjunct Assistant Professor
   3. Stephen DesJardins • Assistant Professor
   4. Lelia B. Helms • Professor
   5. Alan Henkin • Professor
   6. Marti Milani • Adjunct Assistant Professor
   7. Ernest T. Pascarella • Professor
   8. Dorothy Persson • Adjunct Assistant Professor
   9. Chet Rzonca • Associate Professor

Courses:
- Issues and Policies in Higher Education
- Teaching of Adults
- Foundations of Vocational Education
- Introduction to the Law of Student Services
- Education and the World of Work
- The Community College
- Curriculum Development: Application to Community Colleges
- Evaluation: Application to Community Colleges
- Finance and Economics of Higher Education
- The Law and Higher Education
- History and Philosophy of Postsecondary Education
- Introduction to Planning, Policy Analysis and Evaluation
- Organizational Theory and Administrative Behavior
- Education and Public Policy
- Higher Education Management
- Microcomputers in Institutional Research
- Administration of Technical Educational Programs
- Policy, Planning and Implementation in Education
- Legal Issues in Student Services
- Strategic Marketing and Institutional Development

Student enrollments: M.A. (10 full-time, 24 part-time), Ph.D. (15 full-time, 40 part-time); Ed.S. (6 part-time)

Key textbooks/readings:
There are six required/core introductory courses in the higher education doctoral program: history and philosophy, research methods, organizational analysis, management, law, economics and finance, and policy analysis. For masters' students, there is an overview course required: issues and policies in higher education. A broad spectrum of research journals in education, higher education, law, business, management, policy, communications are used as the program is structured to be interdisciplinary in nature.

Northern Iowa, University of, Educational Leadership Program

Address: 508 Schindler Education Center, Cedar Falls, Iowa, 50701-0604, United States

Phone: 319-273-2605
Fax: 319-273-5175
Website: http://www.uni.edu/coe/elcpe/postsecondaryed

Date established: 1970
Major source of funding: University

Organizational focus:
    The Educational Leadership Program provides intensive study involv-
    ing the preparation of personnel for leadership roles in K–12 schools,
    postsecondary institutions, and nonschool settings. Within the Educa-
    tional Leadership intensive study area, individuals with college or
    university administrative or teaching experience may pursue study in
    postsecondary education to prepare for roles with increasing adminis-
    trative or teaching responsibilities in postsecondary education
    organizations. A program of study focusing on postsecondary educa-
    tion, pursued in conjunction with the College of Education doctoral
    core courses, individually designed related studies, internship, and dis-
    sertation research, seeks to prepare its graduates to be scholar/
    practitioners in colleges and universities.

Staff (name • title/rank • specialization):
    1. Carolyn Bair • Assistant Professor • student affairs
    2. Larry W. Keig • Assistant Professor • curriculum, teaching and learn-
    ing
    3. Gerradine Pereault • Associate Professor • leadership studies
    4. Michael D. Waggoner • Professor • organizational theory and lead-
    ership

Courses:
    • Organization and Administration of Postsecondary Education
    • History and Philosophy of Higher Education
    • Introduction to Student Affairs
    • Postsecondary Curriculum and Assessment
    • Teaching in College
    • The Two-Year College
    • College Student Development
    • Communication and Leadership in Postsecondary Education

- Economics of Higher Education
- seminar: Postsecondary Education
- internship: Postsecondary Education

Student enrollments: M.A. (32 full-time, 8 part-time), Ph.D. (10 full-time, 2 part-time)
Key journals:
- *Review of Higher Education*
- *Journal of Higher Education*
- *Research in Higher Education*
- *Journal of College Student Development*

Kansas

Kansas, University of, Higher Education Program

Address: 201 Bailey Hall, University of Kansas, Lawrence, Kansas, 66045, United States
Phone: 785-864-9721
Fax: 785-864-5076
E-mail: stwombly@ukans.edu
Website: http://www.ukans.edu

Major source of funding: University

Organizational focus:
The Program is part of the Department of Teaching and Leadership. Its goal is to prepare administrators for positions within higher education institutions.

Staff (name • title/rank • specialization):
1. Susan Twombly • Professor • higher education curriculum, community colleges, women in higher education, Latin America
2. Lisa Wolf-Wendel • Assistant Professor • women's colleges, diversity, faculty
3. Christopher Morphew • Assistant Professor • state policy, institutional diversity
4. Jerry Bailey • Associate Professor • federal policy
5. Charles Carlsen • President, Johnson County Community College • community colleges

Courses:
- Introduction to Higher Education Administration
- Higher Education in the United States
- Program Planning and Evaluation in Higher Education
- College Student
- Introductionto Student Affairs Administration
- Capstone in Student Affairs
- Governance
- Curriculum and Innovation in Higher Education
- Current Trends in Policymaking and Reform
- Theory and Research in Administration

Student enrollments: M.S. (25 full-time, 5 part-time), Ph.D. (5 full-time, 20 part-time), Ed.D. (25 part-time)

Key textbooks/readings:
- *Higher Education in the U.S.*
- *American Higher Education: A History*
- *Higher Education in Transition*
- *ASHE Reader on Governance*
- *ASHE Reader on College Students*

Key journals:
- *Journal of Higher Education*
- *Review of Higher Education*
- *NASPA Journal*

Kansas State University, College Student Personnel Program

Address: Kansas State University, Bluemont Hall, Room 301, Manhattan, KS, 66506-5312, United States

Phone: 785-532-5541
Fax: 785-532-7304
E-mail: kpbp58@ksu.edu
Website: http://www.educ.ksu.edu/Departments/edpsych

Date established: 1964
Major source of funding: University

Organizational focus:
> Located in the Department of Counseling and Educational Psychology, the Program provides professional preparation of college student personnel workers.

Staff (Name • title/rank):
> 1. Michael Dannells • Professor and Chair

Student enrollments: M.S. (25 full-time, 5 part-time), Ph.D. (2 full-time, 8 part-time)

Key textbooks/readings:
- Rudolf. *The American College and University: A History*.
- Brubacher and Rudy. *Higher Education in Transition*.
- Komives and Woodard. *Student Services: A Handbook*.

Key journals:
- *Journal of College Student Personnel*
- *NASPA Journal*
- *Journal of Higher Education*
- *Research in Higher Education*

Kentucky

Louisville, University of, Administration and Higher Education Program

Address: University of Louisville, Education Bldg. #325, Louisville, KY, 40292, United States

Phone: 502-852-6428
Fax: 502-852-0616
E-mail: pawint01@athena.louisville.edu
Website: http:www.louisville.edu/edu/edad

Date established: 1980
Major source of funding: University

Organizational focus:
> The primary focus of the Program is to prepare students for entry and advancement in careers as higher education administrators. Its secondary purpose is to prepare students to become teacher/scholars in higher education administration.

Staff (name • title/rank • specialization):
1. Paul A. Winter • Assistant Professor of education administration • recruitment and selection of educational personnel

Courses:
- Educational Resource Management in Postsecondary Education
- Organization and Administration of Higher Education
- The American College or University
- Introduction to Research Methods
- Philosophy of Higher Education
- Principles of Education Leadership
- Planning
- Legal Issues in Postsecondary Education
- Internship in Postsecondary Education

Student enrollments: M.A. (4 full-time, 26 part-time), Ph.D. (2 full-time, 38 part-time)
Key journals:
- *Journal of Higher Education*
- *Research in Higher Education*
- *Review of Higher Education*
- *Community College Review*
- *Community College Journal of Research and Practice*

Western Kentucky University, Educational Leadership Program

Address: TPH 417-D, Bowling Green, Kentucky, 42101, United States

Phone: (502) 745-4849
Fax: (502) 745-5445
Website: http://www.wku.edu/Dept./Academic/Education/EDAE/sa/sa-index.htm

Date established: 1991
Major source of funding: University

Organizational focus:
   The Master of Arts in Education degree in student affairs is designed to prepare individuals for entry and midlevel professional positions in student affairs. It is theory based yet applications oriented. Graduates of the program will have the necessary skills and competencies to suc-

ceed in a variety of student affairs units—such as, admissions, housing and residence life, financial aid, orientation, placement, minority student services, advisement, student activities, student life, student conduct, international student affairs.

Students who are successful in the M.A.E. program in student affairs develop proficiency in all areas of student affairs work. Individual students are also provided with opportunities to focus in on specific content areas. The actual program content can be divided into three broad areas: (1) theoretical foundations (historical and evolutionary considerations, theories of student development, theories of organizational development, etc.); (2) parameters of professional practice (ethical, legal and political issues; diversity and multiculturalism; social and moral responsibilities; etc.); and (3) strategies for enhancing administrative effectiveness (leadership training, staff recruitment, training, and evaluation; budgeting and planning; program development, implementation, and assessment; etc.).

Staff (name • title/rank):
1. Aaron W. Hughey • Associate Professor and Program Coordinator
2. Cheryl Chambless • Adjunct Faculty and Director of Admissions
3. Don Dinkmeyer, Jr. • Associate Professor
4. Delbert Haytden • Professor
5. Susan James • Associate Professor
6. Karl Laves • Adjunct Faculty and Clinical Psychologist, Counseling Services Center
7. Cynthia Mason • Assistant Professor
8. Donald Nims • Assistant Professor
9. Vernon Sheeley • Professor
10. John Osborne • Adjunct Faculty and Assistant Vice President for Finance and Administration
11. Stephen Schnacke • Professor and Department Head
12. Fred Stickle • Professor
13. Karen Westbrooks• Assistant Professor
14. Jerry Wilder• Professor and Vice President for Student Affairs

Courses:
• Research Methods
• Introduction to Professional Counseling
• Social and Cultural Diversity in Counseling
• Career Counseling

- Counseling Theories
- Introduction to Student Affairs
- The American College Student
- Leadership in Student Affairs
- Student Development
- Administration of Student Affairs
- Technology in Student Affairs
- practicum
- internship (6 hours)
- Seminar in Career Guidance
- Psychology of Adult Life and Aging
- Psychology of Individual Differences
- Advanced Adolescent Psychology
- Social Psychology of Organizations
- Organizational Psychology

Student enrollments: M.A.E. (40–50)

Key textbooks/readings:
- Susan R. Komives, Dudley B. Woodard, Jr., and Associates. *Student Services: A Handbook for the Profession* (3d edition). Jossey-Bass 1996.
- Margaret J. Barr and Associates. *The Handbook of Student Affairs Administration*. 1993.

Key journals:
- *Journal of College Student Development*
- *College Student Affairs Journal*
- *Journal of Higher Education*
- *Industry and Higher Education*

Louisiana

Louisiana State University, Higher Education Program
Address: 111 Peabody Hall, Baton Rouge, LA, 70803, United States
Phone: (225) 388-6900
Fax: (225) 388-6918
Website: http://asterix.ednet.lsu.edu/~elrcweb/

Date established: 1993
Major source of funding: University

Organizational focus:
    The Higher Education Program, a subset of the Department of Educational Leadership, Research, and Counseling, offers a concentration within the Ph.D. in educational leadership and research. This program prepares experts for posts on junior college, college, and university campuses. Students in this concentration may anticipate taking courses in the foundations of higher education, the economics of university management, gender and race issues in higher education, and so forth. This concentration also provides hands-on experiences through its university-based practicums, preparing students for real-world jobs in the higher education field.

Staff (name • title/rank • specialization):
    1. Becky Ropers-Huilman • Assistant Professor • curriculum and college teaching, race and gender in higher education, qualitative methodology
    2. Bud Davis • Professor • organization in higher education, foundations of higher education, leadership
    3. Richard Fossey • Associate Professor and Associate Dean • law in higher education
    4. Barbara Fuhrmann • Professor and Dean • politics in higher education, curriculum
    5. Kevin Kinser • Assistant Professor

Courses:
    • Foundations of Higher Education
    • Race and Gender in Higher Education
    • Law in Higher Education
    • Finance in Higher Education
    • Curriculum and College Teaching
    • Organization and Administration in Higher Education
    • College Students in the United States

Student enrollments: Ph.D. (5 full-time, 35 part-time)

Key journals:
    • *Review of Higher Education*

New Orleans, University of, Educational Leadership, Counseling, and Foundations Program

Address: 348 Bicentennial Education Center, University of New Orleans, New Orleans, LA, 70148, United States

Phone: 504-280-6661
Fax: 504-280-6453
Website: http://www.uno.edu

Date established: 1956
Major source of funding: University

Organizational focus:
The Department of Educational Leadership, Counseling and Foundations at the University of New Orleans offers programs leading to the M.Ed. and Ph.D. degrees in educational leadership and counseling, offering concentrations in either school administration or higher education. The graduate program in higher education prepares individuals for administrative, research, teaching, student services, and other positions in colleges, universities, public and private agencies, and other organizations involved in the study and practice of leadership and policy in postsecondary education. These programs primarily serve the urban and greater metropolitan area of New Orleans and the south-central and southeastern regions of the United States.

Staff (name • title/rank • specialization):
1. Michael B. Paulse • Professor and Coordinator, Higher Education • economics and finance of higher education, college teaching, curriculum and faculty development, college choice and persistence, educational research methods
2. Joseph B. Berger • Assistant Professor • governance and organizational theory, student services, student development, faculty issues, educational research methods
3. Ted Remley • Professor and Coordinator, Counseling • counseling in higher education, community colleges, legal issues
4. James Meza • Professor and Department Chair • legal aspects of higher education
5. Linda C Tillman • Assistant Professor • issues of race in higher education, faculty mentoring, qualitative research methods, community and technical colleges
6. Marydee Spillett • Assistant Professor • qualitative research methods, student services, student development, student leaders in higher education, women in higher education

7. Barbara Johnson • Visiting Assistant Professor • faculty issues in higher education, historically-black colleges and universities, college choice and persistence, governance and administration

8. Mary Louise Trammell • Adjunct Faculty and Associate Vice Chancellor, Office of Research and Sponsored Programs • history of higher education, legal aspects of higher education, policy analysis

9. Darren Lyn • Adjunct Faculty and Associate Director, Office of Financial Aid • student financial aid policy and administration, student services, persistence

10. James Killacky • Adjunct Faculty • community college organization and administration, governance of higher education, university-community relations

11. Max Reichard • Adjunct Faculty • community college organization and administration, history of higher education, planning in higher education

Courses:
- Student Affairs Administration in Higher Education
- College Student Development
- Student Choice in Higher Education
- Governance in American Higher Education
- History and Philosophy of Higher Education
- Financial Management in Higher Education
- Legal Aspects of Higher Education
- College Teaching
- College Curriculum
- Community and Technical Colleges
- Higher Education Policy Analysis
- Current Issues in Higher Education
- Advanced Theories in Educational Administration
- Leader Behavior in Educational Administration
- Power and Politics in Educational Administration
- Strategic Approaches to Educational Administration
- Seminar in Educational Administration
- Research Seminar in Educational Administration
- Dissertation Research in Educational Administration

Student enrollments: M.A. (20 full-time, 10 part-time), Ph.D. (20 full-time, 10 part-time)

Key textbooks/readings:
- *Governance of American Higher Education: ASHE Reader.*

- Birnbaum. *How Colleges Work.*
- *History and Philosophy of Higher Education: ASHE Reader.*
- *American Higher Education: A History.*

Key journals:
- *Research in Higher Education*
- *Journal of Higher Education*
- *Review of Higher Education*
- *Journal of College Student Development*
- *Chronicle of Higher Education*

Northwestern State University, Student Personnel Services Program

Address: Northwestern State University College of Education, Natchitoches, LA, 71457, United States

Phone: 318-357-6289
Fax: 318-357-6275
Website: http://www.nsula.edu/departments/sps

Date established: 1970
Major source of funding: University

Organizational focus:
The program's main focus is the preparation of student affairs professionals

Staff (name • title/rank):
1. Robert L. Bowman • Associate Professor and Chair
2. Frances C. Pearson • Assistant Professor
3. Vicki E. Bowman • Associate Professor
Courses:
- Introduction to Student Personnel Services
- Dynamics of the Counseling Process
- Counseling Theories
- Internship in Student Personnel Services
- Group Dynamics
- Multicultural and Diverse Populations
- Personnel Administration in Higher Education
- Diagnosis and Treatment in Counseling
- American College Student
- Advanced Group Leadership

- Organization and Administration of Higher Education
- Educational Research
- Legal and Ethical Issues in Higher Education
- Human Growth and Development
- Appraisal of the Individual
- Statistics

Student enrollments: M.A. (75 full-time)

Key journals:
- *Journal of College Student Development*
- *Journal of Higher Education*
- *College Student Affairs Journal*
- *Journal of Counseling and Development*
- *Journal of College and University Student Housing*
- *NASPA Journal*

Maine

Maine, University of, Student Development and Higher Education Leadership Program

Address: College of Education and Human Development, University of Maine, Orono, Maine, 04469-5766, United States

Phone: Masters- 207-581-2485/EdD- 207-581-2416
Fax: 207-581-2423
Website: http://www.ume.maine.edu/~cofed/academic/gradprogs/higheredgr.htm
Date established: 1968
Major source of funding: University
Organizational focus:
   Graduate level professional preparation and development, research and public service related to student development and college and university leadership
Staff (name • title/rank):
   1. Gerald Work • Professor
   2. Suzanne Estler • Associate Professor

Courses:
- Developmental Theory in Higher Education
- Impact of College on Students

- History of Higher Education in the United States
- Seminar in Student Affairs Issues
- Capstone Seminar on Student Affairs
- Seminar on Higher Education in the United States
- Higher Education and the Law
- International Comparative Higher Education
- Higher Education Internship
- Introduction to Educational Research
- Educational Measurement
- Statistical Methods in Education
- Naturalistic Observation Research in Learning Environments
- Qualitative Research: Theory, Design and Practice
- Advanced Statistical Methods in Education
- Seminar in Interpersonal Dimensions of Leadership
- Theories of Administration
- Leadership Styles in Education and Human Services
- Organizational Behavior in Education
- Educational Policy Formulation and Analysis
- doctoral seminar

Student enrollments: M.Ed. (15 full-time, 10 part-time), Ed.D. (9 part-time)
Key textbooks/readings:
- *ASHE Reader on Organizations and Governance in Higher Education*
- *ASHE Reader on College Students*

Key journals:
- *Journal of Higher Education*
- *Research in Higher Education*
- *NASPA Journal*
- *Initiatives* (journal of the NAWE)
- *Administrative Science Quarterly*

Maryland

Maryland at College Park, University of, Higher Education Program

Address: 2110 Benjamin Building, University of Maryland, College Park, MD 20742, USA
Phone: 301-405-3570
Fax: 301-405-3573
E-mail: rb21@umail.umd.edu
Website: http://www.umd.edu/edpa

Date established: 1980
Major source of funding: University

Program focus:
The doctoral program in higher education in the Department of Education Policy and Leadership prepares students for leadership positions in higher education administration, policy analysis, and scholarship. Program graduates obtain senior positions in community colleges, four-year institutions, national and regional higher education associations, state agencies and commissions dealing with higher education, as well as with executive and legislative branches of both state and federal government.

Staff (name • title/rank • specialization):
1. Robert Berdahl • Professor • state and federal politics and policies in higher education, British and comparative higher education
2. Robert Birnbaum • Professor • organization, governance and leadership in higher education, Japanese higher education
3. Sharon Fries–Britt • Assistant Professor • persistence, retention, access issues; college impact; the study of gifted black collegians
4. Frank Schmidtlein • Associate Professor • campus governance, planning and decision making, finance
5. Laura Perna • Visiting Assistant Professor• public policy analysis in higher education, financing higher education, student access and choice
Affiliated faculty:
6. Barbara Finkelstein • Professor • professional culture, cross-cultural education policy, women in higher education
7. Steven Selden • Professor • curriculum theory and development in higher education, conceptual analysis, improvement of college teaching

Courses:
• Professional Seminar in Higher and Adult Education
• Organization and Administration of Higher Education
• Retention Theories and the Impact of College
• Research in Education Policy, Planning and Administration
• State Systems of Higher Education
• Higher Education Finance
• College Teaching
• Special Topics in Education Policy and Administration: Management Innovation in Higher Education
• Research Seminar on Special Education

- Higher Education Law
- Higher Education in American Society
- The Community and Junior College
- Academic Administration
- History of Higher Education in the United States
- Qualitative Research Methods in Education
- Law, Equity, and Diversity in Education
- Higher Education Planning
- Curriculum in Higher Education
- Doctoral Research Critique Seminar

Student enrollments: M.A. (4 full-time, 10 part-time), Ph.D. (65)

Key textbooks/readings:
- *Organization and Administration.*
- M. Peterson, ed. *Higher Education.*
- *Reader in Organization and Governance in Higher Education.* 4rth ed. Lexington, Mass. 1991.
- R. Birnbaum. *How Colleges Work: The Cybernetics of Academic Organization Leadership.* San Francisco: Jossey-Bass, 1999.
- D. E. Walker. *The Effective Administrator.* San Francisco: Jossey-Bass.
- K. E. Eble. *The Art of Administration.* San Francisco: Jossey-Bass, 1978.
- *History of Higher Education American Association for Higher Education, Reader on the History Higher Education.* Simon & Schuster, 1997
- *History of Higher Education Quarterly*

Key journals: All the standard journals in the field of higher education

Massachusetts

Boston College, Higher Education Program

Address: Campion Hall, Room 205, 140 Commonwealth Avenue, Chestnut Hill MA 02467 USA

Telephone: 617-552-4185
Fax: 617-552-1840
Website: http://infoeagle.bc.edu/bc_org/avp/soe/hea/HEA.html

Date established: 1968
Major source of funding: University

Program focus:

The Boston College Program in Higher Education offers master's and doctoral degree study in the field of higher education. The Program prepares professionals in higher education and features a rigorous social science–based approach to the study of higher education. Specializations in higher education administration, student affairs, international higher education, and others, are offered. The Higher Education Program works closely with the Center for International Higher Education.

Staff (name • title/rank • specialization):

1. Philip G. Altbach • J. Donald Monan Professor of Education • comparative and international higher education, the academic profession, student activism, publishing and knowledge distribution
2. Karen D. Arnold • Associate Professor • student development, academic talent development, women in higher education
3. Kathleen A. Mahoney • Assistant Professor • history of higher education, history of religion and education, gender education
4. Ana M. Martínez-Alemán • Assistant Professor • philosphy and theory of higher education; teaching and learning; the impact of race, culture, and gender on college teaching and learning; feminist theory and pedagogy; cross-cultural studies
5. Diana C. Pullin • Professor • law and higher education, public policy
6. Ted I. K.Youn • Associate Professor • organizational analysis of higher education, politics and political institutions in American higher education, the academic profession

Adjunct faculty:

7. Frank Campanella • Executive Vice President of Boston College; Professor in the Carroll School of Management • finance and economics of higher education
8. Anne Marie Delaney • Director of Program Research • institutional research
9. Howard London • Provost, Bridgewater State University • community colleges
10. Jack Warner • Vice Chancellor, Massachusetts Board of Higher Education • student personnel issues

Courses:

- Education Law and Public Policy
- Issues in Higher Education
- Higher Education in American Society

- Organization and Administration of Higher Education
- Student Affairs Administration
- The Community-Junior College
- Adult and Continuing Education
- College Student Development
- Global and Comparative Systems in Higher Education
- Institutional Research: Implementation and Utilization
- The Academic Profession
- Public Policy, Politics, and Higher Education
- Curriculum Development and Design in Higher Education
- Organizational Decision Making in Higher Education
- Financial Management in Higher Education
- Seminar on Law and Higher Education
- Gender Issues and Higher Education
- Seminar in Research in Higher Education
- Internship in Higher Education

Student enrollments: M.A. (30 full-time, 18 part-time), Ph.D. (40)

Boston College, Center for International Higher Education

Address: Campion Hall, Room 207, 140 Commonwealth Avenue, Chestnut Hill MA 02467 USA
Telephone: 617-552-4236
Fax: 617-552-8422
E-mail: highered@bc.edu
Website: http://www.bc.edu/cihe
Date established: 1994
Major source of funding: University; grant funds from various philanthropic organizations

Institutional focus:
   The Boston College Center for International Higher Education has as its primary aim providing information and publications to colleges and universities related to the Jesuit tradition, it also has a broader mission to be a focal point for discussion and thoughtful analysis of higher education. The Center provides information and analysis for those involved in managing the higher education enterprise internationally through publications, conferences, and the maintenance of a database of individuals and institutions. The Center is especially concerned with creating dialogue and cooperation among academic

institutions in the industrialized nations and those in the developing countries of the Third World.

Center publications:
- *International Higher Education* (quarterly newsletter)

The Garland Readings Series in Higher Education:
- Joseph O'Keefe, SJ. *Issues in Catholic Higher Education.*
- Lewis Tyler and colleagues.*Latin American Higher Education.*
- Maresi Nerad. *Graduate Education.*
- Karen Arnold. *Student Development.*
- Ted I. K. Youn. *Organization and Administration of Higher Education.*
- Peter Darvas. *European Higher Education.*
- Philip Altbach and Martin Finkelstein. *The Academic Profession.*
Routledge/Falmer Book Series:
- A. D. Tillett and Barry Lesser, eds. *Science and Technology in Central and Eastern Europe: The Reform of Higher Education.*
- Ruth Hayhoe. *China's Universities, 1895–1995: A Century of Cultural Conflict.*
- Gary Bonvillian and Robert Murphy. *The Liberal Arts College Adapting to Change: The Survival of Small Schools.*
- Charles J. Bierne, SJ. *Jesuit Education and Social Change in El Salvador.*
- James J.F. Forest, ed. *University Teaching: International Perspectives.*
- Jan Sadlak and Philip G. Altbach, eds. *Higher Education Research at the Turn of the New Century: Structures, Issues, and Trends.*
- Billie Wright Dziech and Michael W. Hawkins. *Sexual Harassment in Higher Education: Reflections and New Perspectives.*
 Other books:
- Zaghloul Morsy and Philip G. Altbach, eds. *Higher Education in International Perspective: Critical Issues.* Garland and UNESCO.
- Philip G. Altbach. *Comparative Higher Education: Knowledge, the University, and Development.* Greenwich, Conn.: Ablex, 1998.
- Philip G. Altbach, Robert O. Berdahl, and Patricia J. Gumport, eds. *American Higher Education in the Twenty-first Century: Social, Political, and Economic Challenges.* Baltimore and London: Johns Hopkins University Press, 1999.
- Philip G. Altbach, ed. *Private Prometheus: Private Higher Education and Development in the 21st Century.* Westport, Conn: Greenwood, 1999.

Staff (name • title/rank):
1. Philip G. Altbach • J. Donald Monan Professor of Education
2. Jef Davis • Research Assistant

3.Yoshikazu Ogawa • Research Assistant
4. Kevin Sayers • Research Assistant
5. Roberta Bassett• Managing Editor, *Review of Higher Education*
6. Damtew Teffera • Research Assistant and Coordinator of the African Higher Education Research Handbook Project
7. Francesca Purcel, Research Assistant

Harvard University, Higher Education Program

Address: 435 Gutman Library, Appian Way, Cambridge, Massachusetts, 02138, United States

Phone: 617-495-3447
Fax: 617-496-3095
Website: http://gseweb.harvard.edu/~highered/

Major source of funding: University

Organizational focus:
The Harvard University Graduate School of Education Program in Higher Education is focused on the education/professional development of master's degree, Certificate of Advanced Study, and Doctoral degree students in higher education.

Staff (Name • Rank • Specialization):
1. Judith Block McLaughlin • Director, Higher Education Program, Lecturer • leadership and governance
2. Richard Chait • Professor • governance, faculty and academic affairs
3. Julie Reuben • Associate Professor • history of higher education
4. Stacy Blake • Assistant Professor • multiculturalism, mentoring, organizational behavior
5. James Honan • Lecturer • strategic planning, financial management
6. David Kuechle • Professor • negotiations and mediation, collective bargaining, crisis management
7. Charles Willie • Professor • historically black colleges and universities
8. Gary Orfield • Professor • access to higher education, affirmative action
9. Clayton Spencer • Executive Assistant to President of Harvard University • higher education policy
10. Derek Bok • Professor and former Harvard University President • current criticism of higher education, affirmative action

Student enrollments: Ed.M. (35 full-time,10 part-time), Ed.D. (15 full-time, 15 part-time)

Massachusetts at Boston, University of, New England Resource Center for Higher Education

Address: University of Massachusetts Boston, Graduate College of Education, 100 Morrissey Blvd., Boston, Massachusets, 02125-3393, United States

Phone: 617-287-7740
Fax: 617-287-7747
E-mail: nerche@umb.edu
Website: http://www.nerche.org
Date established: 1988
Major source of funding: University, private foundations
Organizational focus:
> The New England Resource Center for Higher Education (NERCHE) is devoted to strengthening higher education's contributions to society through collaboration. It does this by working on a continuing basis with colleges and universities in New England through think tanks, consultation, workshops, conferences, research, and action projects.

Staff (name • title/rank • specialization):
> 1. Deborah J. Hirsch • Director, NERCHE, Adjunct Associate Professor • higher education policy, practice service learning, faculty professional service
> 2. Catherine A. Bureack • Associate Director, NERCHE, Adjunct Professor • higher education policy, practice service learning, faculty professional service
> 3. Sharon Singleton • Program Associate, NERCHE • higher education policy, practice service learning, faculty professional service

Michigan

Michigan, University of, Center/Program for the Study of Higher and Postsecondary Education

Address: 2117 School of Education Building, 610 E. University Avenue, Ann Arbor, MI, 48109-1259, United States

Phone: 734-764-9472
Fax: 734-764-2510
E-mail: cshpe.info@umich.edu

Website: http://www.umich.edu/cshpe

Date established: 1957
Major source of funding: University
Organizational focus:
    This is a graduate program (doctoral and master's) and a research cen-
    ter. There are 10 full-time faculty representing the range of scholarly
    areas: academic affairs, teaching and learning, public policy, organiza-
    tions behavior and management, finance, college impact, community
    colleges, and research evaluations and assessment. The instructional
    programs are aimed at preparing entry- and midlevel administrators
    and practitioners (master's) and top-level leaders and faculty (doctoral)
    in higher education. The research is diverse in focus and covers the
    scholarly areas noted above. At the moment, faculty and graduate stu-
    dents are working on sponsored projects on institutional
    transformation, curriculum leadership, instruction in verbal teaching,
    learning environments, organizational leadership by chief academic
    officers, racial environment, and its impact on students, college access
    and affordability, strategic planning in community colleges, and state
    and institutional policies regarding student outcome assessment,
    among others. The philosophy is to prepare higher education leaders
    who are able to understand and conduct research by involving them
    in inquiry activities.

Current publications:
    • *Pursuit* (biannual newsletter)
Staff (name • title/rank • specialization):
    1. Elizabeth Barry • Associate Vice President • counsel law and higher
    education
    2. Eric L. Dey • Associate Professor • college student research, statistics
    and research design
    3. Maureen A. Hartford • Adjunct Assistant Professor • management of
    student affairs
    4. Donald E. Heller • Assistant Professor • postsecondary education eco-
    nomics and finance, public policy
    5. Sylvia Hurtado • Associate Professor • college student development,
    social context of higher education/research design methods
    6. Janet H. Lawrence • Associate Professor and Director CSHPE • college
    instruction, faculty, research design

7. Michael T. Nettles • Professor and Executive Director, Frederick D. Patterson Research Institute • public policy, assessment, research design methods

8. Jana Nidiffer • Assistant Professor • history of higher education, women in higher education

9. Marvin W. Peterson • Professor • history of higher education, women in higher education

10. Joan S. Stark • Professor • administrative behavior and personnel, curriculum and academic administration, research design and methodology

11. Teshome G. Wagaw • Professor • postsecondary education in developing nations, comparative postsecondary education

Courses:
- Introduction to Higher Education
- The Community College
- Human Resource Development in Postsecondary Education
- Urban Higher Education
- Theory and Practice of Continuing Education
- Management of Student Affairs and Support Services
- History and Philosophy in Postsecondary Education
- Pscyhological Bases of Postsecondary Education
- Postsecondary Institutions as Complex Organizations
- Curriculum in Postsecondary Education
- Financing Management and Strategy in Postsecondary Education
- Public Policy and Postsecondary Education
- Research and Educational Practice
- Research Design in Higher and Continuing Education
- Introduction to Quantitative Methods in Educational Research
- Quantitative Methods for Non-Experimental Research
- Research Practicum in Higher and Continuing Education
- Administrative Practicum in Higher and Continuing Education
- Independent Study in Higher and Continuing Education
- Topics in Higher and Continuing Education
- Technology in Higher Education
- Personnel Administration in Postsecondary Education
- Community College Governance in Postsecondary Education
- Planning, Analysis and Institutional Research
- The American College Student
- Evaluation and Assessment in Postsecondary Education
- The College and University Professor

- Current Topics in Postsecondary Instruction
- Philosophy of Academic Leadership
- International and Comparative Higher and Continuing Education
- National Economic and Financial Issues in Higher Education
- State Government and Higher Education
- Race, Ethnicity and Gender in Higher Education
- Law and Higher Education
- Managing Change and Quality in Higher Education Institutions
- Program Design and Adult Learning
- Professional Education in College and Universities
- Capital Financing, Asset Management and Fund Raising in Higher Education
- Case Studies in Higher Education Management
- Public Policy Research and Analysis in Postsecondary Education
- Dissertation Research Seminar in Higher and Continuing Education

Student enrollments: M.A. (25–30 full-time, 5 part-time), Ph.D. (50 full-time, 50 part-time)

Key journals:
- all higher education and disciplinary journals

Eastern Michigan University, Educational Leadership Program

Address: 127 Pittman Hall, Ypsilanti, MI, 48197, United States

Phone: (734) 487-0255
Fax: (784) 487-4608
E-mail: James.Barott@emich.edu
Webiste: http://www.emich.edu/public/leadcons/home.html

Major source of funding: University

Organizational focus:
Graduate training at the master's and doctoral level for educational leaders in K–12 and higher education.

Staff (name • title/rank):
1. Charles Achilles • Professor
2. James Baratt • Associate Professor
3. Helen Ditzhazy • Professor
4. Beverly Geltner • Associate Professor

5. Alison Harmon • Associate Professor
6. Donna Schmitt • Professor
7. William Price • Professor
8. Jaclynn Tracy • Associate Professor
9. James Berry •Associate Professor/Department Head

Courses:
   • Education Leadership in a Pluralistic Society
   • Educational Organization
   • Educational Leadership Theory and Practice
   • Introduction to Higher Education
   • Law for Higher Education
   • Collective Negotiations in Education
   • Organization and Administration of Higher Education
   • Organizational Theory
Student enrollments: M.A. (30 part-time), Ph.D. (40 full-time)

Michigan State University, Higher, Adult, and Lifelong Education Program

Address: Educational Administration Department, 421 Erickson Hall, East Lansing, MI, 48824, United States

Phone: 517-355-4544
Fax: 517-353-6393
E-mail: dirkx@pilot.msu.edu

Date established: 1992
Major source of funding: University

Organizational focus:
   Preparation of administrators in higher education and of faculty in higher education administration and adult education.

Staff (name • title/rank • specialization):
   1. James Fairweather • Professor • higher education, institutional research and statistics
   2. Marvin Grandstaff • Professor • philosophy of education
   3. Anna Ortiz • Assistant Professor • student affairs
   4. Marylee Davis • Professor • student affairs, higher education administration, leadership, community colleges

5. Anne Austin • Associate Professor • higher education administration
6. Robert Rhoads • Assistant Professor • student affairs
7. Kathryn Moore • Professor • student affairs leadership, higher
education administration
8. Steven Weiland, • Professor • adult development

Courses:
- Organizational Theory
- Staff and Professional Development
- Human Resources in Education
- Legal, Fiscal, and Policy Environment of Schools
- Research in Educational Administration
- The Concept of the Learning Society
- Adult Learning
- Strategies for Teaching Adults
- Literacy in the Community and Workplace
- Training in Industry
- Adult Career Development
- Foundations of Postsecondary Education
- Academic Programs and Instruction in Higher Education
- Collegiate Contexts for Teaching Learning
- Legal Issues in Higher Education
- The College Student Experience
- Student Affairs
- Workshop in Educational Administration
- Seminar in Educational Administration
- Practicum in Student Affairs
- Master's Thesis Research
- Qualitative Research Methods
- Administrative Behavior in Educational Organizations
- Educational Law
- Field Research in Educational Administration
- Proseminar in Higher, Adult and Lifelong Education
- Seminar in Adult Education
- Education and Work
- Leadership in Postsecondary Education
- Women's Education and Professional Development
- Independent Study
- Special Topics in Higher, Adult and Lifelong Education
- Laboratory and Field Experience in Educational Administration
- Research Practicum in Educational Administration

• Doctoral Dissertation Research

Student enrollments: M.A. (36 full-time, 16 part-time), Ph.D. (12 full-time, 20 part-time)

Minnesota

Minnesota, University of, Educational Policy and Administration Program

Address: 330 Wulling Hall, 86 Pleasant Street, SE, Minneapolis, Minnesota 55455-0221, United States

Phone: 612-624-1006
Fax: 612-624-3377
E-mail: mand@tc.umn.edu
Website: http://edpa.coled.umn.edu/

Date established: 1992
Major source of funding: University

Organizational focus:
    Graduate programs and research on higher education.

Staff (name • title/rank • specialization):
    1. William Ammentorp • Professor • educational leadership, two-year colleges
    2. Melissa S. Anderson • Associate Professor • graduate education, academic misconduct, academic-industry relations, faculty demography, ethical issues in rersearch
    3. James C. Hearn • Professor • organization of postsecondary education, government education policy
    4. Darrell R. Lewis • professor • economics of higher education
    5. Karen Seashore Lewis • Professor • professional and ethical values in graduate education, academic-industry relations
    6. Caroline Sotello Viernes Turner • Associate Professor • diversity in higher education, organization theory, two-year colleges
    7. Carol Boyer • Lecturer • clinical faculty
    8. Darwin Hendel • Lecturer • clinical faculty
    9. Alice Thomas • Adjunct faculty

Courses:
- American Higher Education
- Two-Year Postsecondary Institutions
- The College Student
- The Higher Education Institution: Organization and Environment
- Instruction and Leadership in Higher Education
- Leadership and Administration in Higher Education
- Federal and State Policy
- Financing Higher Education
- Strategic Planning in Higher Education
- Law in Higher Education
- Leadership and Administration in Student Affairs

Student enrollments: M.A. (28), Ph.D. (54), Ed.D. (52)

Key readings/journals:
- J. S. Brubacher and W. Rudy. *Higher Education in Transition: A History of American Colleges and Universities*. New Brunswick, N.J.: Transaction, 1997.
- J. M. Shafritz and S. Ott. Eds. *Classics of Organization Theory*. Chicago: Dorsey, 1987.
- *Journal of Higher Education*
- *Review of Higher Education*
- *Research in Higher Education*

Minnesota, University of, Postsecondary Education Policy Studies Center

Address: 330 Wulling Hall, University of Minnesota, Minneapolis, Minnesota 55455-0221, United States

Phone: 612-624-1006
Fax: 612-624-3377
Website: http://www.coled.umn.edu/pepsc

Date established: 1999
Major source of funding: varied sources of funding

Organizational focus:
Located in the College of Education and Human Development at the University of Minnesota, the Center was created to raise public aware-

ness of critical policy issues in postsecondary education, critique existing and proposed policies, foster better understanding of policy implications, and facilitate discussions about policy development through its research and dissemination activities.

Staff (name • specialization):
1. Melissa S. Anderson • research and technology transfer, state financing policy
2. Carol M. Boyer • strategic planning, state and national policy for postsecondary education
3. John R. Brandl • state finance, education policy, and social policy
4. Robert H. Bruininks • educational accountability, strategic planning and management, school-to-work transition, and inclusion of individuals with disabilities
5. David W. Chapman • international development, strengthening higher education systems in the developing world
6. James C. Hearn • financing policy, the role of information and research in postsecondary policymaking
7. Darwin D. Hendel • evaluation of higher education programs and curricula
8. Darrell R. Lewis • the economics of higher education, productivity and efficiency concerns, equity
9. Alice M. Thomas • teaching and learning in higher education, faculty development and evaluation, assessment in higher education
10. Caroline Turner • diversity and equity among faculty, staff, and students
11. research assistants (doctoral students in the higher education program)

Missouri

Central Missouri State University, Higher Education Student Personnel Program

Address: LOV 404F, Central Missouri State University, Warrensburg, MO, 64093, United States

Phone: 660-543-8628
Fax: 660-543-4167
E-mail: dcs8628@cmsu2.cmsu.edu

Date established: 1967
Major source of funding: University

Organizational focus:
   In the student personnel program at Central Missouri State, there is a major emphasis on student development and a secondary emphasis on student services. Coursework in the behavioral sciences is encouraged when needed for professional development. The program is practice-to-theory-to-practice-focused in the hope students will find the connections between theory and classroom learning and how they live and choose to work.
Staff (name • title/rank • specialization):
   1. David C. Sundberg • Coordinator and Associate Professor • college student personnel administration, counseling psychology, student development, ethics
   2. Tom Edmunds • Senior Vice President for Business • higher education law
   3. Judy Vickrey • Vice President for Finance • junior/community college
   4. Sonny Castro • Assistant Vice President for Student Affairs • personnel administration
   5. Beth Tankersley • Director of Community Awareness • personnel administration, diversity issues
Courses:
   • Higher Education
   • The College Student
   • The Junior/Community College
   • The Law in Higher Education
   • Student Development Theories and Practice
   • College Student Personnel Administration
   • Seminar in Higher Education
   • Practica in CSPA
   • College Teaching
   • Curriculum in Higher Education

Student enrollments: M.A. (15–30), Educational Specialist (3–5)

Key journals:
   • *NASPA Journal*
   • *Journal of Higher Education*
   • *Journal of College Student Development*

Missouri at Columbia, University of, Higher and Continuing Education Program

Address: University of Missouri at Columbia, 211 Hill Hall, Columbia, MO, 65211, United States

Phone: 573-882-8231
Fax: 573-884-5714
E-mail: JonesL@missouri.edu
Website: http://www.coe.missouri.edu/elpawww
Date established: 1950
Major source of funding: University; external grants and contracts
Organizational focus:

The goal of the program is producing leaders who can successfully compete for faculty positions at Research I institutions, as well as those who aspire to practitioner-leader positions in the variety of institutions and organizations in which postsecondary education plays a central role. The faculty believes that to produce scholarly and research-oriented faculty members and practitioner-leaders will require students to have (a) broad grounding in higher and continuing education content; (b) specific emphasis in higher and continuing education content; (c) research preparation; and (d) practical and applied experiences in research and teaching.

The Department of Educational Leadership and Policy Analysis does not publish books or journals. However, it is host to the Association for the Study of Higher Education. Dr. Julie Caplow, a faculty member in the higher and continuing education program, currently serves as the Association's executive director.

Staff (name • title/rank):
1. Barbara Townsend • Professor
2. Julie Caplow • Associate Professor
3. Steven Graham • Associate Professor
4. Irv Cockrield • Professor
5. Joe Donaldson • Associate Professor
6. Janice Dawson-Threat • Assistant Professor

Courses:
- Organizational Analysis
- Educational Policy Studies
- Educational Leadership

- History of Higher and Continuing Education in the U.S.
- Governance and Culture of Higher and Continuing Education
- Curriculum Philosophy and Development
- College Student Culture and Environment
- Budget and Finance in Higher and Continuing Education
- Race, Gender, and Ethnicity in Higher Education
- The Adult Learner
- Program Planning in Higher and Continuing Education
- Instructional Strategies in Higher and Continuing Education
- Foundations of Student Affairs Administration
- Student Affairs Administration: Methods and Programs
- College Teaching
- Introduction to Continuing Education
- Continuing Education for the Professions

Student enrollments: M.A. (40 part-time), Ph.D. (15 full-time, 81 part-time), Ed.D. (20part-time)

Key journals:
- *Review of Higher Education*
- *Journal of Higher Education*
- *Research in Higher Education*
- *Journal of College Student Development*
- *Adult Education Quarterly*
- *Innovative Higher Education*
- *Journal of Continuing Higher Education*

Missouri at Kansas City, University of, Educational Administration and Higher Education Program

Address: University of Missouri-Kansas City, School of Education, 5100 Rockhill Road, Kansas City, Missouri 64110, United States

Phone: 816-235-2716; 816-235-2449
Fax: 816-235-6504
E-mail: palmr@umkc.edu
Website: http://www.umkc.edu

Major source of funding: University

Organizational focus:
    To train individuals for work in higher education administration.

Staff (name • title/rank):

    1. Richard L. Palm • Assistant Professor • student affairs, ethics, finance

    2. J. Douglas Toma • Assistant Professor • law, history

    3. Elizabeth Noble • Associate Professor • assessment, Total Quality Management organization

    4. Ed Underwood • Associate Professor • diversity

    5. Russ Doll • Professor • foundations, history and social structures

    6. Joan Gallos • Associate Professor • leadership organization

Courses:

- Organization and Administration of Higher Education
- History of Higher Education
- Ethics and Values in Higher Education
- Cultural Diversity
- Financial Aspects
- Students Affairs Administration
- College Student
- Student Development Theory
- Community College
- Law of Higher Education
- Assessment and Evaluation
- Total Quality Management
- Internship/Practicum
- Leadership
- Power and Influence
- Sociological Foundations
- Historical Foundations

Student enrollments: M.A. (4 full-time, 36 part-time), Ph.D. (7 full-time, 8 part-time), Ed.Spec. (2 full-time, 13 part-time)

Key textbooks/readings:
- *Student Services Workbook.*
- *Organizational Administration of Higher Education. ASHE Reader*

Missouri at St. Louis, University of, Metropolitan Academy for Education Executives, Higher Education Program

Address: UMSL School of Education, 8001 Natural Bridge Road, St. Louis, Missouri 63121-4499, United States

Phone: 314-516-5944

Fax: 314-516-5942
Website: http://www.umsl.edu/~educate/
Date established: 1999
Major source of funding: University

Organizational focus:
The purpose of the Metropolitian Academy for Education Executives is to provide administrators and faculty members in the St. Louis region's postsecondary institutions with the opportunity to achieve a doctorate degree in higher education while working full or part time.

Staff (name • title/rank • specialization):
1. Sandy MacLean • Adjunct Professor of Education • student affairs administration, college students

Courses:
• Organization and Administration of Higher Education
• History and Philosophy of American Higher Education
• Curriculum in Higher Education
• The College Student
Student enrollments: (20 part-time)

Montana

Montana, University of, Educational Leadership and Counseling Program

Address: School of Education, University of Montana, Missoula, MT, 59812–1053, United States

Phone: 406-243-4969
Fax: 406-243-2916
E-mail: lfoster@selway.umt.edu
Website: www.umt.edu/education.html

Date established: 1991
Major source of funding: University

Organizational focus:
The Program is based upon a conceptual model that emphasizes the development of a comprehensive knowledge and skill base that

will produce reflective and competent leaders for service in K–12 schools and for teaching and administrative roles in higher education.

Staff (name • title/rank • specialization):
1. Len Foster • Associate Professor • higher education administration, faculty issues, college teaching
2. Donald Robson • Professor • college and university administration
3. David Aronofsky • Adjunct Professor • higher education law

Courses:
- Internship in College Teaching
- Internship in Higher Education Administration
- College and University Administration
- The College Professor
- Community College
- Federal and State Higher Education Policy
- College Student
- History of Higher Education

Student enrollments: Ph.D. (5 full-time, 10 part-time)

Key textbooks/readings:
- Frederick E. Balderston. *Managing Today's University: Strategies for Viability, Change and Excellence.* San Francisco: Jossey-Bass.
- Goodchild and Wechster. *ASHE Reader: The History of Higher Education.* Ginn.

Key journals:
- *Review of Higher Education*
- *Chronicle of Higher Education*
- *Journal of Higher Education*
- *Minnesota Review*
- *Harvard Educational Review*
- *Change*
- *Educational Record*

Nebraska

Nebraska, University of, Educational Leadership and Higher Education Program
Address: 1204 Seaton Hall, P.O. Box 770638, Lincoln, NE, 68588-0638, United States

Phone: (402) 472-3726
Fax: (402) 472-4300
E-mail: aseagren@ulinfo.unl.edu
Website: http://hou.edadone.unl.edu/welcome.htm
Major source of funding: University

Organizational focus:
The major purpose of the Program is to provide academic preparation and professional development for those individuals who will serve: (1) as leaders for public and private education institutions, organizations, and agencies not requiring formal administrative certification; (2) as researchers and faculty in areas such educational administration/leadership, policy studies, and law; and (3) as leaders for institutions of higher and postsecondary education in the areas of academic affairs, business affairs, student affairs, and institutional advancement. Graduates will be expected to enter leadership positions in some type of higher or postsecondary education or related agency such as government, foundations, or human service organizations. The Program is also designed to prepare faculty leaders and scholars to teach and research in higher and postsecondary education.

Faculty and staff affiliated with the program will seek first to serve the needs of the state and region but will also give careful consideration to the need for professionals in international and multicultural education. The Program is located in the Department of Educational Administration.

Current publications:
- *The Academic Chairperson's Handbook.*
- *Academic Leadership in Community Colleges.*
- *The Department Chair: New Roles, Responsibilities, and Challenges.*

Staff (name• title/rank • specialization):
1. Marilyn Grady • Professor • administrator preparation, internships, practicums, research
2. Alan Seagren • Professor and Director of the Center for the Study of Postsecondary and Higher Education • finance, administrative issues, professoriate
3. Sheldon Stick • Professor • administrative issues, history of higher education, college teaching
4. Fred Wendel • Professor and Director of Assessment Center • higher education personnel
5. Miles Bryant • Associate Professor • organizational theory, research

6. Larry Dlugosh • Associate Professor and Department Chair • policy development
7. Donald Uerling • Associate Professor • education law
8. Jim Ihrig • Instructor and Assistant Director CSPHE • community college
9. Bill Herrmann • Instructor • student affairs administration

Courses:
- History and Philosophy of Higher Education
- Independent Study
- Higher Education Leadership
- Higher Education Policy
- Higher Education Environment
- Issues in Higher Education
- Higher Education Economics/Finance
- The Community College
- Higher Education Law
- Administrative View of Professoriate
- College Teaching
- College Student Personnel
- Dissertation Proposal Development
- Field Studies
- Doctoral Seminar
- Internship

Student enrollments: M.A. (2 part-time), Ph.D. (75 part-time)

Key textbooks/readings:
- P. Altbach, R. Berdahl, and P. Gumport, eds. *Higher Education in American Society.* 1994.
- A. Levine, ed. *Higher Learning in America: 1980–2000.* Baltimore: John Hopkins Univeristy Press. 1993.

New Jersey

Rowan University, Educational Leadership Department Program

Address: Robinson Building, Glassboro, NJ, 08028, United States
Phone: (609) 256-4701
Fax: (609) 256-4918
Website: http://charlotte.rowan.edu/edlead/

Date established: 1923
Major source of funding: University

Organizational focus:
Rowan University offers a Master of Arts in higher education and an Ed.D. in educational leadership (with a track in higher education).

Staff (name • title/rank • specialization):
1. Herman James • University Professor • higher education administration
2. Carol Matteson • Professor • higher education administration
3. Thomas Monahan • Associate Professor • higher education administration, research procedures
4. Richard R. Smith • Professor • community colleges, teaching and learning, assessment
5. Federico Talley • Administrator • student affairs

Courses:
• Higher Education Administration
• Higher Education in America
• Student Services in Higher Education
• Planning and Resource Allocation in Higher Education
• Legal Issues in Higher Education
• The Nontraditional Student
• Change in Higher Education
• Practicum in Higher Education Administration
• Higher Education Administration Capstone Seminar
• Leadership Seminar I–VI
• Leadership Theory
• Leadership Challenges
• Research for Educational Leadership I–V
• Organizations as Cultures: Theory
• Organizations as Cultures: Applications
• Theories of Change
• Changing Organizations
• Forces of Change in American Society
• The Policy Environment
• Leadership Problems
• Dissertation Proposal

- Electives

Student enrollments: M.A .(12–24 full-time, 12–20 part-time), Ed.D. (12–16 full-time)

Key journals:
- *Review of Higher Education*
- *Journal of Higher Education*
- *Research in Higher Education*
- *Change*
- *Educational Record*
- *Community College Review*
- *Educational Policy*
- *Planning for Higher Education*

New York

New York University, Higher Education Program

Address: 239 Greene Street, Suite 300, New York, NY 10003-6674, United States
13244-2340, United States

Phone: 212 998 5509
Fax: 212 995 4041
Website: http://www.nyu.edu/

Date established: 1960
Major source of funding: University

Organizational focus:
The Program offers the Ph.D., Ed.D., and M.Ed. in college and university administration, urban community college leadership, and student affairs. Program faculty are involved in conducting funded research on higher education policy. The Program is affiliated with the Department of Administration, Leadership, and Technology.

Staff (name • title/rank • specialization):
1. James Bess • Professor • organizational theory
2. Romero Jalomo • Assistant Professor • student retention and transfer, community colleges

3. Teboho Moja • Visiting Professor • international higher education policy, South African higher education
4. Richard C. Richardson Jr. • Professor • higher education policy,
access and equity issues
5. Joshua L. Smith • Professor • urban community college leadership
6. The program also uses administrators and researchers from
within and outside New York University as adjuncts.

Courses:
   • Organizational Theory I and II
   • Current Research in Higher Education
   • The Politics of Higher Education
   • Governance of Colleges and Universities
   • The College Presidency
   • The American College
   • The Community College
   • Students in Higher Education
   • Higher Education and the Law
   • Institutional Assessment in Higher Education
   • Innovations in Higher Education
   • Financing Higher Education
   • Faculty Personnel: Policies, Practices and Problems
   • Foundations of Student Personnel Administration
   • Issues in Instruction
   • Ethnic Groups in Higher Education

Student enrollments: M.Ed. (70), Ph.D. (20 full-time, 30 part-time), Ed.D. (2
full-time , 18 part-time)

Key journals: Those that deal with higher education issues related to policy,
theory, administration, community colleges, and student affairs.

**State University of New York at Albany, Educational Administra-
tion and Policy Studies Program**

Address: University of Albany, State University of New York, School
of Education, 1400 Washington Avenue, Albany, NY, 12222, United
States

Phone: 518-442-5080
Fax: 518-442-5084

E-mail: fred@cnscax.albany.edu
Website: http://www.albany.edu/eaps/
Date established: 1948
Major source of funding: University, grants

Organizational focus:
Graduate programs in the department provide study leading to doctoral (Ed.D.), master's degree (M.A.), and the CAS (Certificate of Advanced Study). The three programs offer students graduate preparation for a wide variety of leadership and staff positions in school- and district-level administration, colleges and universities, and other organizations at local, state, and national levels. In addition, overseas students and others are prepared for educational planning and policymaking positions in foreign countries and with international agencies and foundations.

The programs in educational administration and policy studies include three subfields that allow students to pursue courses related to particular career interests: school administration, higher education administration, and educational policy studies.

Staff (Name):
1. Mark Berger
2. Daniel Levy
3. Kathryn Schiller
4. Anthony Cresswell
5. Raymond O'Connell
6. Gilbert Valverde
7. Frederick Dembowski
8. Gordon Purrington
9. Sandra Vergari
10. Sanford Levine
11. Cornelius Robbins

Courses:
• Introduction to Law and Education
• Introduction to Organizational Analysis
• The Economics of Education
• The Political Economy of Educational Planning and Development
• Macro-Sociology of Education and Administration
• Micro-Sociology of Education and Administration

- Ethics and Education
- Labor Relations and Collective Bargaining
- Politics of Education
- Organizational Development
- Quantitative Methods
- Introduction to Business Management in Education
- Public School Finance
- Current Best Practices in School Business Management
- Seminar in Adult and Continuing Education
- Administration of Institutions of Higher Education
- Two-Year College in American Education
- Administration of College Staff Policies
- Politics of Higher Education
- Introduction to Educational Management
- Comparative Education
- Educational Public Relations
- Personnel Administration in Public Schools
- Educational Administration in Federal and State Governments
- Programs and Services for the Handicapped
- Law and Special Education
- Seminar in Educational Administration
- Institute in Education
- Management Skills Practicum
- Advanced Organizational Analysis
- Advanced Social Analysis
- Introduction to Research Methods in Educational Administration and Policy Studies
- Research Practicum in Educational Administration and Policy Studies
- Leadership and Administration
- The Principalship
- Administrative Planning in Higher Education
- Politics of Private and Independent School and College Administration
- Seminar on Labor Management Relations in Education
- Advanced School Business Management
- Public School Finance (Advanced)
- Advanced Seminar in the Politics of Education
- Higher Education Finance
- Higher Education and the Law
- Research Colloquium on Higher Education

- Seminar on College Persistence
- Seminar in the Administration of the Community College
- Advanced Study in Educational Management
- Theory in Educational Administration
- Computer Applications in Educational Administration and Policy Studies
- Education and Social Change in Developing Nations
- Law and the School Administrator
- Educational Policy and the Law
- Advanced Seminar in Educational Administration
- Seminar in Administrative Analysis I
- Seminar in Administrative Analysis II
- Research and Independent Study in Administration
- Seminar in Administrative Research

Student enrollments: M.A. (70), Ph.D. (80), Nondegree (63), CAS (33)

State University of New York at Buffalo, Educational Leadership and Policy Program

Address: 468 Baldy Hall, University at Buffalo, State University of New York, Buffalo, NY, 14260, United States

Phone: 716-645-2471
Fax: 716-645-2481
Website: http://www.GSE.Buffalo.edu/

Major source of funding: University

Organizational focus:
   The department focuses on preparing scholars and educational professionals and leaders to work creatively in a range of educational institutions and settings. These include public and private elementary and secondary schools; colleges and universities; business and industry; international agencies and nongovernmental organizations; local, state and federal governments; and philanthropic and social welfare institutions.
   There are several programs within the department. These include educational administration (Ph.D., Ed.D., and Ed.M.), specialist in educational administration diploma, social foundations (Ph.D.), general education (Ed.M.), higher education concentration at the master's

and doctoral level, including master's degree in student services administration, and finally a school diploma in critical thinking.

The focus in higher education stresses an interdisciplinary approach to the study of postsecondary education and all academic programs are individually designed. While students are exposed to the theories of administration, as well as to the practical issues that higher education administrators face in today's colleges and universities, the Program is designed to provide a well-grounded understanding of the nature and problems of higher education.

Staff (name • title/rank • specialization):
1. William Barba • Assistant Professor • history of higher education, academic collective bargaining, law and higher education
2. Dennis Black • Adjunct Assistant Professor and Vice President, Student Affairs • law and higher education, college student services and development
3. William Cummings • Professor • comparative higher education
4. D. Bruce Johnstone • University Professor and former SUNY Chancellor • economics, finance, and governance of higher education; curriculum ; international comparative higher education
5. Albert Pautler • Professor • curriculum and instruction, instructional leadership
6. Barbara Ricotta • Adjunct Lecturer and Dean of Students • college student services and development
7. Ronald Stein • Associate Professor and Vice President for University Relations and Development • philosophy of higher education, ethical issues in higher education
8. Stuart Steiner • Adjunct Professor and President, Genesee Community College • community college issues
9. Robert Wagner • Adjunct Assistant Professor and Vice President for University Services • finance in higher education
10. Rachele Pope • Visiting Associate Professor • multicultural education
11. Lynn Ilon • Assistant Professor • economics of education, global education, comparative international education

Courses:
• Higher Education in the United States
• Historical Bases of Higher Education
• Organization and Governance
• The Financing of Higher Education

- The American College Student
- Philosophy of Higher Education
- Community Junior College
- Comparative Higher Education
- Race and Class in Higher Education
- Law and Higher Education
- Critical Issues in Higher Education
- Fundamental Concepts of HED Leadership
- Curriculum in Postsecondary education
- Student Development (master's)
- Practicum in Student Services
- Internship
- Organization Administration and Issues in College Student Services
- Quantitative Methods
- Nature of Inquiry
- Quantitative Research Methods

Student enrollments: M.A. (18 full-time, 34 part-time), Ph.D. (25 full-time, 17 part-time)

Key journals:
- *ASHE Reader on History of American Higher Education*
- *ASHE Reader on Foundations of American Higher Education*
- *Review of Higher Education*
- *Journal of Higher Education*
- *Chronicle of Higher Education*

Key textbooks and readings:
   The materials vary from year to year. Current basic texts include:
   - James L. Bess, ed. *Foundations of American Higher Education*. ASHE Reader Series. Simon & Schuster, 1991.
   - David W. Breneman, Larry L. Leslie, and Richard E. Anderson, eds. *Financing in Higher Education: Reader on Finance in Higher Education*. ASHE Reader Series. Needham Heights, 1993.

Syracuse University, Higher Education Program

Address: Higher Education Program, School of Education, 350 Huntington Hall, Syracuse, NY
13244-2340, United States

Phone: 315-443-4763
Fax: 315-443-9218

E-mail: HIED@sued.syr.edu

Date established: 1931
Major source of funding: University

Organizational focus:
The Higher Education Program at Syracuse University seeks to bridge the borders between theory, research, and practice through the adaptation of collaborative models of graduate education. In both master's and doctoral degree programs, students and faculty work together on a variety of projects in which theory and research are employed to the solution of important issues of practice—in particular the education and degree attainment of students in both two- and four-year college settings. The Program seeks to build an inclusive community of discourse about theory and practice by drawing upon the skills of faculty and student affairs professionals from across campus and from nearby institutions of higher education.

Staff (name • title/rank):
1. Vincent Tinto • Program Chair and Distinguished University Professor
2. Catherine McHugh Engstrom • Coordinator of Master's Program and Assistant Professor
3. Joan Burstyn • Professor

Courses:
• Understanding Educational Research
• Advanced College Student Development
• The American College and University
• Principles and Practices of Student Affairs Administration
• Legal Issues in Higher Education
• Independent Study
• Internship in Higher Education
• Issues and Practices in Financing Higher Education
• Enhancing Student Attainment
• Gender and Race in Higher Education
• Research on the College Student
• Introduction to College Student Development
• Organization and Administration in Higher Education
Key journals:
• Review of Research in Education

- Journalof Higher Education
- NASPA Journal
- Journal of College Student Development
- Review of Educational Research
- Review of Higher Education
- American Educational Research Journal

Ohio

Bowling Green State University, Higher Education and Student Affairs Program
Address: 330 College of Education and Human Development, Bowling Green, OH, 43403, United States

Phone: 419-372-7382
Fax: 419-372-9382
E-mail: hesa@mailserver.bgsu.edu
Website: http://edap.bgsu.edu/HESA/

Date established: master's 1970, doctoral 1990
Major source of funding: University

Organizational focus:
   The higher education doctoral program serves the postsecondary education community. The combined resources of Bowling Green State University, the Department of Higher Education and Student Affairs, the Higher Education Program Faculty, and a regional network of cooperating colleges and universities are committed to the preparation of higher education leaders. Preparation for this field at Bowling Green State University is distinguished by an emphasis on five program characteristics:
      • a commitment to education leadership grounded in expressed principles, ideals, ethics, and values;
      • a zeal for involvement and advocacy in the higher education profession;
      • a holistic perspective of higher education that reflects an understanding of the interests and concerns of the internal campus environment, external constituents, and the global community;
      • expertise in a discipline-based academic speciality, in addition to a command of a core professional studies in higher education; and
      • appreciation for both quantitative and qualitative tools of inquiry, emphasizing an understanding of their application to an array of

problems, challenges, issues, and practices in higher education.

Staff (name • specialization):
1. Leigh Chiarelott • higher education curriculum, teacher education and the psychopolitical climate, curriculum theory
2. Michael D. Coomes • federal higher education policy analysis, knowledge production and utilization in the student affairs profession
3. Robert Debard • two-year colleges, transfer students, budgeting and financial management, organizational behavior and development
4. Donald D. Gehring • legal issues in higher education, alcohol, the presence of the federal government in higher education
5. Patricia M. King • intellectual development of college students and adults, moral development, ethical issues in college student affairs and higher education
6. William E. Knight • institutional research, assessment, planning, research methods, financial issues, governance, history of American higher education

Courses:
- Governance and Organization of Higher Education
- Administration of Higher Education
- Curriculum in higher Education
- Law in Higher Education
- Budget Administration in Higher Education
- The American College Student
- History and Philisophy of Higher Education
- Issues in Higher Education
- Organization and Administration of the Two-year College
- Leadership in Higher Education
- Planning in Higher Education
- Women in Higher Education
- College and University Teaching
- Comprative Higher Education

Student enrollments: M.A. (70 full-time), Ph.D. (35–40 full-time, 12 part-time)

Miami University, College Student Personnel Program

Address: Department of Educational Leadership, 350 McGuffey Hall, Miami University, Oxford, OH, 45056, United States

Phone: (513) 529-6825
Fax: (513) 529-1729
E-mail: rogersjl@muohio.edu
Website: http://www.muohio.edu/csp/

Date established: 1963
Major source of funding: University

Organizational focus:
   The focus of our program is to prepare master's level students to work in student affairs positions in colleges and universities.

Current publications:
   • *Perspectives* (annual journal)

Staff (name • title/rank • specialization):
   1. Marcia B. Baxter Magolda • Professor • student development theory
   2. Alicia Chavez • Assistant Professor • diversity development in higher education
   3. Peter Magolda • Associate Professor • education anthropology, qualitative program evaluation
   4. Judy L. Rogers • Associate Professor • leadership theory and development

Courses:
   • Introduction to College Student Personnel
   • Student Development Theory I
   • Educational Leadership and Organizational Development
   • Higher Education in the United States
   • Group Interventions Skills in College Student Personnel
   • Professional Development in College Student Personnel
   • Student Development Theory II
   • Student Cultures in the University Environment
   • College Student Personnel Administration
   • College Student Development: Inquiry and Assessment
   • Fieldwork Inquiry in College Student Cultures
   • Program Evaluation and Assessment in Higher Education

- Seminar in Student Development
- Seminar in Student Cultures
- Seminar in Student Affairs Administration
- Student Affairs in the New Millennium
- Practicum in College Student Personnel

Student enrollments: M.A. (42 full-time, 3 part-time)

Ohio State University, Higher Education and Student Affairs Program

Address: 301 Ramseyer Hall, Ohio State University, 29 W. Woodruff Avenue, Columbus, OH, 43210, United States

Phone: 614-292-7700
Fax: 614-292-7020

Date established: 1948
Major source of funding: University

Organizational focus:
The Program's focus is on the preparation of leaders and professors in higher education and student affairs.

Staff (name • title/rank • specialization):
1. Leonard Baird • Professor • attrition and retention, person-environment interaction; impact on college students
2. Philip T. K. Daniel • Associate Professor • school law, higher education law; special education law
3. Ada Demb • Associate Professor • corporate boards, governance issues, decision making in administration, the changing roles of presidents and provosts in universities
4. Wayne K. Hoy • Professor • organizational culture, leadership issues, characteristics of healthy schools, student achievement
5. Susan R. Jones • Assistant Professor • women's identity development, service learning, student affairs administration
6. Helen Marks • Assistant Professor • school organization, school restructuring, teacher empowerment, community service learning, student outcomes, issues of equity
7. Daniel Miller • Assistant Professor • organizational theory, human relations, community development
8. Brad Mitchell • Associate Professor • educational policy analysis, organizational change, how policy influences the culture and leader-

ship of educational organizations

9. Robert F. Rodgers • Associate Professor • adult psychosocial and cognitive development, interaction between personality type and development, Jungian psychology

10. Mary Ann Donowitz Sagaria • Associate Professor • administration, leadership, academic women's colleges and universities as workplaces, gender issues in higher education

11. Scott R. Sweetland • Assistant Professor • school finance, political economy of education

12. I. Phillip Young • personnel selection and contract negotiations in college systems

13. Cynthia Uline • Assistant Professor • philosophical applications to administrative practices, ethics in educational decision making and leadership

14. Franklin B. Walter • Visiting Professor • superintendent-in-residence

Courses:
- Organization Theory
- Personality, Human Development, and Leadership
- Social and Political Contexts of Education
- Administration of Higher Education
- Administration of Academic Affairs in Higher Education
- Impact of College on Students
- Legal Aspects of Higher Education
- Analyzing Data in Educational Research
- Legal Research in Educational Administration
- Leadership in Educational Administration
- Introductionto Student Affairs
- Practice of College Student Development
- Group Interventions of Higher Education
- History of Universities
- Understanding Educational Organizations
- Theory and Practice of Student Development: Intellectual Development
- Theory and Practice of Student Development: Moral Development
- Administration of Higher Education
- Interaction of Student Environment
- Introduction to Counseling
- Administration of Academic Affairs
- Case Studies in Higher Education

Student enrollments: M.A. (50 full-time, 5 part-time), Ph.D. (30 full-time, 10 part-time)

Ohio University, Higher Education Program

Address: Ohio University, McCracken Hall, Athens, OH, 45701, United States
Phone: 740-593-4440 (Program) 740-593-0847 (Center)
Fax: 740-593-0477
E-mail: moden@ohiou.edu (program); youngb@ohiou.edu (Center)

Date established: 1969 (Program), 1981 (Center)
Major source of funding: University (Program), private foundations (Center)

Organizational focus:
> The Program's focus is to provide master's and doctoral education through traditional and innovative delivery methods for faculty and administrators, and to provide services to two-year and colleges in Appallachia and developing nations.

Staff (name • title/rank • specialization):
1. Victoria Guthrie • Professor • college students
2. Richard Miller • Professor • organization issues
3. Gary Moden • Professor • finance and assessment
4. Robert Young • Professor • curriculum and teaching
5. Charles Ping • President Emeritus • international and contemporary issues
6. Fred Dressel • Professor • student affairs
7. Michael Williford • Administrator, Director of Institutional Research

Courses:
- Introduction
- History and Philosophy
- Contemporary Issues
- Legal Issues
- College Teaching
- Curriculum Issues
- Assessment
- Governance
- Management

- Politics and Policy
- Student Affairs
- College Student Development
- Learning Environment
- Multicultural Develpment
- Administration of Student Affairs
- Institutional Research
- Issues in Higher Education

Student enrollments: M.A. (40 full-time, 20 part-time), Ph.D. (18 full-time, 22 part-time)

Key journals:
- *ASHE Readers*
- *Journal of Higher Education*
- *Chronicle of Higher Education*
- *Review of Higher Education*
- *Higher Education Abstracts*
- *Journal of College Student Development*

Toledo, University of, Higher Education Program/John H. Russel Center for Educational Leadership

Address: 2801 West Bancroft, Toledo, OH, 43606-3390, United States

Phone: 419-530-2461(Program); 419-530-2155 (Center)
Fax: 419-530-4912 (both)
E-mail: skatsin@utnet.utoledo.edu; dmanns@utnet.utoledo.edu
Date established: Program, 1963; Center, 1967
Major source of funding: University; private gifts

Organizational focus:
The Program in Higher Education offers graduate study at the master's and doctoral levels to prepare persons for administrative and teaching leadership roles at public and private two- and four-year institutions of higher education. Students are provided with a platform on which to develop their own sense of vision and understanding of issues related to leading, not merely managing, institutions and people. Students are encouraged to appreciate the contextual differences among and between institutions in the world's most diverse system of higher education. The Program is especially tailored to serve

the needs of adult learners and professionals already in the field who hold full-time positions—via courses delivered in the late afternoon and evenings.

Current publications:
- a quarterly newsletter

Staff (name • title/rank • specialization):
1. Penny Poplin Gosetti • Assistant Professor • campus cultures, student affairs, women in higher education
2. Stephne G. Katsinas • Professor • higher education history, policy, lay governance
3. Ronald D. Opp • Associate Professor • faculty issues, assessment, community colleges
4. Frank E. Horton • Professor • lay governanace, policy, urban higher education, strategic planning
5. C. Jack Maynard • Associate Professor • curriculum, teacher education
6. David L. Meabon • Associate Professor • student affairs, campus community, student fees
7. Mary Ann Heinrichs • Professor • general education, women in higher education
8. Richard R. Perry • Professor • independent colleges, institutional research, legal issues
Student enrollments: M.A. (15 full-time, 2 part-time), Ph.D. (6 full-time, 9 part-time)

Courses:
- History of Higher Education
- Research in Higher Education

Key textbooks/readings:
- Brubaker. *The American College or University*.
- Kougez and Posner. *Leadership Theory*.
- *Research in Higher Education*
- *Journal of Higher Education*
- *Review of Higher Education*
- *Community College Review*
- *NASPA Review*

Oklahoma

Oklahoma, University of, Adult and Higher Education Program

Address: 820 Van Vleet Oval, ECH 227, Norman, OK, 73019, United States
Phone: (405) 325-4202
Fax: (405) 325-2403
Website: http://www.ou.edu/education/elps/edah/

Major source of funding: University

Organizational focus:
   The Program prepares graduates to assume leadership, administrative, teaching, and training positions in a variety of
   organizational settings. Graduates compete for positions as train-
   ers, adult educators, program planners, distance education
   specialists, administrators, and instructors in adult education organizations, colleges and universities (including community
   colleges and vocational schools), governmental and military agencies, and business and industry. The program is located in the
   Department of Educational Leadership.

Staff (name • title/rank • specialization):
   1. David Tan • Associate Professor and Director • institutional research, planning, leadership, assessment, the college student,
   research methodology and statistics
   2. Rosa Cintron • Assistant Professor • student personnel, community college, history, multiculturalism
   3. Jerome Weber • Professor • college administration, athletic administration
   4. Connie Dillon • Professor • distance education
   5. Robert Fox • Professor • instructional strategies, higher education and
   society, continuing professional education
   6. Huey Long • Professor • adult learning, self-directed learning
   7. Irene Karpiak • Assistant Professor • critical literature in adult
   and higher education, continuing higher education
   8. Gary Green • Professor • training and development

Courses:
   • Planning in Higher Education
   • Institutional Research in Higher Education

- Research on the College Student
- Financial Management in Higher Education
- Student Personnel Services in Higher Eduation
- Assessment in Adult and Higher Education
- Research in Adult and Higher Education
- Administration of Adult and Higher Education
- Issues in Adult and Higher Education
- Critical Literature in Adult and Higher Education
- American Community/Junior College
- Leadership Development
- Adult Learner
- Legal Aspects of Higher Education

Student enrollments: M.A. (50–70), doctorate (60–90) on the main campus in Norman. M.A. program, in a contract with U.S. Department of Defense, at five military sites (about 100)

Key journals:
- *Research in Higher Education*
- *Journal of Higher Education*
- *Planning in Higher Education*
- *Journal of College Student Development*

Oklahoma State University, Educational Leadership Program

Address: 203 Willard Hall, Stillwater, OK, 74078, United States

Phone: 405-744-9893
Fax: 405-744-7758
Website: www.osu.edu/homepages

Major source of funding: University

Organizational Focus:
The Program focuses on the preparation of professionals in higher education administration and college teaching. Concentrations are offered in higher education administration and academic leadership at both the M.S. and Ed.D. level. The college teaching degree is also an Ed.D.

Staff (name • title/rank • specialization):
1. David Webster • Associate Professor • rankings

2. Michael Mills • Assistant Professor • policy
3. Adrienne Hyle • Associate Professor • change
4. Kelly Ward • Assistant Professor • higher education

Courses:
- Educational Ideas
- Planning and Change
- Politics
- Organizational Theory
- Leadership
- Seminar
- Academic Department
- Higher Education Finance
- Effective Teaching
- Impact of College on Students
- Higher Education Law
- Administration of Higher Education
- Community Junior College
- Critical Issues

Key journals:
- *Journal of Higher Education*
- *Review of Higher Education*

Oregon

Oregon, University of, Higher Education Program

Address: College of Education, Eugene, OR, 97403, United States

Phone: (541) 346-5171
Fax: (541) 346-5174
E-mail: Kenkemp@oregon.uoregon.edu
Website: http://darkwing.uoregon.edu/delta/
Date established: 1876
Major source of funding: University

Organizational focus:
The instructional program leads to the M.S .and Ph.D. degrees. The department of Education Leadership, Technology, and Administration houses the ERIC Clearinghouse for Educational Administration.

Staff (name • title/rank • specialization):
1. Ken Kempner • Associate Professor • comparative education, higher education policy
2. Steve Goldschmidt • Associate Professor • law
and planning
3. Dan Williams • Vice President • leadership and
administration
4. Shirley Clark • Vice Chancellor • leadership and
governance

Courses:
- • Higher Education Governance I, II, III
- • Philosophy of Higher Education
- • Higher Education in Developing Countries
- • Community College Administration

Student enrollments: M.A. (15 full-time, 10 part-time),
Ph.D. (5 full-time, 20 part-time)

Key journals:
- • *Journal of Higher Education*
  - • *Review of Higher Education*
  - • *Higher Education*

**Portland State University, Postsecondary, Adult and Continuing Educa-
tion Program**

Address: PO Box 751, Portland, OR, 97207, United States

Phone: 503-725-4754
Fax: 503-725-8475

Date established: 1992
Major source of funding: University

Organizational focus:
The Postsecondary, Adult and Continuing Education Program is a specialization area in both the master's program in Educational Policy,
Foundations, and Administrative Studies, and the doctoral program
in Educational Leadership (Ed.D.) in the Graduate School of Educa-

tion. The program serves students focusing on higher education administration, student services in higher education, training and development, and community college education.

Staff (name • title/rank • specialization):
1. Mary Kinnick • Professor • higher education administration, student affairs, evaluation and assessment
2. Janine Allen • Adjunct Associate Professor • student affairs
3. Vasti Torres • Adjunct Assistant Professor • student affairs
4. Janet Bennett • Adjunct Professor • training and development
5. Shirley Anderson • Adjunct Associate Professor • community college education

Courses:
- Student Services Foundations I, II and III
- Contemporary Issues in Postsecondary Education
- The Community College
- Planning and Budgeting in Postsecondary Education
- Policy and Governance in Postsecondary Education
- Adult Learning
- Developmental Perspectives on Adult Learning
- Course Design and Evaluation
- Assessing Adult Learning

Student enrollments: M.A./M.S. (90), Ed.D. (35 part-time)
Key journals:
- *Journal of Higher Education*
- *Research in Higher Education*
- *Review of Higher Education*
- *Journal of College Student Development*
- *Adult Education Quarterly*
- *Educational Evaluation and Policy Analysis*

Pennsylvania

Indiana University of Pennsylvania, Student Affairs in Higher Education Program

Address: 226 Stouffer Hall, IUP, Indiana, PA, 15705, United States

Phone: 724-357-1251
Fax: 724-357-7821
E-mail: LUNAR@GROVE.IUP.EDU
Website: http://www.iup.edu/st

Date established: 1971
Major source of funding: University

Organizational focus:
   To prepare students for entry-level positions in U.S. two- and four-
   year colleges and universities.

Current publications:
   • *Development* (biannual alumni newsletter)

Staff (name • title/rank • specialization):
   1. Holly A. Belch • Assistant Professor • student affairs administration
   2. Linda M. Hall • Associate Professor • student affairs administration
   3. Ronald Lunardini • Associate Professor • student affairs administration
   4. John A. Mueller, Assistant Professor, student affairs administration
   5. Ron Thomas, Professor Emeritus

Courses:
   • Student Development in Higher Education
   • Contemporary Issues in Higher Education
   • Management of Organizational Behavior
   • The American College Student
   • Cultural Pluralism

Student enrollments: 62 full-time, 3 part-time

Key journals:
   • *Journal of College Student Development*
   • *NASPA Journal*

Kutztown University, Student Affairs in Higher Education Program

Address: Kutztown, PA, 19530, United States

Phone: 610-683-4204
Fax: 610-398-1585
E-mail: bucci@kutztown.edu
Website: http://www.kutztown.edu/acad/graduate

Date established: 1991
Major source of funding: University

Organizational focus:
   To prepare students for professional careers in student services in higher
   education institutions.

Staff (name • title/rank):
   1. Deborah Barlieb • Assistant Professor
   2. Frank A. Bucci • Professor and Program Coordinator
   3. Joanne Cohen • Assistant Professor
   4. Margaret A. Herrick • Associate Professor and Department Chairperson
   5. Sandra McSwain • Professor

Student enrollments: M.A. (6 full-time, 46 part-time)

Courses:
   • Methods of Research
   • Education and Psychology Tests and Measurement
   • Social Interpretation of Education

Key textbooks:
   • A. Rentz. (1998). *Student Affairs Practice in Higher Education*. Charles
   C. Thomas, 1998.
   • R. M. Kaplan and D. P. Saccuzzo. *Psychological Testing*. Brooks/Cole.
   • Gerald Kranzler. *Statistics for the Terrified*. Prentice Hall.
   • Mark Mitchell and Janine Jolley. Research Design Explained. 3d ed..
   Holt, Rinehart, & Winston.

Pennsylvania, University of, Higher Education Program

Address: 4200 Pine Street, 4th Floor, Philadelphia, PA, 19188, United States
Phone: 215-898-2444

Fax: 215-898-9876
E-mail: feld@underground.irhe.upenn.edu (Steve Feld, Instructor and Academic Coordinator)
Website: http://www.upenn.edu/gse/Academics/HED/index.html

Date established: 1984
Major source of funding: University

Organizational focus:
The Program trains students in higher education administration. The goal is to prepare School of Education graduates for senior-level administrative positions within higher education, positions in higher education consulting and in higher education policymaking agencies and organizations, and to prepare researchers and professors of higher education administration.

Staff:
Three full professors, five adjunct professors, three lecturers/instructors, two coordinators.
Specializations include: finance, market economics, history, organizational management, student life, management of change, outcomes/assessment.

Courses:
- Contemporary Issues in Higher Education
- Higher Education Systems
- Governance in Higher Education
- History of American Higher Education
- Quantitative Research Methods (doctoral)
- Methods of Institutional Research Strategic Planning
- Administration of Student Life
- Enrollment Management
- Developments in Higher Education: Residential Colleges
- Management in Higher Education
- Law in Higher Education
- Public Policy Issues in Higher Education
- Proseminar in Research and Analysis in Higher Education (2 semesters)
- Readings in Higher Education (2 semesters)
- Access and Choice in American Higher Education
- Case Studies in Higher Education Administration
- Teaching and Learning in Postsecondary Education
- Economics of Higher Education

- Finance in Higher Education
- Budget and Resource Allocation

Student enrollments: M.S.Ed. (15 full-time, 22 part-time), Ed.D. (15 full-time, 25 part-time), Ph.D. (8 full-time, 20 part-time)

The Pennsylvania State University, Center for the Study of Higher Education

Address: 403 South Allen Street, Suite 104, University Park, PA, 16801-5252, United States
Phone: 814-865-6346
Fax: 814-865-3638
Website: http://www.ed.psu.edu/cshe

Date established: 1969
Major source of funding: federal government, private foundations, University

Organizational focus:
    The Center provides studies, analyses, and reports relevant to decision making in higher education and, in doing so, aids in the formulation of higher education policy. The Center has provided guidance, support, and research on issues, topics, and problems central to the higher education policy of the federal government, of the various states, of the Commonwealth of Pennsylvania, and of Pennsylvania State University.

    The purpose of the Center is to examine issues that affect the policies and practices of postsecondary institutions and their implications for leadership, planning, and general administration.

Current publications:
    - *Annual for Higher Education*
    - *New Directions for Institutional Research*

Staff (name • title/rank • specialization):
    1. Alberto F. Cabrera • Associate Professor and Senior Research Associate • college student adjustment and persistence, minorities in higher education, the effects of student financial aid, quantitative research methodologies
    2. Carol L. Colbeck • Assistant Professor and Research Associate • organizational and disciplinary influences on faculty work behavior, the impact of

faculty teaching efforts on student learning, curricular reform

3. Roger L. Geiger • Professor and Head of the Higher Education Program • history of higher education

4. Robert M. Hendrickson • Professor and Chair of the Department of Education Policy Studies • organizational theory, administration, law of higher education

5. Robert Marine • Research Associate • complex service and data systems, process evaluation, technology applications in higher education

6. James L. Ratcliff • Professor and Senior Scientist • assesment and evaluation, curriculum, and program development; community college education

7. Patrick T. Terenzini • Professor and Senior Scientist • impact of college on students, student retention, institutional research and planning, the assessment of student learning outcomes

8. James Fredricks Volkwein • Professor, Senior Scientiest, and Director • government regulations and university autonomy, planning strategies and models, performance measures, academic program evaluation and accreditation, assmessment of student learning and growth

Courses:
- Higher Education in the United States
- Curricula in Higher Education
- Administration in Higher Education
- The History of American Higher Education
- Higher Education Students and Clientele
- Legal Issues in Higher Education
- Organizational Theory and Higher Education
- Qualitative Methods in Educational Research

Student enrollments: M.A. (10), Ed.D./Ph.D. (90)

Key journals:
- *Journal of Higher Education*
- *Research in Higher Eduation*
- *Annual for Higher Education*
- *New Directions for Institutional Research*

The Pennsylvania State University, Higher Education Program

Address: 403 South Allen Street, Suite 115, University Park, PA, 16801-5202, United States

Phone: 814-863-2690
Fax: 814-865-0543
E-mail: HIEDE@PSU.EDU
Website: http://www.ed.psu.edu/hied/default.htm
Date established: 1950
Major source of funding: University

Organizational focus:
   The Program focuses on the preparation of individuals who are capable of researching, analyzing, and managing critical problems in postsecondary education.

Current publications:
   • *History of Higher Education Annual*

Staff (name • title/rank):
   1. Alberto F. Cabrera • Associate Professor of Education and Research Associate, Center for the Study of Higher Education
   2. Carol L. Colbeck • Assistant Professor of Education and Research Associate, Center for the Study of Higher Education
   3. Roger L. Geiger • Professor of Education, Higher Education Program
   4. Robert M. Hendrickson• Professor of Education and Head, Department of Education Policy Studies
   5. David Post• Professor of Education and Senior Research Associate, Center for the Study of Higher Education
   6. James Ratcliff• Professor of Education and Director, Center for the Study of Higher Education
   7. Patrick Terenzini• Professor of Education and Senior Scientist, Center for the Study of Higher Education

Courses:
   • Educational Mobility in Comparative Perspective
   • Ethnicity, National Identity, and Education
   • Higher Education in the United States
   • College Teaching
   • Curricula in Higher Education

- Community junior College and the Technical Institute
- Education for the Professions
- Administration in Higher Education
- The History of American Higher Education
- Higher Education Students and Clientele
- Curriculum Design and Evaluation in Higher Education
- Legal Issues in Higher Education
- Organizational Theory and Higher Education
- Research Design: Implications for Decisions and Policy in Higher Education
- Qualitative Methods in Educational Research
- Comparative Higher Education
- Research Topics
- Internship in Higher Education
- Individual Studies
- Special Topics
- D.Ed Thesis Research
- Ph.D. Dissertation
- D.Ed. Thesis Research
- Ph.D. Dissertation

Student enrollments: M.A. (1 full-time, 7 part-time), Ph.D. (15 full-time, 30 part-time), D.Ed. (5 full-time, 40 part-time)

Pittsburgh, University of, Higher Education Administration Program
Address: 5S01 Forbes Quadrangle, 230 S. Bouquet Street, Pittsburgh, PA, 15260, United States

Phone: (412) 648-7100
Fax: (412) 648-1784
Website: http://www.pitt.edu/~soeforum

Date established: 1961
Major source of funding: University

Organizational focus:
    The University of Pittsburgh is a Carnegie Research I University and member of the Association of American Universities. The Higher Education Administration Program, located in the Department of Administrative and Policy Studies, offers master's and doctoral de-

gree programs oriented toward students who are committed to pursuing careers in higher education management, policy, and finance.

Staff (name • title/rank • specialization):
1. James E. Mauch • Professor • comparative higher education, administration, research
2. Glenn M. Nelson • Associate Professor • administration, student affairs
3. Eugenie Potter • Assistant Professor • philosophy, ethics
4. John C. Weidman • Professor • comparative higher education, policy, administration
5. John L. Yeager • Associate Professor • comparative higher education, strategic planning, budget

Courses:
- Administrative and Policy Core I
- Administrative and Policy Core II
- Higher Education Administration
- Politics and History of Higher Education
- Higher Education Strategic Planning
- Higher Education Budget and Finance
- Higher Education Human Resource Management
- Higher Education Academic Program Management
- Higher Education Organizational Development
- Legal Issues in Higher Education
- Student Services Administration
- Diversity in Higher Education
- Data Base Management
- Ethical Issues in Higher Education
- Internship in Higher Education
- Student, Campus, and Society
- Seminar in College Teaching
- Comparative Higher Education
- Project Planning in Higher Education
- Policy Studies in Higher Education
- Advanced Seminar in Higher Education
- Introductionto Educational Evaluation
- Planning and Use of Evaluation by Administrators
- Institutional Assessment and Accreditation in Higher Education

Student enrollments: M.Ed. (2 full-time, 18 part-time), Ed.D. (5 full-time, 65 part-time)

Shippensburg University, Counseling and Student Personnel Program

Address: Shippensburg Unviersity, Department of Counseling CEC, 1871 Old Main Drive, Shippensburg, PA, 17257, United States

Phone: 717-532-1668
Fax: 717-530-4056
E-mail: tlhozman@ark.ship.edu
Website: http://ark.ship.edu
Date established: 1960
Major source of funding: University

Organizational focus:
The Department of Counseling teaches the necessary skills for the professional practice of counseling and student personnel work. The Program also facilitates the conceptualization of a professional role, one that is flexible enough to grow as new knowledge and developments occur. The counseling program is a careful balance of theory with practice. Students are required to complete a practicum and a minimum of two internships.

The Department offers the following graduate degree specializations in counseling: Master of Education degree and certification as elementary or secondary school counselors, Master of Science degree with specialization in community or mental health counseling, and Master of Science degree with specialization in college counseling or student personnel services. The Department of Counseling is fully accredited by the Middle States Association of Colleges and Secondary Schools and the National Council for Accreditation of Teacher Education (NCATE). The Department if also authorized by the State Board of Counseling.

Staff (name • title/rank):
1. Anthony F. Ceddia • President of the University
2. Robert B. Bartos • Dean of Graduate Studies and Dean, College of Education and Human Services
3. Renee M. Payne • Assistant Dean of Graduate Studies
4. Paul F. Dempsey • Assistant Dean of Graduate Studies and Registrar

5. Thomas L. Hozman • Counseling Department Chair
6. Jan L. Arminio • Professor
7. Mary O. Bradshaw • Psychological Counselor
8. Ford W. Brooks • Professor
9. Andrew L. Carey • Professor
10. Kurt L. Kraus • Professor
11. Kathryn A. Kurdt • Psycholofical Counselor
12. David L. Lovett • Director of Counseling Services
13. Rebecca M. LaFountain • Professor
14. Beverly L. Mustaine • Professor
15. Norman R. Sharp • Professor
16. Michelle Stefanisko • Counseling Psychologist

Student enrollments: M.A. (155 full-time, 75 part-time)

Key textbooks/readings:
   • S. T. Glassing. Counseling: A Comprehensive Profession. 3rd ed. Englewood, Calif.: Prentice Hall, 1996.
   • "The Student Learning Imperative." Special issue. *Journal of College Student Development* 37 (1996).
   • S. R. Kimonos and D. B. Woodward. *Student Services: A Handbook for the Profession*. San Francisco: Jossey-Bass, 1996.
   • *Points of View*. Washington, D.C.: National Association of Student Personnel Administrators, 1989.

Key journals:
   • *Journal of Counselor Education and Supervision*
   • *Journal of Counseling and Development*
   • *The Professional School Counselor*
   • *Journal of Individual Psychology*
   • *Journal of Addiction and Offender Counselors*
   • *Journal of College Student Development*
   • *Journal for Specialization in Group Work*

South Carolina

South Carolina at Columbia, University of, Higher Education Administration and Student Personnel Services Program

Address: University of South Carolina, Columbia, SC, 29208, United States

Phone: (803) 777-5240

Fax: (803) 777-3090
Website: http://www.ed.sc.edu/zedlp.htm
Date established: 1963
Major source of funding: University

Organizational focus:
The higher education programs prepare individuals for careers in higher education administration and college student personnel services. The doctoral program prepares scholar-administrators for higher-level administration positions in universities. The master's degree program prepares individuals for entry-level positions in higher education institutions—such as residence hall management, admissions, financial aid, student services, career planning and placement, records and registration, student activities, international education and institutional development.

Current publications:
• *Carolina View* (journal)

Staff (name • title/rank • specialization):
1. Betsy Barefoot • Clinical Professor • student affairs
2. John Gardner • Adjunct Professor • first year (Freshman)
3. Paul Fidler • Associate Professor • student affairs
4. Jim Hudgins • Clinical Professor • community college
5. Tim Letzring • Assistant Professor • law of higher education
6. Gene Luna • Clinical Professor • higher education administration
7. Jim Rex • Professor • institutional development
8. Katherine Reynolds • Assistant Professor • history/biography
9. E. Michael Sutton • Assistant Professor • student affairs
10. Michael F. Welsh • Associate Professor • higher education administration
11. Richard Wertz • Associate Professor • finance

Courses:
• Higher Education in America
• Student Personnel Services in Higher Education
• The American College Student
• Ideas of American Higher Education
• The Community/Technical/Junior College
• Organizational Change in Higher Education
• Financial Aspects of Higher Education

- Legal Aspects of Higher Education
- Principles of College Teaching
- Organization, Administration, Governance
- Leadership in Higher Education

Student enrollments: M.A. (80 full-time, 10 part-time), Ph.D. (5 full-time, 45 part-time), other (25 part-time)

Key textbooks/readings:
- S. R. Komives and D. B. Woodward, Jr. *Student Services: A Handbook for the Profession*. 3d ed. San Francisco: Jossey-Bass, 1996.
- A. L. Rentz. *Student Affairs Practice in Higher Education*. Springfield, Ill.: Charles C. Thomas, 1996.
- F. Rudolph. *The American College and University: A History*. Athens: University of Georgia Press, 1990.

Key journals:
- *Review of Higher Education*
- *Journal of Higher Education*
- *Journal of the First Year Experience*
- *Case Research Journal*
- *History of Ed. Journal*
- *NASPA Journal*
- *College Student Affairs Journal*
- *Journal of College Student Development*
- *Academe*

Tennessee

Memphis, University of, Higher and Adult Education Program

Address: 113 Patterson, Memphis, TN, 38152-6172, United States

Phone: 901-678-2368
Fax: 901-678-3215

Date established: 1975
Major source of funding: University
Organizational focus:
   We offer a doctoral degree in higher and adult education.

Staff (name • title/rank • specialization):
1. Robert O. Riggs • Coordinator and Professor • finance and law
2. Barbara K. Mullins • Professor • adult learning
3. Patricia J. Murrell• Professor • professional education
4. John R. Petry • Professor • evaluation, learning theories,
5. James. L. Penrod • Professor • strategic planning, information systems
6. John C. Smart • Professor • legal issues, academic leadership, community college

Courses:
- Overview of Higher Education
- Higher Education Administration
- History of Higher Education
- Higher Education Law
- Higher Education Finance
- College Teaching
- Research in Higher and Adult Education
- Adult Learning and Leadership
- Developing and Funding Leadership Programs
- Administration of Adult and Continuing Education

Student enrollments: Ed.D. 5 (full-time, 50 part-time)

Key journals:
- *Journal of Higher Education*
- *Review of Higher Education*
- *Research in Higher Education*
- *Adult Education Quarterly*
- *International Journal of Lifelong Education*

Texas

Baylor University, Collegiate Scholars of Practice Program

Address: Baylor University, Department of Educational Administration, School of Education, Waco, TX, 76798-7312, United States
Phone: (254) 710-6107
Fax: (254) 710-3117
E-mail: chester_hastings@baylor.edu
Website: http://www.baylor.edu/Graduate_School/

Date established: 1990
Major source of funding: University

Organizational focus:
The Program is designed to meet the needs of working men and women with demonstrated leadership ability and a strong commitment to the education profession and to improving higher education. Our three and one-half year Ed.D. program is delivered via a unique monthly cohort format.

Staff (name • title/rank • specialization):
1. Chester R. Hastings • Professor and Chief Advisor • community college, student services, curriculum and instruction
2. James L. Williamson • Professor and Chair, Department of Educational Administration • policy, interprofessional collaboration, administration
3. Weldon Beckner • Professor • ethics, philosophy, history
4. Betty Jo Monk • Associate Professor • leadership
5. Robert C. Cloud • Professor • community college, governance, organization, law
6. Douglas Rogers • Associate Professor • technology
7. Mark Bateman • Associate Professor • research

Courses:
- Trends in Educational Thought
- Educational Evaluation
- Research in Educational Administration
- Technology in Educational Administration
- Competency Assessment and Evaluation
- Advanced Studies in Educational Leadership
- The Community College
- International and Comparative Education
- The College Student
- Organization and Administration of the Community College
- Community Relations
- Student Services in Higher Education
- Seminar: Education (Washington)
- Business and Finance in Higher Education
- Seminar: Politics, Policy, and Governance of Education
- Inter-professional Education and Practice
- Curriculum and Instruction in the Community College
- Seminar: American Educational Thought

• Higher Education Law
Student enrollments: Ed.D. (2 full-time, 30–40 part-time)

Key textbooks/readings:
• M. Apple. *Official Knowledge: Democratic Education in a Conservative Age.*
• C. Barnard. *The Functions of the Executive.*
• W. Bennis. *On Becoming a Leader.*
• D. Berliner and B. Biddle. *The Manufactured Crisis: Myths, Fraud, and the Attack on America's Public Schools.*
• E. Boyer. *Scholarship Reconsidered: Priorities of the Professoriate.*
• J. Dewey. *The Child and the Curriculum* and *School and Society.*
• M. Fullan. *Change Forces: Proving the Depths of Educational Reform.*
• C. Glassick, M. Huber, and G. Maeroff. *Scholarship Assessed: Evaluation of the Professoriate.*
• J. Goodlad and R. McMannon. *The Public Purpose of Schooling.*
• R. M. Kanter. *The Change Masters.*
• D. Schon. *The Reflective Practitioner.*
• A. N. Whitehead. *The Aims of Education.*

Key journals:
• *Chronicle of Higher Education*
• *Phi Delta Kappan*
• *Community College Journal*
• *Journal of College Student Development*

Dallas Baptist University, Higher Education Program

Address: 3000 Mountain Creek Parkway, Dallas, TX, 75211-9299, United States
Phone: (214) 333-5200
Fax: (214) 333-5551
Website: http://www.dbu.edu

Date established: 1898
Major source of funding: University

Organizational focus:
The purpose of Dallas Baptist University is to provide Christ-centered, quality higher education in the arts, sciences, and professional studies at both the undergraduate and graduate levels to traditional age and adult

students in order to produce servant-leaders who have the ability to integrate faith and learning through their respective callings.

Staff (name • title/rank):
1. Michael J. Rosato • Dean, College of Education; Director, Higher Education Program

Courses:
- College and University Administration
- Research Methods in Higher Education
- Ethics and Leadership Theory: Servant Leadership
- History and Philosophy of Higher Education
- Legal Aspects and Finance in Higher Education
- Readings in Higher Education
- Practicum in Higher Education

Student enrollments: M.Ed. (1 full-time, 14 part-time)

Key textbooks/readings:
- Higher Education in American Society.
- *The Idea of a Christian College*.

Houston, University of, Institute for Higher Education Law and Governance

Address: 202 TU II, University of Houston Law Center; 4800 Calhoun, Houston, TX, 77204-6370, United States

Phone: 713-743-2075
Fax: 713-743-2085
E-mail: ihelg@www.law.uh.edu
Website: http://www.law.uh.edu/LawCenter/Programs/IHELG

Date established: 1982
Major source of funding: University; grant and contract funds from various foundations

Organizational focus:
The Institute for Higher Education Law and Governance (IHELG) is the only research institute in the United States devoted to scholarship and practice of higher education law as a field of study. The Institute sponsors scholarship activities, research projects, colloquia, confer-

ences, round tables, and workshops on higher education legal and finance issues; sponsors a research monograph series (totaling over 220 studies); and trains postdoctoral fellows, University of Houston Law Center (UHLC) law students, and University of Houston doctoral students in college law and administration. Its specialized library holds over 2,000 volumes.

Current publications:

IHELG publishes a working paper Research Monograph Series, averaging one such study per month. Virtually all are reprinted as refereed journal or law review articles or as books or book chapters. (All titles are available from the IHELG website.)

Staff (name • title/rank):
1. William B. Bates • Director
2. Michael A. Olivas • Professor of Law
3. Nancy Snyder-Nepo • Research Assistant
4. Dennis Duffy • Research Fellow and UH General Counsel
5. Laura Rothstein • Professor, UHLC Law Foundation
6. Craig Joyce • Professor, UHLC Law Foundation
7. Amaury Nora • Professor, UHLC Law Foundation
8. Nestor Rodriguez • Professor, UHLC Law Foundation
9. Augustina H. Reyes • Professor, UHLC Law Foundation

Courses:
• Higher Education Law Seminar
• Intellectual Property
• Special Education Law
• Constitutional Law Seminar

Key textbooks/readings:
• Michael A. Olivas. *The Law and Higher Education: Cases and Materials on Colleges in Court*. 2d ed. Carolina Academic Press, 1997.
• William A. Kaplin and Barbara Lee. *The Law of Higher Education*. 3d ed.(Jossey-Bass, 1996.

Key journals:
• *Journal of College and University Law*
• *Journal of Education*
• *Journal of Legal Education*
• *Journal of Higher Education*
• *Review of Higher Education*
• *Research in Higher Education*

North Texas, University of, Higher Education Program

Address: College of Education, University of North Texas, Denton, TX, 76203, United States
Phone: 940-565-2045
Fax: 940-565-2905
Website: http://www.unt.edu/highered

Date established: 1960
Major source of funding: University

Organizational focus:
The Program in Higher Education awards the master's degree in student services administration and Ed.D. and Ph.D. degrees in higher education. The Program in Higher Education additionally sponsors the *Community College Journal of Research and Practice.*

Staff (name • title/rank • specialization):
1. Jack Baier • Professor • student services administration, finance, planning
2. Paul Dixon • Professor • administration, policy studies, research and statistics
3. John Eddy • Professor • student services administration, history, philosophy, general administration
4. Bonita Jacobs • Assistant Professor • student development administration
5. D. Barry Lumsden • Professor • learning and assessment, adult development, the community college
6. Ron Newsom • Associate Professor • teaching and learning, history, philosophy
7. Pamela Hill • Adjunct Faculty • student development, minorities and women in higher education
8. Pete Lane • Adjunct Faculty • institutional advancement
9. Richard Rafes • Adjunct Faculty • legal issues in higher education

Courses:
• Foundations of Student Development Administration
• Internship
• Teaching and Learning
• Publishing
• Perspectives
• Research on Higher Education

- General Administration
- Academic Administration
- Resource Development
- Studies in Higher Education
- Student Development Administration
- Policy Studies
- Comparative International Systems
- The Professoriate
- The Role of Higher Education in a Democracy
- Planning
- Legal Aspects
- Finance
- Studies in Higher Education: Effective College Teaching
- The Adult Learner
- Seminar in College Student Personnel Work

Student enrollments: M.A. (7 full-time, 10 part-time), Ph.D. (18 full-time, 72 part-time)

Key textbooks/readings:
- Ortega y Gasset, Jose. *Mission of the University.*
- Edward Shils. *The Calling of Education: The Academic Ethic and Other Essays on Higher Education.*
- Arthur Levine. *Higher Learning in America 1980–2000.*
- Lawrence Levine. *The Opening of the American Mind.*
- Clark Kerr. *The Uses of the University.*

Key journals:
- *AAHE Bulletin*
- *Academe*
- *Alternative Higher Education*
- *Black Issues in Higher Education*
- *Change*
- *Chronicle of Higher Education*
- *College Student Journal*
- *College Teaching*
- *Community College Review*
- *Community College Journal of Research and Practice*
- *Innovative Higher Education*

- *Journal of College Student Development*
- *Journal of College Student Personnel Development*
- *Journal of Higher Education*
- *Metropolitan Universities*
- *Research in Higher Education*
- *Review of Higher Education*
- *Journal of Blacks in Higher Education*

Texas A and M University, Higher Education Administration and Student Affairs Administration in Higher Education (SAAHE) Program

Address: Texas A and M University, Educational Administration Department, 511 Harrington Tower, College Station, TX, 77843-4226 United States

Phone: 409-845-2716
Fax: 409-862-4347
E-mail: b-cole@tamu.edu

Date established: 1969
Major source of funding : University
Organizational focus:

The Program's main purpose is preparing higher education and student affairs professionals for administration in public and private institutions of higher education. A secondary purpose is preparing a small number of teachers and researchers who are focused on higher education or student affairs.

Staff (name • title/rank • specialization):
1. Yvonna S. Lincoln • Professor • qualitative research, history and philosophy of higher education (foundations), organizational theory, college teaching
2. D. Stanley Carpenter • Professor • student affairs administration, introduction to research methods, administration of higher education institutions
3. Bryan R. Cole • Professor and Department Head • higher education law, quality management in higher education
4. Carol Logan Patitu • Assistant Professor • the American college student, student services, practicum supervision, multicultural education in student affairs programming

5. Dean C. Corrigan • Professor • public policy and higher education, statewide coordination and planning
6. Ed J. Davis • Professor and President, TAMU Development Foundation • finance
7. Brent Patterson • Adjunct Associate Professor • the law in student affairs administration
8. William J. Kibler • Adjunct Associate Professor and Deputy Vice Chancellor for Student Affairs • the law in student affairs administration, planning and programming in student affairs
9. Jan Winniford • Adjunct Assistant Professor • internship and practicum supervision, student judicial affairs

Courses:
- History and Philosophy of Higher Education
- Introduction to Higher Education Research Methods
- Organization and Administration of Higher Education
- Case Studies in Higher Education Administration
- Finance of Higher Education
- Public Policy and Higher Education
- Higher Education Law
- Total Quality Management in Higher Education
- Organizational Theory in Higher Education

Student enrollments: M.A. (15 full-time, 35 part-time), Ph.D. (20 full-time, 50 part-time), Ed.D. (10 full-time, 50 part-time)

Key textbooks/readings:
- Birnbaum. *How Colleges Work.*
- Christopher Lucas. *Crisis in the Academy.*
- Christopher Lucas. *Higher Education in the United States.*
- Goodchild and Wechsler, eds. *History of Higher Education.*

Key journals:
- *Review of Higher Education*
- *Journal of Higher Education*

Texas A and M University at Commerce, Secondary and Higher Education Program
Address: Texas AandM University, Commerce, TX, 75429, United States

Phone: 903-886-5607
Fax: 903-886-5603

E-mail: jon_travis@tamu-commerce.edu; bob_munday@tamu-commerce.edu
Website: http://www.tamu-commerce.edu

Date established: doctoral degree, 1962; Center for Community College
   Education, 1967
Major source of funding: University

Organizational focus:
   The Program prepares graduates for faculty positions in secondary
   schools, colleges, and universities, and to trains administrators for colleges and universities. The Center for Community College Education
   is both an extension of the graduate degrees in higher education and
   an outreach service for the area community colleges.

Current publications:
   • *Models for Improving College Teaching.* (faculty resource)
   •*The Center Page* (newsletter)

Staff (name • title/rank • specialization):
   1. Jon Travis • Associate Professor and Director, Center for Community College Education • community colleges, college teaching,
   qualitative research, higher education administration
   2. Robert Munday • Professor and Department Head • philosophy of
   education, college teaching, higher education administration
   3. William Campion • Associate Professor • community colleges, higher
   education administration
   4. William Ogden • Professor • history of education
   5. James Tunnell • Professor • community colleges, higher education
   administration
   6. Robert Windham • Professor • curriculum, higher education administration

Courses:
   • Philosophy of Education
   • The American Community College
   • The Community College Curriculum
   • Analysis of Teaching in Higher Education
   • Effective Teaching and Learning in Higher Education
   • History of Education in the United States
   • Institutional Effectiveness and Outcomes Assessment
   • Advanced Practicum in Supervision and Curriculum

- Curriculum Development in Higher Education
- Fundamental Theories in Community College Instructional Leadership
- Seminar in Instructional Leadership
- Issues in Higher Education
- Higher Education and the Law
- Finance and Governance in Higher Education
- Administration in Higher Education
- Research Methods
- Advanced Research Methodology: Interpretive Inquiry
- Research Collaquium

Student enrollments: M.S. (50–100), Ph.D. (150–200)

Key textbooks/readings:
- H. Ozman and S. Craver. *Philosophical Foundations of Education*. 6th ed. Englewood Cliffs, N.J.: Prentice-Hall, 1999.
- A. M. Cohen and F. B. Brawer. *The American Community College*. 3d ed. San Francisco: Jossey-Bass, 1996.

Key journals:
- *Community College Journal*
- *Community College Review*
- *Community College Journal of Research and Practice*
- *Review of Higher Education*
- *Journal of Higher Education*
- *Change*
- *College Teaching*
- *Journal on Excellence in College Teaching*
- *Innovative Higher Education*
- *Research in Higher Education*
- *Thought and Action*

Texas Tech University, Higher Education Program

Address: Texas Tech University, College of Education, Box 41071, Lubbock, TX, 79404-1071, United States

Phone: 806-742-2393
Fax: 806-742-1997x239 or 302
E-mail: ismit@ttacs.ttu.edu
Webiste: http://www/edu/ttu/edu/edweb/edhe

Date established: 1970
Major source of funding: University

Organizational focus:
The purpose of the program is to prepare individuals for leadership roles in colleges, universities, local, state, and federal agencies; and business and industry. Degree programs include: an M.Ed. in higher education (majors: administration and student affairs) and an Ed.D. in higher education (majors: university administration, community college leadership/teaching/and students affairs)

Current publications:
• *Higher Education Program* (biannual newsletter)

Staff (name • title/rank • specialization):
1. Albert B. Smith • Professor and Coordinator, Higher Education Program Area
2. Bonita Butner • Assistant Professor of Higher Education • student affairs
3. Brent Cejda • Assistant Professor of Higher Education • university administration
4. John Murray • Associate Professor of Higher Education • community college leadership/teaching
5. E. Dale J Cluff • Professor and Dean of Libraries
6. Robert H. Ewalt • Associate Professor and Vice President for Student Affairs
7. Fred Hartmeister • Assistant professor and Coordinator, Educational Leadership
8. Troy Johnson • Adjunct Assistant Professor and Assistant Dean of the Graduate School
9. Suzanne G. Logan • Adjunct Assistant Professor and Associate Vice Provost • outreach and extended studies
10. Rebecca Owens • Adjunct Assistant Professor and Director of Program for Academic Support Services
11. Michael Shonrock • Adjunct Assistant Professor and Dean of Students
12. Patricia S. Yoder-Wise • Adjunct Professor and Dean of the School of Nursing

Courses:
• Seminar in Higher Education

- The History of Higher Education in the United States
- American Higher Education
- Comparative Higher Education
- Critical Issues in Higher Education
- Organization and Governance in Higher Education
- The Community Junior College
- Community College Leadership
- The Administration of Higher Education
- Institutional Planning in Higher Education
- Development and Finance in Higher Education
- Higher Education and the Law
- Student Services in Higher Education
- Issues in Student Affairs
- The American College Student
- Assessment of Student Outcomes in Higher Education
- College Teaching
- College and University Curriculum
- Internship in Higher Education
- Higher Education Research Seminar

Student enrollments: M.A. (20 full-time, 15 part-time), Ed.D. (10 full-time, 60 part-time)

Key textbooks/readings:
- J. L. Bess, ed. *Foundations of American Higher Education ASHE Reader Series*. Needham Heights, Mass.: Ginnn, 1993.
- F. E. Balderson. *Managing Today's University: Strategies for Viability, Exchange, and Excellence*. San Francisco: Jossey-Bass, 1995.

Key journals:
- *Journal of Higher Education*
- *Community College Review*
- *Research in Higher Education*
- *Community College Journal of Research and Practice*
- *NASPA Journal*
- *Journal of College Student Development*

Utah

Utah Education Policy Center (UEPC)

Address: 1705 E. Campus Center Drive, Room 339, Salt Lake City, Utah, 84112–9254, United States

Phone: 801-581-6714
Fax: 801-585-6756
Website: http://www.gse.utah.edu/policy/policy2.htm

Date established: 1970
Major source of funding: University; foundation and research grants

Organizational focus:
Utah Education Policy Center (UEPC) conducts policy research studies for state agencies, local school districts, the higher education board and other clients. UPEC also provides policy research experience as required in academic programs (Ed.D. degree) as well as of Ph.D. students.

Current publications:
• *Annual Yearbook on Education in Utah.*
• periodic policy papers on selected educational policy issues

Staff (name • title/rank):
1. Anthony W. Morgan • Professor and Co-Director of UPEC
2. Patrick Galven • Associate Professor and Co-Director of UPEC
3. Hal Robbins • Policy Analyst
4. Bob Johnson • Associate Professor
5. Ann Hinckley • Research Assistant

Student enrollments: Ed.D. (10–12 part-time)
Utah, University of, Educational Leadership and Policy Program

Address: 1705 E. Campus Center Drive, Room 339, Salt Lake City, Utah, 84112-9254, United States
Phone: 801-581-6714
Fax: 801-585-6756
Website: http://www.gse.utah.edu/edadm/edadm.htm

Major source of funding: University; private foundation research grants
Organizational focus:

The Program is part of an academic department offering professional preparation programs and degrees at the master's and doctoral (Ed.D. and Ph.D.) levels. Academic degree programs, research, and professional service components include all levels of education from elementary to university levels.

Staff (name • title/rank • specialization):

1. Anthony W. Morgan • Professor • policy, planning; finance, comparative higher education
2. L. Jackson Newell • Professor • history, curriculum, academic administration
3. David P. Gardner • Professor • history, policy, politics
4. Paul Brinkman • Adjunct Professor • economics and finance of higher education

Courses:
- History of Higher Education
- Policy
- Finance
- Governance and administration
- Student Affairs administration

Student enrollments: M.Ed. (6), Ph.D. (4), Ed.D. (6)

Virginia

Virginia Polytechnic Institute and State University, Higher Education and Student Affairs Program

Address: Virginia Tech, College of Human Resources and Education, Blacksburg, VA, 24061-0302, United States
Phone: 540-231-9705
Fax: 540-231-7845
Website: http://www.chre.vt.edu/~/elpshe/

Date established: 1972
Major source of funding: University

Organizational focus:

The master's program in student affairs administration is designed to prepare professionals for entry into the student affairs field. Our doctoral programs are designed to prepare professionals for educational leadership roles in higher education institutions. Our doctoral programs have three specializations available to students: academic and student affairs administration, institutional planning and research, and policy studies in higher education.

Staff (name • title/rank • specialization):
1. Don G. Creamer • Professor and Program Coordinator of Higher Education and Student Affairs • policy studies, organization development
2. Joan B. Hirt • Associate Professor • professionalization in student affairs
3. Steven M. Janosik • Associate Professor • policy studies, higher education law

Courses:
- Student Development in Higher Education
- Theory and Appraisal of College Student Development
- Program Interventions for Promoting College Student Development
- The American College Student and the College Environment
- Practicum in Student Affairs
- Seminar: Research in Student Affairs
- Governance and Policy in Education
- College and University Administration
- Higher Education in the United States
- Higher Education Law
- Financial Administration in Higher Education
- Organization Development in Education
- Policy Studies in Education
- Theories of Educational Organizations
- Institutional Planning and Research
- Institutional Effectiveness and Student Outcome Assessment
- Problems in Education: Practice of Educational Research and Assessment
- Seminar: The State Role in Education
- Seminar: Staffing Practices in Education

Student enrollments: M.A. (28 full-time, 1 part-time), Ph.D. (10 full-time, 8 part-time)

Virginia, University of, Center for the Study of Higher Education

Address: University of Virginia, Curry School of Education, Charlottesville, VA, 22903, United States

Phone: 804-924-3880
Fax: 804-924-0747
E-mail: highered@virginia.edu
Website: http://curry.edschool.virginia.edu/curry/dept/edlf/he/

Date established: 1969
Major source of funding: University

Organizational focus:

The Center for the Study of Higher Education is an instructional, research, and service unit of the Curry School of Education. The Center's instructional programs provide college, university, and adult educational leaders the opportunity to explore established and emerging practices in postsecondary education, to analyze current issues and challenges, and to think critically about educational and institutional priorities and commitments.

In addition to courses, the Center sponsors workshops, seminars, and short institutes as well as research reports and occassional papers that provide college and university administrators and other education leaders with fresh perspectives on developments in postsecondary education.

Current publications:
- *Virginia Education Review*
- *The Quarterly* (newsletter)

Staff (name • specialization):
1. David W. Breneman • economics, the liberals arts college
2. Jay L. Chronister • administration, economics and finance of higher education, faculty issues
3. Annette Gibbs • student affairs administration, governance and management of colleges and universities
4. Elizabeth Flanagan • adult learners
5. Raymond M. Haas • administration and planning in higher education

6. Samuel E. Kellams • college student development, curriculum, multicultural issues in higher education
7. Patricia Lampkin • student affairs administration
8. Robert M. O'Neil • legal aspects of college administration
9. Alton L. Taylor • institutional analysis and planning in higher education
10. Jennings L. Wagoner • history of higher education, policy studies

Courses
   • History of Higher Education
   • The College Student
   • Curriculum in Higher Education
   • Governance and Management of Colleges and Universities
   • Student Affairs in Higher Education
   • Organization and Adminstration of Student Affairs Programs in Higher Education
   • Economics and Finanace of Higher Education
   • Management and Planning in Higher Education
   • Legal Aspects of College Administration
   • The Adult Learner
   • The Community College
   • The American Professoriate
   •Seminar in Higher Education

Student enrollments: Ed.D./Ph.D. (15–20 full-time, 15–20 part-time)

Washington, D.C.

ERIC Clearinghouse on Higher Education

Address: One Dupont Circle, Suite #630, Washington DC 20036, United States
Telephone: 800/773-3742
Fax: 202-452-1844
Website: http://www.eriche.org

Date established: 1967
Major source of funding: government

Organizational focus:
   Research and literature dissemination, publication, question and answer service, and original research

Current publications:
- ASHE-ERIC Higher Education Report Series (8 monographs per year)
- *ERIC Digests* (10 per year)
- bibliographies
- book reviews
- electronic newsletter

Staff (name • title/rank • specialization):
1.Adrianna Kezar • Director and Assistant Professor • leadership, organizational theory, diversity and multiculturalism
2. Karen Kellogg • Associate Director • student affairs, research on students, administration
3. Two part-time graduate students

The World Bank, Tertiary Education Thematic Group (TETG)

Address: 1818 H Street, NW, Washington DC 20433, USA

Telephone: 202-473-5444
Fax: 202-614-0944
Website: http://www.worldbank.org

Date established: 1944
Major source of funding: member countries

Organizational focus:
The Tertiary Education Thematic Group (TETG) of the Human Development Network (HDN) of the World Bank serves to link professionals within the Bank who manage and administer loan projects related to tertiary education reform and enhancement througout the six world regions served by the institution. This Thematic Group shares lessons learned in the field and generates knowledge through internal training programs and publications.
Current publications: multiple publications of all types

Staff (name • specialization):
1. Jamil Salmi • Latin America and the Caribbean
2. Lauritz Holm-Nielsen • Latin America and the Caribbean
3. William Saint • Sub-Saharan Africa
4. Francis Steier • Middle East and North Africa
5. Benoit Millot • Middle East and North Africa

6. Hena Mukherjee • South Asia
7. Shashi Shrivastava • South Asia
8. Peter Moock • East Asia
9. Fredrick Golladay • Europe and Central Asia
10. Richard Hopper • Human Development Anchor

West Virginia

West Virginia University, Higher Education Administration Program

Address: West Virginia University, 508 Allen Hall, Morgantown, WV, 26506, United States

Phone: 304-293-3707
Fax: 304-293-2279
E-mail: rhartnet@wvu.edu

Date established: 1975
Major source of funding: University

Organizational focus:
The Program's focus is on student personnel, academic, and financial/managerial higher education at the doctoral level, and general higher education administration at the master's level. The Program is part of the Department of Educational Leadership Studies.

Staff (name • title/rank • specialization):
1. Richard Hartnett • Professor • international higher education, history of higher education, theory of administration
2. Elizabeth Jones • Assistant Professor • student affairs, curriculum, evaluation
3. Ernest Goeres • Professor, Associate Dean, Budgeting/Finance
4. Scott Kelley • Professor, Vice President Administration, Finance
Courses:
• Theory of Administration
• Development of Higher Education Administration
• Higher Education Administration
• Leadership
• Introductionto Student Personnel
• College Student
• Higher Education Finance

Student enrollments: M.A. (5 full-time, 25 part-time), Ph.D. (4 full-time, 50 part-time)

Key journals:
- *Journal of Higher Education*
- *Education AdministrationQuarterly*
- *Administrative Science Quarterly*
- *Review of Higher Education*
- *Higher Education*
- *Academe*
- numerous student affairs journals
- *Comparative Education*
- *Journal of Education Administration* (Australia)

Wisconsin

Wisconsin at La Crosse, University of, College Student Development and Administration Program

Address: 149 Graff Main Hall, UW-La Crosse, La Crosse, WI, 54601, United States

Phone: 608-785-8063
Fax: 708-785-6575
Website: http://www.uwlax.edu/Graduate/index.html
Date established: 1969

Major source of funding: University

Organizational focus:
The purpose of the Program is to train master's degree candidates in student development in higher education.
Staff (name • title/rank):
1. Larry Ringgenberg • Director, Student Activities and Coordinator, College Student Development and Administration
2. Mary Beth Vahala • Assistant Director, Student Activities
3, Tom Hood • Dean of Students
4. Michael Miyamoto • Assistant Dean of Students

5. Don Campbell • Director of Continuing Education
6. Jon Hageseth • Director, Counseling and Testing and Director, Health Center
7. Andrea Goudie • Counseling and Testing
8. Jodie Rindt-Wagner • Counseling and Testing
9. Andy Ziemelis • Counseling and Testing
10. Ann Korschgen • Director, Career Services
11. Nick Nicklaus • Director, Residence Life

Courses:
- Student Development Theory I
- Higher Education and the Student Personnel Function
- Research and Evaluation
- Advising and Helping Relationships
- Multicultural Groups, Special Populations and Environmental Interactions
- Student Development Theory II
- Student Affairs Administrative Practica
- Student Affairs Programming Practica
- Administration in Higher Education
- Legal Aspects of Student Affairs
- Organizational Theory
- Internship
- Capstone Seminar

Key journals:
- *College Student Development Theory and Practice for the 1990s*. ACPA, 1990.
- *College Student Affairs Administration*. ASHE, 1998.
- *NASPA Journal: Journal of Student Affairs Administration, Research and Practice*
- *Journal of College Student Development*

Wisconsin-Madison, University of, Higher Education Program

Address: University of Wisconsin-Madison 1025 West Johnson Street Madison, WI, 53706-1796, United States
Phone: 608-262-3107
Fax: 608-265-3135

Date established: 1974

Major source of funding: University

Organizational focus:
The Education Administration Department offers the Master of Science degree, the Ph.D. degree, and a specialist certificate in educational administration. All three degrees are intended to increase professional knowledge and skills essential for educational leadership, and to prepare persons for leadership positions at all levels of education: preschool, elementary, secondary, special education, vocational and technical schools, and colleges and universities, both public and private.

Staff (name • title/rank):
1. Clifton Conrad • Professor
2. Jacob Stamper • Professor
3. Chris Gulve • Assistant Professor
4. Allen Phelps • Professor

Courses:
• Introduction to Higher Education
• Organization and Administration of Higher Education
• Curriculum in Higher Education

Student enrollments: M.A. (5 full-time, 20 part-time), Ph.D. (10 full-time, 65 part-time)

Key journals:
• *ASHE Reader*
• *Journal of Higher Education*
• *Review of Higher Education*

Venezuela

UNESCO, International Institute for Higher Education in Latin America and the Caribbean

Address: Apartado 68394, Caracas, 1062A, Venezuela

Phone: (582) 2860721-0516
Fax: (582) 2860326-2039

Date established: 1978
Major source of funding: UNESCO; external contributions

Institutional funding:
The Program of the International Institute for Higher Education in Latin America and the Caribbean (IESALC), is focused around the following four central themes:
• lifelong high-quality higher education;
• higher education for a sustainable human development;
• higher education management; and
• reformulation of international cooperation.

Current publications:
• *Educación superior y sociedad* (journal)
• *Towards a New Higher Education.*
• *Higher Education in the XXIst Century: The Vision of Latin America and the Caribbean.*
• *Higher Education in the Caribbean.*

Vietnam

Asian Institute of Technology (AIT)

Address: 21 Le Thanh Tong, Hanoi, 84–4, Vietnam

Phone: +84-4-8253493
Fax: +84-4-8253658
Website: http://www.asdu.ait.ac.th/aitcv/aitcv.html

Date established: 1993
Major source of funding: international donors (Finland 40%, Sweden 12%, Denmark 12%, Belgium 12%), training and consultation activities

Organizational focus:
Th goal of the Institute is to offer higher education and retraining with academic programs, short-term training, consultation and information dissemination.

Courses:
Industrial Systems Engineering Program (for the master's degree)

Student enrollments: M.A. (25 full time)
National Institute for Educational Development (NIED) (Vien Nghien cuu Phat Trien Giao Duc)

Address: 106 Tran Hung Dao, Hanoi, Vietnam

Phone: 84-4-8253390, 84-4-8253292 (General Director)
Fax: 84-4-8261993
E-mail: lam.nied@netnam.org.vn

Date established: 1988
Major source of funding: client contracts

Organizational focus:
The National Institute for Educational Development (NIED) is an educational research and development institution. It has an autonomous legal and financial status and provides research and development services in education, training, and development. NIED's primary functions include:
- research and development for educational development;
- educational policy preparation;
- strategic planning for education;
- management; and
- postgraduate training in educational development.

Current publications:
- *Educational Development.* (a set of 9 books on educational policy)

Staff (name • title/rank):
1. Dang Ba Lam • Professor and General Director
2. Mac Van Trang • Professor and Editor-in-Chief of the *Review*
3. Nguyen Tien Dat • Professor
4. Nguyen Cong Giap
5. Phan Kha
6. Pham Thanh Nghi
7. Phan Tung Mau
8. Nguyen Ba Thai
9. Pham Quang Sang
10. Tran Khanh Duc

Student enrollments: M.A. (150 full-time)

Courses:
- Foreign Language (English)
- Philosophy
- Computer Science
- Methodology of Scientific Research
- Psychology
- Philosophy
- Computer Science
- Methodology of Scientific Research
- Psychology
- Pedagogy
- Sociology
- Economics of Education and Training
- Theory of Organization and Management
- The Public Administration in Education
- Methods for Researchers in Education
- Policy and Strategy in Education and Training
- Administration Processes in Educational Institutions
- Management of Financial and Physical Resources in Education and Training
- Human Resources Management
- Systems of Educational Management Information
- Socioeconomic Requirements of Education
- Experience and Achievements of Other Countries in Education and Training
- Organization and Implementation of Educational Research Projects

CHAPTER 4

Journals in Higher Education
An International Inventory

Yoshikazu Ogawa

Africa

South African Journal of Higher Education
2/yr
Editor: Philip Higgs
Publisher: South African Association for Research and Development in Higher Education, University of South Africa, P.O. Box 392, Pretoria 0001, Republic of South Africa
Journal Web site: http://www.saardhe.ac.za/sajhe/98123.html

Asia

Daigaku Ronshu (Research in Higher Education)
(In Japanese)
1/yr
Publisher: Research Institute for Higher Education, Hiroshima University 2-2, Kagamiyama 1, Chome, Higashi-Hiroshima 739-8512 Japan
Publisher's Web site: http://www.hiroshima-u.ac.jp/

Yoshikazu Ogawa is a graduate assistant in the Center for International Education at Boston College. He has been a researcher at the Center for Higher Education at Hiroshima University, Japan.

Gaodeng Jiaoyu Yanju (Journal of Higher Education)
(In Chinese)
Editor: Yao Qihe
Publisher: Huazhong University of Science and Technology, Wuhan
430074, Hubei Province, China
Editorial office: Editorial Department of Journal of Higher Education
Publisher's Web site: http://www.hust.edu.cn/new/english/
main.htm

Jiaoyu Yanjiu (Educational Research)
(In Chinese)
12/yr
Editor: Lian Riuqing
Publisher: China National Institute for Educational Research
Editorial office: Editorial Department of Educational Research, 46
Beisanhuan Zhonglu, Beijing 10088, China
Publisher's Web site: www.cnier.edu.cn

Journal of Higher Education (India)
4/yr
Editor: Shri V. Appa Rao
Publisher: University Grants Commission, Bahadurshah Zafar Marg,
New Delhi 110002 India
Publisher's Web site: http://www.ugc.ac.in/

Journal of Higher Education and Professional Training
12/yr
(In Vietnamese)
Editor: Van Dinh Ung
Publisher: 49 Dai Co Viet St., Hanoi, Vietnam

Koutou-Kyouiku Kenkyu (Japanese Journal of Higher Education
Research)
(In Japanese)
1/yr
Editor: Masakazu Yano
Publisher: Tamagawa University Press, 6-1-1 Tamagawa Gakuen,
Machida, Tokyo, 194-8610, Japan
Editorial office: Tokyo Institute of Technology, 2-12-1 Ookayama
Meguro-ku, Tokyo 152-8552, Japan
Publisher's Web site: http://www.tamagawa.ac.jp/SISETU/UP/
index-e.html

Kyoto Daigaku Koutou-kyouiku Kenkyu (Kyoto University Research in Higher Education)
(In Japanese)
1/yr
Editors: Masao Ishimura
Publisher: Research Center for Higher Education, Kyoto University, Yoshidahonmachi, Sakyo-ku, Kyoto 606-8501, Japan
Publisher's Web site: http://www.kyoto-u.ac.jp/index-e.html

Renda Fuyin Baokan Zilao/Higher Education Renda Duplicating Documents
(In Chinese)
12/yr
Editor: Xie Zili
Publisher: China Renda Social Sciences Information Center, Renmin University
Editorial office: Editorial Department of Higher Education, China Renda Social Sciences Information Center, 3 Zhangzizhong Road, Beijing 100007, China
Publisher's Web site: http://www.ruc.edu.cn/english/index.htm

Shanghai Gaojiao Yanjiu (Shanghai Research in Higher Education Journal)
(In Chinese)
12/yr
Editor: Hu Ruiwen
Publisher: Shanghai Institute of Educational Science, Shanghai Education Commission
Editorial office: Editorial Department of Shanghai Research in Higher Education Journal, 21 Chaling Beilu, Shanghai 200032, China

University News
52/yr
Publisher: Association of Indian Universities, 16 Kotla Marg, New Delhi 110 002, India
http://www.aiuweb.org/univnew.htm

Xuewei Yu Yanjiusheng Jiaoyu (Academic Degrees and Graduate Education)
(In Chinese)
6/yr
Editor: Wang Yue
Publisher: China Academic Degree and Graduate Education Society of the State Council, Peoples Republic of China
Editorial office: Editorial Department of Academic Degrees and Graduate Education, Beijing Technology University, Beijing 100081, China
Publisher's Web site: http://www.publist.com/cgi-bin/show?PLID=4312053

Zhongguo Gaodeng Jiaoyu (Chinese Higher Education)
(In Chinese)
12/yr
Editor: Zhang Dimei
Publisher: Ministry of Education, Peoples Republic of China
Editorial office: Editorial Department of Chinese Higher Education, 10 North Road, Wenhui Yuan, Haidan, Beijing 100088, China
Publisher's Web site: http://www.publist.com/cgi-bin/show?PLID=4188147

Zhongghu Gaojiao Yanjiu (China Higher Education Research)
(In Chinese)
6/yr
Editor: Wang Ge
Publisher: Chinese Association of Higher Education
Editorial office: Editorial Department of China Higher Educatison Research, 35 Damucang Hutong, Xidan, Beijing 100816, China

Europe

Active Learning
2/yr
Editor: Joyce Martin
Publisher: University of Oxford, 13 Banbury Road, Oxford OX2 6NN, UK
Journal Web site: http://www.cti.ac.uk/publ/actlea/

Alma Mater
(In Russian)
6/yr

Publisher: People's Friendship University of Russia
Editorial office: ul. Mikluklo-Maklaya 6, 117198 Moscow, Russia
Publisher's Web site: http://med.pfu.edu.ru/_new/english/win/
index_e_n.html

Assessment and Evaluation in Higher Education
4/yr
Editor: William A. H. Scott
Publisher: Carfax Publishing Ltd., Rankine Rd., Basingstoke, Hants RG24
8PR, UK
Editorial office: Departmemt of Education, University of Bath, Bath BA2
7AY, UK
http://www.tandf.co.uk/journals/alphalist.html

Aula: revue pro vysokoskolskou a vedni politiku
(In Czech)
4/yr
Editor: Helena Sebkova
Publisher: Centrum pro Studium Vysokého Skolstvi, U. Luzickeho
seminare 13/90, 118 00 Prague 1, Czech Republic
Publisher's Web site: http://rvs.upce.cz/nova/stale/struktura/
predsed/materialy/csvs1999.htm

Beiträge zur Hochschulforschung (Review of Higher Education)
(In German)
4/yr
Publisher: Bayerisches Staats-Institut für Hochschulplanung
Prinzregentenstr. 24, 80538 Munich, Germany
Journal Web site: http://www.ihf.bayern.de/publikationen.htm

Bildungsforschung und Bildungspraxis (Education et recherche/
Educazione e ricerca)
(In German, French, Italian)
3/yr
Editor: Gianni Ghisla
Publisher: Universitaetsverlag Freiburg Schweitz, Pérolles 42, CH-1700
Fribourg, Switzerland
Journal Web site: http://www.phs.unisg.ch/BBER/BUB98_3/
menu_d.html

CRE Action
(In English and French)
6/yr
Editor: Andris Barblan
Publisher: Association of European Universities, 10 rue Consel General,
CH 1211, Geneva 4, Switzerland
Journal Website: http://www.unige.ch/cre/publications/
cre_action_welcome.htm

DUZ: Das Unabhängige Hochschulmagazin
(In German)
6/yr
Editor: Marco Finetti
Publisher: RAABE, Postfach 301155, 53191 Bonn, Germany
Editorial office: DUZ Redaktion, Johannesstr. 72, 53225 Bonn, Postfach
301155, 53191 Bonn, Germany
Journal Web site: http://www.raabe.de/bn_duz.html

European Journal of Education
4/yr
Editor: Tony Becher
Publisher: Carfax Publishing Ltd., Rankine Rd., Basingstoke, Hants RG24
8PR, UK
Editorial office: European Institute of Education and Social Policy,
Universite de Paris IX Dauphine, 1, Place du Marechal de Lattre de
Tassigny F-75116 Paris, France
http://www.carfax.co.uk/eje-ad.htm

Fondazione RUI: Revista di cultura universitaria
(In Italian)
3/yr
Publisher: Unione Stampa Periodica Italiana, Viale Ventuno Aprile 36,
00162 Rome, Italy
Journal Web site: http://www.fondazionerui.it/pubbl.html

Forschung und Lehre
12/yr
Editor: Felix Grigat
Publisher: Geschäftsstelle des Deutschen Hochschulverbandes
Rheinallee 18, 53173 Bonn, Germany
Journal Web site: http://www.forschung-und-lehre.de/

Forum Akademickie
(In Polish)
12/yr
Editor: Andrzej Swic
Publisher: Academicka Oficyna Wydawnicza, ul.Tomasza Zana 38a, 20-601 Lublin 17, Poland
Journal Web site: http://www.forumakad.pl/

Higher Education
8/yr
Editors: Grant Harman, Dai Hounsell, Gary D. Rhoades, and Ulrich Teichler
Publisher: Kluwer Academic Publishers, PO Box 322, 3300 AH, Dordecht, The Netherlands
Editorial office: Kluwer Academic Publishers, POB 990, 3300 AZ Dordrecht, The Netherlands
Journal Web site: http://www.wkap.nl/journalhome.htm/0018-1560

Higher Education in Europe
4/yr
Senior Editor: Leland Conley Barrows
Publisher: Carfax Publishing, Rankine Road, Basingstoke, Hante RG248PR, UK
Editorial office: UNESCO-CEPES, 39 Stirbei Voda, R-70732, Bucharest, Romania
Publisher's Web site: http://www.tandf.co.uk/journals/alphalist.html

Higher Education Management
3/yr
Editor: Professor Maurice Kogan
Publisher: OECD Publications, 2 rue André Pascal, 75775 Paris Cedex 16, France
Editorial office: 48 Duncan Terrace, London, N1 8AL, UK
Publisher's Web site: http://electrade.gfi.fr/cgi-bin/OECDBookShop.storefront

Higher Education Policy
4/yr
Editor: Guy Neave
Publisher: Elsevier Science Ltd., Box 800, Kidlington, Oxford OX5 1DX, UK
Editorial office: International Association of Universities (IAU), 1, rue

Miollis, Paris, France
Publisher's Web site: http://www.elsevier.nl/inca/publications/store/3/
0/9/1/0/index.htt

Higher Education Quarterly
4/yr
Editors: Gareth Williams, Peter Wright, Malcolm Tight, and Gareth Parry
Publisher: Blackwell Publishers, 108 Cowley Road, Oxford, OX4 1JF UK
Editorial Office: Institute of Education, University of London, UK
Publisher's Web site: http://www.blackwellpublishers.co.uk/asp/
journal.asp?ref=0951-5224

Higher Education Review
3/yr
Editor: John Pratt
Publisher: Tyrell Burgess Associates, Ltd., 34 Sandilands, Croydon CR0
5DB, UK
Publisher's Web site: http://www.srhe.ac.uk/cvcp983.htm

History of Universities
(In English, French, German, Italian and Spanish)
1/yr
Editor: Caureuce Brockliss
Publisher: Oxford University Press, Walton St. Oxford OX2 6DP, UK
Publisher's Web site: http://www.oup.co.uk/isbn/0-19-822001-4

Hochschule Ost
(In German)
4/yr
Editor: Peer Pasternack
Publisher: Universität Leipzig, PF 920, 04009 Leipzig, Germany
Publisher's Web site: http://www.uni-leipzig.de/~hso/vorstellung.htm

Das Hochschulwesen (Higher Education)
(In German)
4/yr
Editors: Rudolf Ederer, Bianca Meurer
Publisher: Luchterhand Verlag, Postfach 2352, 56513 Neuweid, Germany
Publisher's Web site: http://www.luchterhand.de/HLV_HOME.NSF/
Frames?OpenForm

Industry and Higher Education
6/yr
Editor: John Edmondson
Publisher: IP Publishing, Ltd., 4-5 Coleridge Gardens, London NW6
3QH, UK
Publisher's Web site: http://www.ippublishing.com/
general_industry.asp

International Higher Education
2/yr
Publisher: TEXT Consortium Ltd., University of Derby, Kedleston Rd.
Derby DE22 1GB, UK
Publisher's Web site: http://www.bc.edu/bc_org/avp/soe/cihe/
direct1/Newslet3.html

Journal of Further and Higher Education
3/yr
Editor: Jennifer Rowley
Publisher: Carfax Publishing Ltd., Rankine Rd. Basingstoke, Hants RG24
8PR, UK
Editorial office: Edge Hill College of Higher Education, St. Helens Rd.
Ormskirk Lancashire, L39 9NP, UK
Publisher's Web site: http://www.tandf.co.uk/journals/alphalist.html

Journal of Higher Education Policy and Management
2/yr
Editors: Vin Massaro and Gavin Moodie
Publisher: Carfax Publishing
Rankine Road, Basingstoke, Hants RG24 8PR, UK
Publisher's Web site: http://www.tandf.co.uk/journals/alphalist.html

Le Monde de L'Education, de la Culture, et de la Formation
(In French)
12/yr
Publisher: Le Monde, 21 Bis, Rue Claude Bernard, 75242 Paris Cedex 05,
France
Journal Web site: http://wwww.lemonde.fr/mde/

Magistr
(In Russian)
12/yr

Editor: R. A. Kazakova
Publisher: Research Institute for Higher Educatsion, 1, 3ʳᵈ Kabelnaya St.,
111024 Moscow, Russia
Journal Web site: http://www.cuni.cz/cuni/ruk/ipc/magistr.htm

Minerva
4/yr
Publisher: Kluwer Academic Publishers, POB 322, 3000 AH Dordrecht,
The Netherlands

Nauka i Szkolnictwo Wyzsze
(In Polish)
2/yr
Editor: Maria Wojcicka
Publisher: Centrum Badan Polityki Naukowej i Szkolnictwa Wyzszego,
00-046 Warsaw, ul., owy Swiat 69, Poland
Publisher's Web site: http://chemeng.p.lodz.pl/dry/Zylla.html

OHZ: Österrichische Hochschulzeitung
(In German)
Publisher: Österrichische Hochschulzeitung, Hohenstaaufengasse 5, A-
1010 Vienna, Austria
Publisher's Web site: http://www.archinform.de/start.htm?page=/ort/
3093.htm

Perspectives: Policy and Practice in Higher Education
4/yr
Editor: Celia M. Whitchurch
Publisher: Harvey
Publisher: Carfax Publishing
Rankine Road, Basingstoke, Hants RG24 8PR, UK
Editorial office: The Association of University Administrators, School of
Medicine King's College, London, SE1 9RT, UK
Publisher's Web site: http://www.taylorandfrancis.com/JNLS/per.htm

Quality in Higher Education
3/yr
Editor: Lee Harvey
Publisher: Carfax Publishing
Rankine Road, Basingstoke, Hants RG24 8PR, UK
Editorial office: Center for Research into Quality, Baker Building, Univer-

sity of Central England in Birmingham, 90, Aldridge Road, Perry Barr, Birmingham, B4 2TP UK
Publisher's Web site: http://www.tandf.co.uk/journals/carfax/13562517.html
Reflections on Higher Education
Editor: Robert Wood
Publisher: 2 Gaveston Dr., Berkhansted, Herts HP4 1JE, UK
http://www.bbk.ac.uk/asd/bourne.htm

Research into Higher Education Abstracts
3/yr
Editor: Ian McNay
Publisher: Carfax Publishing
Rankine Road, Basingstoke, Hants RG24 8PR, UK
Editorial office: School of Post-compulsory Education and Training, University of Greenwich, Southwood Site, Eltham, London SE9 2UG, UK
Publisher's Web site: http://www.tandf.co.uk/journals/carfax/13562517.html

Research in Post-compulsory Education
3/yr
Publisher: Triangle Journals Ltd., POB 65, Wallingford, Oxford OX10 0YG, UK
Publisher's Web site: http://www.triangle.co.uk/rpe/00.htm

Studies in Higher Education
3/yr
Editor: Mantz Yorke
Publisher: Carfax Publishing
Rankine Road, Basingstoke, Hants RG24 8PR, UK
Editorial office: Centre for Higher Education Development, Liverpool John Moores University, I.M. Marsh Campus, Barkhill Road, Aigburth, Liverpool L17 6BD, UK
Publisher's Web site: http://www.tandf.co.uk/journals/carfax/13562517.html

Teaching in Higher Education
4/yr
Publisher: Carfax Publishing
Rankine Road, Basingstoke, Hants RG24 8PR, UK

Publisher's Web site: http://www.tandf.co.uk/journals/carfax/
13562517.html

Tertiary Education and Management
4/yr
Editor: Roddy Begg
Publisher: Jessica Kingsley Publisher, 116 Pentonville Rd., London
N1 9JB UK
Editorial office: University of Aberdeen, Regent Walk, Aberdeen
AB24 3FX Scotland
Publisher's Web site: http://www.jkp.com/catalogue/highered/

Thema: Tijdschrift voor hoger onderwijs and management (Journal
of Higher Education and Management)
(In Dutch)
4/yr
Editor: Hans ten Brinke
Publisher: Elsevier, Postbus 16400, 2500 BK The Hague, The Netherlands

Tijdschrift voor hoger onderwijs (Journal of Higher Education)
(In Dutch)
4/yr
Editor: H. H. C. M. Christiaaans
Publisher: Uitgeverij Lemma, Newtonlaan 57, 3502 GH Utrecht, The
Netherlands
Publisher's Web site: http://www.utwente.nl/cheps/publications/
lang.shtml#DP

Times Higher Education Supplement
52/yr
Editor: Auriol Stevens
Publisher: The Times Supplements Limited, Admiral House, 66-68
E.Smithfield, London E1 9XY, United Kingdom
Journal Web site: http://www.thesis.co.uk/tp/999/PRN/NAV/
index_HGN.html

Universitas: studi e documentazione di vita universitaria
(In Italian)
4/yr

Editor: P. G. Palla
Publisher: Fratelli Palombi Editori, Via dei Gracci 181-182, 00192
Rome, Italy
Publisher's Web site: http://193.205.24.18:4001/ALEPH/ITA/BOC/
BOC/BOC/FULL/0301221?

Vyssheye Obrazovanie v Rossii (Higher Education in Russia)
(In Russian)
6/yr
Publisher: Moscow State University of Printing Arts
Editor: Boris G. Yakovlev
Editorial office: Sadovaya-Spasskaya ul. D6, kom 309, 103045 Mos-
cow, Russia

Zeitschrift für Hochschuldidaktik: Beitrage zu Studium,
Wissenschaft, und Beruf
(In German)
4/yr
Editor: Martin Lischka
Publisher: StudienVerlag Innsbruck-Wien
Andreas Hofer Strasse 38,Postfach 104, A-6010 Innsbruck, Austria
Editorial office: Osterreichische Gesellschaft für
Hochschuldidaktik,Strozzigasse 2, A-1080 Wien, Austria
Publisher's Web site: http://link.springer.de/link/service/journals/
94191/index.htm

Latin America

Docencia post-secundaria
(In Spanish)
4/yr
Editor: Ricardo Beltran Rojas
Publisher: Ediciones Educativas, Av. Patria No. 120, Lomas del Valle,
Box 1-440, 44100 Guadalajara, Jal., Mexico
Publisher's Web site: http://www.cidi.oas.org/edu40anivInvest.htm

Educacion Superior y Sociedad (Higher Education and Society)
(In Spanish)
4/yr

Editor: Jose Silvio
Publisher: Centro Regional Para La educacion Superior en America
Latina y el Caribe, Apartado Postal 68-394, Caracas Venezuela
Journal Web site: http://hemeroweb.eafit.edu.co/humani/
EducacSupSocied/educacin.htm

Pensamiento Educativo
(In Spanish)
2/yr
Editor: Ricardo Rojas Valdés
Publisher: Facultad de Educación, Pontificia Universidad Católica de
Chile, Casilla 114-D Macul, Santiago, Chile
Journal Web site: http://www.puc.cl/educacion/indc_rpe.htm

Pensamiento universitario
(In Spanish)
3/yr
Editor: Pedro Krotsch
Publisher: Casilla de Correo 333, Sucursal 12 (b), c.p. 1412, Buenos Aires,
Argentina
Journal Web site: http://www.pue.upaep.mx/formhum/25107.html

Perfiles Educativos
(In Spanish)
3/yr
Editor: Angel Diaz Barriga
Publisher: Centro de Estudios sobre la Universidad, Ciudad
Universidad, Mexico, DF, Mexico
Journal Web site: http://www.unam.mx/cesu/perfiles.html

Revista Cubana de Educación Superior
(In Spanish)
4/yr
Editor: Jesús Maria del Portal
Publisher: Dirección de Información Cientifica y Humanistica, Calle 1,
No. 302, Vadado, Havana, Cuba
Journal Web site: http://www.oei.es/n3833.htm http://www.oei.es/
n3833.htm

Revista de la Educación Superior
(In Spanish)
4/yr
Editor: Alfonso Rangel Guerra
Publisher: Asociación Nacional de Universidades e Instituciones de
Educación Superior, Tenayuca 200, Col. Sta. Cruz Atoyac, 03310 Mexico
DF, Mexico
http://www.oei.es/n3836.htm

Revista educación superior y sociedad
(In Spanish)
2/yr
Publisher: CRESALC, Apartado 68394, Caracas 1062-A, Venezuela
Publisher's Web site: http://www.iesalc.unesco.org.ve/pubiesalc1.htm

Revista Latino-americana de Estudios Educativos
(Latin American Review of Educational Studies)
(In Spanish)
3/yr
Editor: Maria del Carme Baldonedo, Cenrto de Estudios Educativos, A.C,
Av Revolucion 1291, Col Tlacopac, C.P. 01040 Mexico
Journal Web site: http://www.oei.es/revista.htm

U-2000: Cronica de la educación Superior
(In Spanish)
Weekly
Editor: Tonatiuh Ramirez Peraza
Publisher: Servicio de Investigación y Desarrollo Educativo S. C.,
Cumbres de Acultzingo No. 26-501, 03020 México DF, México
Journal Web site: http://www.estadistica.unam.mx/dgesii/memoria93/
dgelu.htm

Universidad Futura (University Futures)
(In Spanish)
4/yr
Editor: Eduardo de La Garza
Publisher: Grupo editorial EON, Av México-Coyoacan 421,XOCO, Col
General Anaya México, D.F
Editorial address: Adriana Corona, Av. San Pablo 180. C.P. 02200, Col
Reynosa Tamaulpias, Azcapotzolco México DF, México

Publisher's Web site: http://www.uaq.mx/servicios/consulta/hemeroteca/edu.html

Universidades
(In Spanish)
1/yr
Publisher: Union de Universidades de América Latina, Ciudad Universitaria, Apartado Postal, 70232, Del. Coyoacán, 04510 México DF, Mexico
Journal Web site: http://www.rediris.es/recursos/centros/univ.es.html
Universitas 2000
(In Spanish)
3/yr
Publisher: Fondo Editrorial para el Desarrollo de la Educación Superior, Apartado 62532, Caracas 1060-A, Venezuela
Journal Web site: http://www2.gratisweb.com/universitas_2000/universitas2000.htm

North America

AAHE Bulletin
10/yr
Editor: Vicky Hendley
Publisher: American Association for Higher Education, One Dupont Circle NW, Suite 360, Washington, DC 20036 USA
Publisher's Web site: http://www.aahe.org/bulletin/bulletin.htm

About Campus
6/yr
Editors: Charles C. Schroeder and Patricia King
Publisher: Jossey-Bass, 350 Sansome St. 5th Fl., San Francisco, CA 94104 USA
Publisher's Web site: http://www.josseybass.com/JBJournals/abc.html

Academe
4/yr
Editor: Ellen Schrecker
Publisher: American Association of University Professors, Suite 500, 1012 Fourteenth Street, NW, Washington, DC USA

Publisher's Web site: http://www.aaup.org/acahome.htm

Academic Questions
4/yr
Editor: Brandford P. Wilson
Publisher: Transaction Periodicals Consortium, Rutgers University, 35 Berrue Cir., Piscataway, NJ, 08854 USA
Editorial office: National Association of Scholars, NAS, 221 Witherspoon Street, 2nd Floor, Princeton, NJ 08542 USA
Publisher's Web site: http://www.nas.org/aq.htm
Assessment Update: Progress, Trends, and Practices in Higher Education
6/yr
Editor: Trudy W. Banta
Publisher: Jossey-Bass, 350 Sansome St. 5th Fl., San Francisco, CA 94104 USA
Publisher's Web site: http://www.josseybass.com/JBJournals/au.html

Black Issues in Higher Education
26/yr
Editor: Cheryl Fields
Publisher: Cox, Matthews, and Associates, Inc., 10520 Warwick Ave., Suite B-8, Fairfax VA 22030, USA
Journal Web site: http://www.blackissues.com

Canadian Journal of Higher Education
(La revue canadienne d'enseignement supérieur)
(In English and French)
3/yr
Editor: Glen Jones
Publisher: University of Manitoba, CJHE (Center for Higher Education Research and Development), c/o CSSHE, 220 Sinott Building, 70 Dysant Road, University of Manitoba, Winnipeg, MB R3T 2N2 Canada
Publisher's Web site: http://www.catchword.com/rpsv/catchword/csshe/03161218/contp1.htm

Canadian Journal of University Continuing Education
Revue canadienne de l'éducation permanente universitaire
2/yr
Editors: Gwenna Moss, Bert Wolfe
Publisher: Canadian Association for University Continuing Education,

Extension Division, 117 Science Place,, University of Saskatchewan, Saskatoon, SK S7N 5C8, Canada
Publisher's Web site: http://strategis.ic.gc.ca/SSGF/mi00606f.html

Change
6/yr
Executive Editor: Theodore J. Marchese
Publisher: Heldref Publications, 1319 Eighteenth Street, NW, Washington DC 20036 USA
Publisher's Web site: http://www.heldref.org/

College and University
4/yr
Editor and Chair: Roman S. Gawkoski
Publisher: American Association of Collegiate Registrars and Admission Officers, One Dupont Circle, NW, Suite 520, Washington DC 20036 USA
Publisher's Web site: http://www.aacrao.org/pub-frame.html

College Board Review
4/yr
Editor: Paul Barry
Publisher: College Board Publications, Two College Way, Forrester Center, W.V. 25438 USA
Editorial Office: The College Board, 45, Columbus Avenue, New York, NY 10023 USA
Publisher's Web site: http://www.collegeboard.org/frstlook/html/index000.html

College Student Affairs Journal
2/yr
Editor: Diane L. Cooper
Publisher: Southern Association for College Student Affairs, 402 Aderhold Hall, The University of Georgia, Athens, Georgia 30602 USA
Publisher's Web site: http://www.sacsa.org/journal.html

College Teaching
4/yr
Editor: Louise M. Dubley
Publisher: Heldref Publications, 1319 Eighteenth St., NW, Washington DC 20036 USA
Publisher's Web site: http://www.heldref.org/

Community College Journal
6/yr
Editor: Cheryl Gamble
Publisher: American Association of Community College, National Center for Higher Education, One Dupont Circle NW Suite 410, Washington, DC 20036 USA
Publisher's Web site: http://www.aacc.nche.edu/books/journal/journalindex.htm

Community College Journal of Research and Practice
4/yr
Editor-in Chief: D. Barry Lumsden
Publisher: Taylor & Francis, 325 Chestnut Street, Philadelphia, PA 19106 USA
Editorial office: P.O. Box 311337, Denton, Texas 76203 USA
Publisher's Web site: http://www.taylorandfrancis.com/program-main.html

Community College Review
4/yr
Editor: George B. Vaughan
Publisher: Department of Adult and Community College Education, College of Education Psychology, NC State University, Box 7801 Raleigh, NC 27695 USA
Journal Web site: http://www2.ncsu.edu/ncsu/cep/acce/ccr/ccreview.htm

Continuing Higher Education Review
3/yr
Editor: Michael Shinazel
Publisher: University Continuing Education Association, One Dupont Circle, Suite 615, Washington DC 20036, USA
Editorial office: University of Wisconsin-Milwaukee, 161 W. Wisconsin Ave., Suite 6000, Milwaukee, WI 53203, USA
Publisher's Web site: http://www.nucea.edu/

Convergence
4/yr
Publisher: International Council for Adult Education, 792 Bathurst St., Suite 500, Toronto M5R 2R4, Canada
Publisher's Web site: http://www.web.net/icae/english/converge.htm

Current Issues in Catholic Higher Education
4/yr
Editor: Paul J. Gallagher
Publisher: Association of Catholic Colleges and Universities, One
Dupont Circle, Washington DC 20036 USA
Publisher's Web site: http://www.accunet.org/Services/pub-auth.htm

Higher Education Abstracts
4/yr
Editor: Bonny McLaughlin
Publisher: Claremont Graduate University, 231 E. Tenth St., Clarmont,
CA 91711, USA
Publisher's Web site: http://www.cgu.edu/inst/hea/hea.html

Hispanic Outlook in Higher Education
26/yr
Editor: Adalyn Hixson
Publisher: Hispanic Outlook in Higher Education Publisher, 210 Route 4
East, Suite 310, Paramus,NJ 07652 USA
Journal Web site: http://www.hispanicoutlook.com/index.html

History of Higher Education Annual
1/yr
Editor: Roger Geiger
Publisher: Higher Education Program, Pennsylvania State University,
403 S. Allen Street, University Park, PA 16801 USA
Publisher's Web site: http://www.ed.psu.edu/hied/annual/default.htm

IGLU: Inter-American Journal of University Management
(In Spanish, French, English)
2/yr
Editor: Pierre Cazalis
Publisher: Inter-American Organization for Higher Education/
Organisation Universitaire Interaméricaine, 2954 Boulevard Laurier,
bureau 090, Sainte-Foy, Québec, G1V 4T2, Canada
Publisher's Web site: http://www.oui-iohe.qc.ca/INDX/en-index.htm

Innovative Higher Education
4/yr
Editor: Ronald D. Simpson, the University of Georgia
Publisher: Human Science Press, Inc.

Editorial office: Office of Instructional Development, Instructional Plaza, University of Georgia, Athens, Georgia 30602 USA
Journal Web site: http://www.isd.uga.edu/ihe/ihe.htm

International Educator
4/yr
Editor: Eric Kronenwetter
Publisher: NAFSA: Association of International Educators, 1307 New York Ave., NW, Washington DC 20005 USA
Publisher's Web site: http://www.nafsa.org/publications/ie/default.html

International Education Forum
2/yr
Editor: V. N. Bhatia
Publisher: Association of International Education Administrators, POB 645120, Washington State University, Pullman, WA 99164 USA
Publisher's Web site: http://www.aieaworld.org/

International Higher Education
4/yr
Editor: Philip G. Altbach
Publisher: Center for International Higher Education, 207 Campion Hall, Boston College, Chestnut Hill, MA 02467 USA
Publisher's Web site: http://www.bc.edu/bc_org/avp/soe/cihe/publications/publications.htm

Journal of Blacks in Higher Education
4/yr
Editor and Publisher: Theodore Cross, 200 W 57th Street, 15Th flr., New York, N.Y 10019 USA
Journal Web site: http://www.jstor.org/journals/10773711.html

Journal of College Admission
4/yr
Editor: Elaina C. Loreland
Publisher: National Association for College Admission Counseling, 1631 Prince Street, Alexandria, VA 22314 USA
Publisher's Web site: http://www.nacac.com/submission.html

Journal of College Student Development
6/yr
Editor: Gregory S. Blimling
Publisher: American College Personal Association
Editorial office: Student Development Office, Appalachian State University, Boone, NC 28608 USA
Journal Web site: http://www.appstate.edu/www_docs/jcsd/welcome.htm

Journal of College and University Law
2/yr
Editor-in-Chief: Laura Rothstein
Publisher: F. B. Rothman and Co., 10368 W. Centennial Rd., Littleton CO 80127 USA
Editorial office: National Association of College and University Attorneys, Suite 620, One Dupont Circle, NW, Washington DC 20036 USA
Publisher's Web site: http://www.nacua.org/publications/jculorder.htm

Journal of College Student Development
6/yr
Editor: Gregory Blimling
Publisher: American College Personnel Association, One Dupont Circle, NW Suite 300, Washington, DC 20036-1110, USA

Journal of Computing in Higher Education
2/yr
Editor: Carol MacKnight
Publisher: Norris Publishers, Box 2593, Amherst MA 01004, USA
Journal Web site: http://www-unix.oit.umass.edu/~carolm/jche/

Journal of Continuing Higher Education
3/yr
Editor: Barbara E. Hanniford
Publisher: Association for Continuing Higher Education (ACHE), Trident Technical College, PO Box 118067, CE-M, Charleston, SC 29423-8067 USA

Journal of General Education
4/yr
Editors: Jeremy Cohen and John J. Romano
Publisher: The Pennsylvania State University Press

Editorial office: Center for the Study of Higher Educator, The Pennsylvania State University, 403 S. Allen Street, Suite 104, University Park, PA 16801 USA
Publisher's Web site: http://www.psu.edu/psupress/titles/jnrl_titles/jge.html

Journal of Marketing for Higher Education
4/yr
Editor: Thomas J. Hayes
Publisher: Haworth Press. 10 Alice St., Binghamton, NY 13904 USA
Journal Web site: http://bubl.ac.uk/journals/bus/jmfhe/

Journal of Studies in International Education
4/yr
Editor: Hans deWit
Publisher: Sage Publications, 2455 Teller Rd., Thousand Oaks, CA., USA
Lingua Franca: The Review of Academic Life
6/yr
Editor-in-Chief: Jeffrey Kittay
Publisher: Lingua Franca, Inc., 22 West 38th Street, New York, NY 10018 USA
Journal Web site: http://www.linguafranca.com/

Metropolitan Universities
4/yr
Publisher: Marilyn Mattsson R & P, Towson State University, 7800 York Rd, Ste. 301, Towson, MD 021204 USA

NASPA Journal
4/yr
Editor: Larry D. Roper
Publisher: National Association of Student Personnel Administrators, 1875 Connecticut Avenue, NW Suite 418, Washington, DC 20009 USA
Editorial Office: 632 Kerr Administration Building, Oregon State University, Corvallis, OR 97331 USA
Publisher's Web site: http://www.naspa.org/marketplace/publications/journal/JOURNAL.HTM

New Directions for Higher Education
4/yr
Editor: Martin Kramer
Publisher: Jossey-Bass, 350 Sansome St., San Francisco, CA 94104, USA
Publisher's Web site: http://www.josseybass.com/JBJournals/
ndhe.html

New Directions for Institutional Research
4/yr
Editor: J. Fredericks Volkwein
Publisher: Jossey Bass, 350 Sansome St., San Francisco, CA 94104, USA
Editorial office: Center for Higher Education, Pennsylvania State University, University Park, PA, USA
Publisher's Web site: http://www.josseybass.com/JBJournals/ndir.html

New Directions for Teaching and Learning
4/yr
Editors: Marilla D. Svinicki
Publisher: Jossey-Bass, 350 Sansome St., San Francisco, CA 94104 USA
Publisher's Web site: http://www.josseybass.com/JBJournals/ndtl.html

Planning for Higher Education
4/yr
Editor: Rod Rose
Publisher: Society for College and University Planning, 311 Maynard Street, Ann Arbor, MI 48105 USA
Publisher's Web site: http://www.scup.org/phe.htm

Research in Higher Education
6/yr
Editor: John C. Smart
Publisher: Human Science Press, 233 Spring Street, New York, N.Y. 10013 USA
Editorial office: Department of Leadership, 113 Patterson Building, The University of Memphis, Memphis, TN 38152 USA
Publisher's Web site: http://www.wkap.nl/journalhome.htm/0361-0365

Review of Higher Education
4/yr
Editor: Philip G. Altbach
Publisher: Johns Hopkins University Press, POB 19966, Baltimore, MD 21218 USA

Editorial office: Campion Hall, Boston College, Chestnut Hill, MA 02467 USA
Publisher's Web site: http://www.press.jhu.edu/press/journals/rhe/ rhe.html

Teaching in Higher Education
4/yr
Publisher: Carfax Publishing Ltd., Rankine Rd., Basingstoke, Hants RG24 8PR, UK
Editorial office: Co. 875-81 Massachusetts Ave., Cambridge, MA 02139 USA
Publisher's Web site: http://www.tandf.co.uk/journals/carfax/ 13562517.html

Thought and Action: The NEA Higher Education Journal
2/yr
Editor: Con Lehane
Publisher: National Education Association, 1201 16th Street NW, Washington DC 20036 USA
Publisher's Web site: http://www.nea.org/he/tanda.html

Trusteeship
6/yr
Editor: Daniel J. Levin
Publisher: Association of Governing Boards of Universities and Colleges, One Dupont Circle Suite 400, Washington, D. C. 20036 USA
Publisher's Web site: http://www.agb.org/periodicals.cfm

Universités
(In French)
4/yr
Editors: Michel Guillou, Jean Claude Castelain
Publisher: Agence francophone pour l'enseignement supérieur et la recherche, B.P. 400 succ., Côtes-des-Neiges, Montréal, Québec, Canada H3S 2S7.
Publisher's Web site: http://www.serveurs-nationaux.jussieu.fr/ LDAPshow/

University Affairs/Affaires Universitaires
10/yr
Editor: Christine Tausig Ford
Publisher: Association of Universities and Colleges of Canada,600-350

Albert Street, Ottawa, Ontario K1R 1B1, Canada
Journal Web site: http://www.cmpa.ca/ed8.html

University Business
6/yr
Editor: Jeffrey Kittay
Publisher: University Business, 22 W. 38th Street, New York, NY 10018
USA
Journal Web site: http://www.universitybusiness.com/0007/
0007toc.html

OCEANIA

Australian Universities' Review
4/yr
Editor: Simon Marginson
Publisher: National Tertiary Education Union, PO Box 1323, South
Melbourne, Vic., Australia 3205
Publisher's Web site: http://www.edunions.labor.net..../services/
publics/aur/aur.html

Higher Education Research and Development
3/yr
Editors: Elaine Martin and Peter Ling
Publisher: Carfax Publishing Ltd., Rankine Rd., Basingstoke, Hants RG24
8PR, UK
Editorial office: HERD, c/o EPI Group, RMIT, GPO2476V, Melbourne,
Vic. 3001, Australia
Publisher's Web site: http://www.tandf.co.uk/journals/
frameloader.html?http://www.tandf.co.uk/journals/carfax/
07294360.html

HERDSA Review
3/yr
Editor: Roger Landbeck
Publisher: HERDSA, POB 516, Jamison, ACT 2614, Australia
Publisher's Web site: http://www.herdsa.org.au/journal.htm

Journal of Institutional Research in Australasia
2/yr
Editors: Ian Dobson and Angelo Calderon
Publisher: Monash University, Clayton, Vic., Australia
Journal Web site: http://129.96.222.99/aair/jira.htm

COUNTRY INDEX

APPENDIX

The Questionnaire:
Instructions
International Survey of Higher Education
Programs, Centers,
and Institutes

Eligibility Requirements

To be included in the higher education inventory, programs, centers, and institutes should meet the following requirements. If you do not believe that your program, center, or institute meets these qualifications, we would still like to hear from you. Please return the enclosed questionnaire with as much information about your organization as possible.

Higher education/postsecondary programs (focusing primarily on graduate teaching):
* At least one FTE (full-time equivalent) faculty member focusing on higher education. This might mean two or more teaching staff who have only a partial commitment.
* At least four graduate/postgraduate-level courses (master's and/or doctoral) that relate to higher education—the definition can be fairly broad. In general, a program should offer the terminal degree (i.e., the most advanced degree available, usually the doctorate), although providing a formal degree is not mandatory.

Higher education centers and institutes:
* A center or institute is primarily focused on research, policy analysis, or related activities, although it may offer some academic courses. It must have at least one full-time professional staff member, and at least two professional support (For example, director, professor, lecturer, researcher, or administrator. Do not include secretaries.) It should have an assigned budget. A center or institute may be housed in a univer-

sity, government, agency, private institution, or be freestanding. Funding may come from a variety of sources.

Response Instructions

You may return the questionnaire by mail, e-mail, or by filling out an electronic version of the questionnaire on the Center for International Higher Education WWW page.

- **Mail Instructions**. Type responses on the enclosed questionnaire. Immediately return completed form via airmail to: Center for International Higher Education, 207 Campion Hall, Boston College, Chestnut Hill, MA 02467 USA;
- **E-mail Instructions**. E-mail correspondingly numbered responses to <highered@bc.edu>. You need not retype the questions;
- **WWW Instructions**. Log on to <http://www.bc.edu/bc_org/avp/soe/cihe/hesurvey.html>. Follow on-screen instructions.

Higher Education Questionnaire

Please type if returning by mail.
Use additional pages as necessary.
Responses should be based on the most current information available at the time of mailing.

Check one of the following:

_____ This is a program (i.e., it mainly focuses on teaching and professional preparation).

_____ This is a center or institute (i.e., it is mainly concerned with research, policy analysis, or related activities).

_____ We fit neither category, but we are concerned with higher/postsecondary education.

(1) What is the formal name of your organization (in English and in your national language)?

(2) Address:

(3) Telephone number(s):

(4) Fax number(s):

(5) E-mail address:

(6) World Wide Web address:

(7) What is the focus of your organization? Please be as specific as possible in describing its main purpose(s) and program(s).

(8) When was your organization established?

(9) What is your organizational location (for example, School of Social Sciences, government agency, private organization, independent research center, etc.)?

(10) What is your major source of funding (university, government, etc.)?

(11) If your organization publishes books, journals, a newsletter, etc., please specify and list recent titles by type.

(12) Please list the names, ranks, and areas of specialization for all members or professional staff in the field of higher education at your organization (For example, director, professor, lecturer, researcher, or administrator. Do not include secretaries.) While these individuals need not be involved on a full-time basis, their participation should be significant.

(13) If applicable, please list the number and names of classes (courses) given in a typical academic year in higher education. Indicate which are master's (M.A.) or doctoral (Ph.D.) level courses. DO NOT include undergraduate (i.e., first-degree) courses.

(14) If applicable, how many students are typically involved in your program?

M.A. _____ full-time _____ part-time _____

Ph.D. _____ full-time _____ part-time _____

Other _____ full-time _____ part-time _____

Please specify "other" degree or certificate:

(15) If applicable, please list the key textbooks and or/readings that are used in your two main introductory courses in the field of higher education? If possible, please also send relevant syllabi.

(16) What are the main journals used in courses or research?

Thank you very much for taking the time to fill out this questionnaire. If you have any brochures or other publications that describe your organization, please send them to us. Please mail this form and any additional materials to: Center for International Higher Education, 207 Campion Hall, Boston College, Chestnut Hill, MA 02467 USA.